典瑞流芳

民國大出版家 夏瑞芳

A Pioneer Remembered

-A Biography of

How Zoen Fong

趙俊邁 著
汪班 袁曉寧 譯
By C.M. Chao
Translated by Ben Wang & Yuan Xiaoning

臺灣商務印書館

典瑞流芳：民間大出版家夏瑞芳／趙俊邁
著；汪班. 袁曉寧譯. -- 初版. -- 臺北市：
臺灣商務, 2014. 06
　　面；　　公分
　　ISBN 978-957-05-2932-6（平裝）

1. 夏瑞芳　2. 傳記

782.882　　　　　　　　　　　005658

典瑞流芳　民國大出版家夏瑞芳

作者◆趙俊邁

譯者◆汪班　袁曉寧

發行人◆施嘉明

總經理◆王春申

副總編輯◆沈昭明

主編◆葉幗英

校對◆趙俊邁　汪班

封面設計◆吳郁婷

出版發行：臺灣商務印書館股份有限公司

10046台北市中正區重慶南路一段三十七號

電話：(02)2371-3712　傳真：(02)2375-0274

讀者服務專線：0800056196

郵撥：0000165-1

E-mail：ecptw@cptw.com.tw

網路書店網址：www.cptw.com.tw

網路書店臉書：facebook.com.tw/ecptwdoing

臉書：facebook.com.tw/ecptw

部落格：blog.yam.com/ecptw

局版北市業字第 993 號

初版一刷：2014 年 6 月

定價：新台幣 450 元

推薦序

趙俊邁先生撰寫的這本介紹夏瑞芳先生傳記「典瑞流芳」（並汪班、袁曉寧二先生的英譯版，更是相得益彰），極有文獻和歷史價值；細讀之後，不但對這位鮮為人知的創辦商務印書館的文化巨人，在推廣教育、知識、學問各方面的不朽成就能有所了解，更能看到中國清末民初混亂複雜的政治社會背景。同時作者也精闢地分析了夏瑞芳在百年前，正當英年有為而罹遭殺害的前因後果。這是我近年來看過的一本特別傑出、引人入勝的傳記，對中國文化教育史以及中國現代史有興趣的讀者如我，確是一本不可不讀的好書！

白先勇 於聖塔芭芭拉

目錄

代序

從二〇一四年的曼哈頓穿越到一九一四年的黃浦灘

二〇一二年夏，曼哈頓中城聯合國大樓中文教學部辦公室裡，空間本不寬敞，加上小會議桌、幾把椅子、書架等擺設，剩餘空間愈顯狹仄，這天，卻擠進五個人，其中有中文教學組組長何勇先生、資深教授汪班先生、華美人文學會首席顧問段女士，還有作者以及當天的主角史濟良先生。

辦公室裡的小會議桌上，堆滿了發黃的老照片和一些中、英文書冊、雜誌、影印文件。

五個人聚精會神的討論著，聲量不高但透著嚴謹、靜肅，主題圍繞著一個印刷出版界的傳奇人物、一段近代文化傳播史中幾乎被遺忘卻影響深遠的歷史。

這位傳奇人物就是商務印書館創辦人之一、第一任總經理夏瑞芳，他和鮑咸昌兄弟等

四人於一八九七年在上海江西北路南首德昌裡（中國墾業銀行原址）創建了商務印書館。

「商務」不僅經營印刷業務，且擴而廣至出版領域，以出版中、英文教科書為主要項目，在民智初開的中國土地上，灌溉了一個世紀的文明滋養、影響了跨世紀的文化發展。

眼前的資料，無系統的散亂在桌上，顯得很雜亂，但在場每個人都專注地拾起片段的文字或照片，透過這些從蛛網封塵中重現的時光定格中，穿梭回十九世紀末年的上海灘，再走進商務印書館原始的「小作坊」，尋找一些夏瑞芳在亂世中奮鬥的汗漬足跡！

夏瑞芳在「商務」的角色，相當於今日的 CEO，他廣納賢能之士，共創大業，開中國印刷事業之先河。適逢滿清末年、民國建立、中華民族百廢待興的大時代，他洞察局勢、放眼民族未來，於是和夥伴張元濟、蔡元培等定下商務「從教育著手，改變中國」的方針大計。

一九一四年一月十日，夏瑞芳於公司總發行所門前遭到「暗殺黨」狙擊，中槍後不能言語，緊急送往仁濟醫院，搶救無效，與世長辭，得年四十三歲。

刺殺原因，傳說不一，但最被接受的說法，是民國初創，政局渾沌，軍閥擁兵惡鬥，史稱「二次革命」之際，上海討袁總司令陳其美要當地商家仕紳支持，夏瑞芳自認是在商

不言政，意欲與政爭劃清界線，並請租界巡捕保護商家生命財產，因他在地方上頗具影響力，討袁軍隊主事者為殺雞儆猴，乃暗殺之。

夏瑞芳被刺辭世，距他創立「商務印書館」僅十七年，但他奠定的基礎，讓「商務」雖經歷風風雨雨，仍屹立於上億萬讀者的心中，從不動搖。在兩岸三地「商務」已成為近代中國讀書者的共同回憶！

中國近代的教育改革，是晚清以來各項改革運動中最有成效的；而促進這項改革最有力的，是各種新式教科書的編製和普及；當時全中國編印教科書貢獻最大的，就是「商務印書館」。因此近代有人如此評價：若說，北大是「五四」新文化運動的策源地；那商務印書館就是近代中國文化傳播的搖籃和中心。

夏瑞芳的智慧和遠見，尤其他豁達大度、知人善用、百折不撓的特性，因緣際會，為商務印書館開拓百年基業，深深影響著近代中國的文化教育出版事業，嘉惠後世淵遠流長！

清末民初，一家民營且無鉅資支撐的小印刷廠，能有如此成就，其傲人之處，不單單只是這些「第一」，其深層意義乃在於「昌明教育、開啟民智」，這是為民族播種、為社

會立命的偉大貢獻，立下了近代中國的文明基石。

無論哪個偉大的時代，在當下時空裡，必有許許多多了不起的人物，分別（不約而同的）在各個角落、階層、事業、領域中，發揮其經世才能、產生無比威力、成就長遠影響。有的轟然驚天動地，如成吉思汗、拿破崙、華盛頓、孫中山等屬，有的靜似春雨潤物，如老莊、孔孟、亞里斯多德、居里夫人、達文西、蔡元培等屬，而夏瑞芳可歸類於後者。

如何將這些如此重要卻長久被遺忘的人物，重新拉回到現代人的眼前？這是當天五人會議的討論焦點，其中的主角史濟良正是夏瑞芳的外孫，「我一心掛念的，就是讓我們家族的下一代不要忘了這位祖輩！」史濟良語氣中透著焦慮和沉重！

四位聽者則有著共同感慨：「豈容青史埋荒煙」？於是，五人共識形成：「應該把這位人物重新定位，同時回顧中國近代歷史，讓新一代的年輕人認識、體會乃至瞭解自己的民族國家，尤其是對海外的華裔子弟，更該提供他們瞭解自己母國近代歷史的機會。」

大夥決議，把從二○一二年的曼哈坦穿梭到一八九七年上海灘的冥想，化作文字、排成文章公諸天下，也就是編寫一本有關夏瑞芳的傳記，而且是中英對照，讓海內外懂中文

或不懂中文的西方讀者，都有同樣機會「看到夏瑞芳」。

此書動筆之初，採「意在筆先」的寫作規範，也就是，為文佈局及取材，盡量擴大歷史角度，不厭其詳期能包括近代中西歷史關係，讓年輕讀者瞭解滿清末年至民國建立之初多災多難的歷程，比較今日所處世界，體悟自己的角色位置。

行文筆調，力求輕鬆易懂，在文學性的追求中添加可讀性，以爭取年輕讀者的青睞！

筆者從事新聞工作半生，寫作態度，謹守記者報導原則，力求嚴謹於史實，絕不穿鑿附會、揣測戲說。然而，夏瑞芳留在世上的資料，十分貧乏，因此在豐富傳記的內容上，難度很大，為彌補此一缺口，必須多採集「商務」在當時的歷史、近代史和印刷史的記載。

諸如，《商務印書館九十年》和《商務印書館一百年》、〈商務一一〇年大事記〉、上海地方誌、中國近代史、《The Birth of a Republic》以及方鵬程先生的《飛躍六十・邁向未來──台灣商務印書館六十周年／商務印書館一一〇周年》等文獻、著作，都是我蒐找資料的「葵花寶典」。

本書在二〇一四年中出版，特此紀念夏先生逝世一〇〇周年！

撰稿歷兩年餘，二○一二年秋，愛妻舊疾復發，住院開刀、醫治、後又經半年多的化療，期間，愛妻不斷提醒不能停筆、鼓勵用心寫書，陪伴愛妻或在病房、或化療室，作者不曾停筆（的確拿筆記本，用筆書寫，回家後再上電腦存記）。

藉此書紀念我的最愛，至情至性的妻子石語年！

人生有陰晴圓缺、顛簸坎坷，必須堅強勇敢面對、持健康樂觀的心態，才能撥雲見日、柳暗花明。

特為附記。虔誠祝願世間眾生福壽康寧，得安穩樂！

趙俊邁　謹記　於紐約

前言並致謝

史濟良（夏瑞芳先生嫡外孫）

以恰當的文字來記載報導一件史實，一位人物的經歷，或一種思想見地，都是有相當難度的寫作任務。至於要給家外祖父夏瑞芳先生（商務印書館創辦人）立傳，介紹他老人家在文化、學術和出版上的種種遠見以及對後世不可泯滅的重大影響，更是極為艱鉅的挑戰，而完成本書「典瑞流芳」的著名作家趙俊邁先生以他精湛的文筆，加上仔細深刻的多方研究、考證，竟能將一百多年前家外祖父成家立業的點點滴滴，據實寫了出來，不但真實，而且流暢動人。作者對百餘年前的動盪時代，以及對夏瑞芳先生高超品行與卓越成就，都有精闢的見解與分析，在在顯示出俊邁先生在撰寫傳記寫作上驚人的才華。

我除了感謝趙俊邁先生大力創作這部傳記的貢獻，美國紐約人文學會的三位負責人何勇，汪班二位先生，與周克芸女士，最先認識到夏瑞芳先生的不朽偉業，產生了撰寫這

本傳記的初衷，更邀請到趙俊邁先生執筆，全心致力於這本傳記成書問世，也使我銘感五內。

同時我也要感謝史丹福大學的胡佛研究中心歷史資料部門同意本書印出其珍藏具有歷史性的、一世紀以前上海有關商務印書館與夏瑞芳先生的寶貴照片（由攝影家 F. Stafford 先生拍攝，此組照片是由 Stafford 先生令孫 R. Anderson 教授捐贈於胡佛研究中心。）此外，《東成西就》一書（英文題目為 *East & West*。二〇一二年香港三聯書店出版有限公司出版）雙語作者羅元旭先生在大作中介紹了一些我前所不知、有關夏瑞芳先生的事蹟。羅先生還細述了家父在紐約工作經過，以及上世紀抗日戰爭中，家父在中國西南的工作情況，由於我當時年僅十歲，家父的經歷我拜讀了羅先生的大作才得以知曉。僅此向元旭先生致謝！

此外，我必須深深感謝唐小腴女士，是小腴女士介紹我認識人文學會，小腴女士並向人文學會建議舉辦一場夏瑞芳先生紀念會，從而促使本書撰寫與出版。我也要感謝上海宋路霞女士，讓我能與家外祖父夏瑞芳先生童年故鄉青浦許多前所不識的親戚團聚。

更不能不提的是我的七位夏氏後裔表親，他們給予本傳記成書莫大的贊同，鼓勵與贊

助。還有表兄江成賢先生在成書過程中，給予我多項極寶貴的建議。

我也要誠摯地感謝臺灣商務印書館熱烈支持並同意出版這本傳記，紀念我外祖父夏瑞芳老先生畢生大力創辦商務印書館。我向臺灣商務印書館致敬！

最後，我要將本傳記獻給先慈母。慈母故於二〇〇六年，享百年高壽。慈母在世，對我細述過一些外祖父生平事蹟，並每每曉諭於我：人生在世，愛護家庭，協助家人，是為至要，也是先慈畢生為人準則。母親訓教致使我終身敬愛母親家族的九位長輩，以及與我同輩的八位夏氏後裔表親。春暉慈語，永記於心，是我決定為外祖父立傳的動機。我慶賀本傳記出版，並衷心祝禱慈母與外祖父夏氏家族典瑞長存，流芳百世！

楔子

民初暗殺疑案　涉陳其美蔣介石

民國三年（一九一四年）一月十日下午六點多，上海租界區發生一樁槍擊暗殺事件，引起相當大的震撼，遇害的是商務印書館總經理夏瑞芳，中彈後送醫急救無效，年僅四十三歲與世長辭。

夏瑞芳遇刺，成為民國初年諸多暗殺疑案之一，其出殯喪禮轟動上海灘；而此案涉及的軍政人物，包括陳其美、袁世凱及蔣介石。

夏瑞芳號粹方，為商務印書館創辦人之一，他以特殊的經營長才，將「商務」從家庭作坊式的印刷廠，發展成中國最大的出版企業。一九一四這一年，商務印書館創立已有十七年，可以說，在夏瑞芳的苦心經營及張元濟等夥伴共同努力下，已完全走上健全的軌

道；該館當時除在上海的印刷所、編譯所、發行所外，還在全國各地設立了二十一個分館、四個支館、一個支店，資本達二佰萬元，員工七百五十人。

夏瑞芳造就的事業，不止於「商務」的成功，影響所及，還包括了教育、傳播、文化等方面的貢獻，對中華民國初建的社會文明發展影響巨大，是改變清末民初中國教科書現代化的重要推手！

刺客的黑暗槍聲　震驚上海灘

這不是月黑風高的夜晚，卻是漫天風雨如晦；這不是明火執杖的對陣，卻是背地暗箭傷人；這不是江湖恩仇的因果，卻是黑暗權力陰謀。

結束一天的忙碌，夏瑞芳輕鬆地走出位於上海公共租界區河南路，俗稱棋盤街的商務印書館總發行所門口，接他的馬車已經停在路邊，正等著載主人回家，如往日般與家人團聚，共用溫馨的晚餐；對夏瑞芳而言，這是他繁忙工作後最期待的天倫之樂。

今天拉車的馬匹異於平常的有些焦躁，不停地踢踏著四蹄，還不時仰頭暗暗地深沉地嘶吼，冥冥中似乎露出動物的特殊感應，顯得有些不安和躁動，駕車的小夥子雙手緊拽著

韁繩，雙臂的肌肉如網球似的凸起，他極力控制著馬嚼子：「老闆，今天吾伲的馬，有些搗蛋，不過，不要緊，阿拉管得住」。

年輕車伕叫胡友慶，他用上海腔和正要登車的主人說，話聲未落，突然從對街闖出一蒙面漢直奔而來，手中持著一把烏漾漾的手槍，還沒看清怎麼回事，槍口已對著夏瑞芳噴出火舌，車旁的夏瑞芳猝不及防，臉孔扭曲成一團，雙手搗著胸口，掌指間汩汩冒出腥紅的鮮血，他中彈了。夏瑞芳忍痛想奔回公司大門，他血流如注、步履踉蹌，沒兩步，就頹然倒下！

寧靜的黃昏，轟然的槍聲，驚起路樹上剛歸巢的鴉雀，呼拉呼拉振翅四下紛亂飛去，槍聲也驚動了「商務」的員工，眾人奔到大門外探看究竟，赫然看到倒在血泊中的夏總經理。

夏瑞芳掙扎著想爬起來，但體氣已虛，力不從心了。

商務印書館的員工們忙成一團，有人急忙打電話給醫院，有人扶起血泊中的夏瑞芳，他努力的堅持最後的生命，虛弱的眼神看到自己的員工，心知自己不行了，想對他們交代幾句話，可是嘴唇困難的動了動，一點聲音也沒發出來！

司閽的老工友趕緊調用車輛將夏總送往仁濟醫院，這所離商務發行所最近，也是最權威的、唯一的西醫醫院，位於英租界西邊的麥家圈。

傷者一送到，醫院的醫師和護士立刻展開急救。

另外一批員工分頭走告夏的家人，公司重要負責人，如張元濟、鮑氏家族、高夢旦等人。

鮑、高、張等人紛紛急忙趕往醫院探視；遺憾的是，當眾人抵達醫院的時候，夏瑞芳已然在愛妻的哀傷中與世長辭！一代出版界巨人，敵不過邪惡的子彈，成為民國初年政治暗殺的犧牲者！

小車伕奮不顧身　忠勇追兇

當員工搶救夏先生的同時，十五六歲的馬車伕奮力「唊」的一聲，手中皮鞭狠抽在馬屁股上，唰的！馬車奔出追趕打黑槍的兇手。

兇手往南邊逃竄，馬車伕追兇，一路叫喊「抓兇手」……，馬匹怒奔、車駕飛騰，衝撞如飛矢，路人見狀，早嚇得四處走避，追到群賢社門口，兇手跑得已精疲力竭，於是向

空中放了兩槍，企圖嚇阻緊追不捨的來人，槍響的當兒，車伕已然趕到，俐落的飛躍下了車轅，揉身撲向兇手，兩人頓時扭打一處，打不過青壯的小胡，兇手惡向膽邊生，一不作二不休，舉起槍朝著對方腦袋扣下板機，小胡心感不妙，抬手推開兇手的腕子，千鈞一髮的偏頭急閃，子彈貼著小胡的耳後飛過，擦破毛皮，鮮血直流，染紅了他的面頰和頸子；兇手顧不得是否打中了對方，轉身又逃，但見一臉是血的小車伕，如影隨形的緊追了上來，被驚動的巡捕，老遠就吹著刺耳的哨子，可是因為跑的上氣不接下氣，哨音是斷斷續續，一搭沒一搭的籲嘘著。

廣東路（當地人也叫五馬路）口有一崗哨，那天站崗的是編號五一一的華人巡捕，槍聲讓他警覺出了大事兒，緊接著看到兩個人一前一後朝他的崗哨方向奔來，前面的一個手上還拎著一把槍，五一一看的真切，貓下身子藏在哨棚子後側，待槍手氣喘如牛的跑到近前，他虎的一下竄出，雙手牢牢環抱住對方的腰，兇手大驚，發現抓他的是個巡捕，趕緊把手中的兇器往道旁一扔，想撇清自己；沒料到身後的小車伕正好趕到，彎腰撿起路邊的那把槍，他憤怒已極、怒不可遏，情緒失控下開槍就打，一個隨之趕來的洋巡捕差點中彈，氣急敗壞的，以為兩人是同黨，就把他們一塊逮捕，送進巡捕房的牢裡。

後來查明了真相，兇手僅一人，名叫王慶瑞，將他留在租界受審；商務則派人將護主追兇的小胡保了出來。

案發第二天，上海灘所有報紙的頭條，都是報導這則新聞，報眉出版日期印著「中華民國三年一月十一日星期日」的上海「申報」，其「本埠新聞」版的頭條大標題是：棋盤街又出暗殺案，旁註三個小標：

- 商務書館經理被害
- 小馬伕拼命窮追
- 巡捕抱住行兇人。

找幕後黑手　底深不可測

如此大案，震驚整個上海灘，夏瑞芳的喪禮極為隆重，商務印書館特編印一套厚厚的線裝哀輓錄，內有祭文，追悼文、輓聯、帳子，外地唁電等，其中國學大師章太炎（炳麟）的輓聯是：

尋竅有殊功，不使精神隨物禍；捐軀付公論，獨留肝膽照人寰。

出殯當日，沿途數千人自動自發為他送行，場面哀傷感人。

蔡元培特為夏瑞芳立傳，文中有：

「君信仰基督教，內行甚修，接人甚和易，宜若可以盡其天年，而卒被暗殺，倘所謂天道無知者邪？君雖歿，而君所創設之事業，方興未艾，其於教育之影響，則輾轉流布而不能窮其所屆，雖謂君永久不死可也。」

董事會決定為夏瑞芳塑造一座銅像，為後來者追思紀念，但被未亡人鮑翠玉婉辭了，翠玉反而勸鮑咸昌等自家兄弟和張元濟、高夢旦等老友：「吾儕把這錢省下來，送給學校、幼稚園、孤兒院豈不好哉？這是瑞芳生前熱心的事體呀！」

翠玉和瑞芳鶼鰈情深，生有一子，單名鵬，女兒八人。幾經思慮再與眾親友討論之後，翠玉最後決定在先夫貧困的家鄉清浦建一所學校來紀念他，於是有了「夏氏小學」。

在夏瑞芳遭暗殺後，親友義憤填膺，想找出幕後黑手，但當時軍閥橫行、肆無忌憚，

尤其暗殺行為，讓一般百姓嚇得噤若寒蟬，敢怒不敢言，兇手王慶瑞在租界受審時供稱，有人以巨資僱他行兇，審問過程中，發現案情背景複雜，謎樣根柢深不可測；因而兇手遭槍決後，商務方面也不敢追究幕後主使人，此案就此不了了之。

夏瑞芳招禍的原因，當時流傳多種版本，後來，可以從《張元濟年譜》中找到較為真實的答案：

「乃因先前出於維護商界利益，曾聯合諸商抵制滬軍都督陳其美駐兵閘北，陳嫉恨之，嗾使人暗殺。」

另一個曾在商務工作多年的胡愈之說，主使暗殺夏瑞芳的是當時滬軍都督陳英士。

曾任清朝湖南布政使、寓居上海的前清遺老鄭孝胥，也在商務印書館工作過，他的日記中說：

「夏遇刺前已接到警告書，此即黨人復閘北搜扣軍火之仇也」。

閘北一詞，源於蘇州河上的兩座水閘。康熙年間建老閘，雍正十三年在老閘西面又建

一新聞。老閘和新閘周圍形成了兩個市集，聚集了些買賣人氣，至上海開埠以後，新閘、老閘北面急速發展，開始出現「閘北」之名。

一八九九年公共租界不斷擴張，閘北地區東面已與租界毗連，西面和南面與租界也僅隔一條蘇州河。閘北道路縱橫，人口稠密，其繁華堪比租界，工商業和文化事業也漸漸興起。

一九○四年，商務印書館在閘北寶山路購地三百畝開設總廠，廠方還在印書館附近建造東寶興里、西寶興里等住宅群，租給本廠職工和遷往閘北的移民居住。

一九三二年，一二八淞滬戰役中，閘北遭日軍攻擊，受到重創，商務印書館盡被焚燬。

順帶，值得一提的：一九三七年，抗日戰爭時，名傳千古的謝晉元八百壯士死守的四行倉庫，就在閘北。

二次革命護商務　惹閘北恩仇

「閘北搜扣軍火之仇」的主角有陳其美、袁世凱、蔣介石。

起因是一九一三年「二次革命」時，夏瑞芳為了保護閘北寶山路的商務印書館，與陳其美結下恩仇。

這個事件，發生於中國近代史上的「二次革命」期間，也就是俗稱的「討袁之役」，辛亥革命民國建立後，中華大地上滿目瘡痍，各地武裝勢力趁機坐大，漫天陰霾籠罩大江南北的上空，爭權奪利的烽火大有一觸即發之勢。

曾在小站練兵的袁世凱，武昌起義後，再度出山任清朝國務總理大臣，與革命軍討價還價，在南北議和後，又開始與孫中山爭著當大總統。（他後來搞帝制當了幾天皇帝，最後在全國百姓唾罵聲中嗚呼哀哉！）

袁世凱與革命軍對抗中，一方面以爭取外國的支援及國內部分軍閥的保持中立為手段，另一方面集結軍隊和革命軍展開爭戰。中山先生為使南北早日統一，避免國民再遭塗炭，一九一二年，民國元年二月將臨時大總統寶座讓給了袁世凱。

第二年（一九一三年）三月二十日發生了宋教仁被刺身亡的政爭巨案，埋下國民革命軍征討北洋軍的導火線。

宋教仁是國民黨代理事長，他主張責任內閣制，並到處演講宣揚將總統改為沒有實權

的虛位領袖，這使得大總統袁世凱很不痛快。

二十日當天，宋教仁在上海火車站搭車北上時，遭到刺客槍擊，送醫院急救無效，於二十二日凌晨去世，年僅三十二歲。袁世凱被認為是暗殺的陰謀者，而他本人並未承認。

當時孫中山在日本考察，聽到消息火速回國，一到上海就召集黃興、陳其美等親信開會，主張以武力討伐袁世凱，但因黨內意見不同，未果。沒多久袁世凱勢力養成，把廣東胡漢民、江西李烈鈞、安徽柏文蔚等中國國民黨三個都督予以免職。此時孫中山忍無可忍，認為再不採取積極行動，袁世凱就要滅黨了，於是命令李烈鈞起兵討伐，這就是歷史上所稱的「二次革命」。

李烈鈞舉兵後，黃興在南京、陳其美在上海、譚延闓在湖南也起義討袁；而許多小說和影視劇中，與義妓小鳳仙譜出千古浪漫戀曲的蔡鍔（松坡）都督，當時在雲南是保持中立的，那會兒，他還沒遇上小鳳仙呢。直到一九一五年末，袁世凱要當皇帝了，蔡鍔才從小鳳仙的溫柔鄉裡驚醒，冒著危險逃出袁世凱監禁，從北京輾轉回到雲南，發動護國起義。

一九一三年，民國二年七月十八日，陳其美宣佈上海獨立，任命黃興為上海討袁軍總

司令。

陳其美召小弟蔣志清來滬組織敢死隊，蔣志清就是後來的蔣介石，當時他還只是個二十六歲的小夥子。他於一九一八年改名中正，字介石。

蔣介石是陳其美門下，二人關係密切，早在辛亥革命期間，上海光復，陳其美用商團的捐款組成滬軍第五團，任命蔣為團長，隸屬黃郛的第二師。陳、黃、蔣三人是換帖拜把的兄弟，陳是大哥，蔣最年少。

陳其美，字英士，浙江吳興人，民國初年政治風雲人物；一九○六年赴日本入警監學校，同年加入同盟會，辛亥革命初期為孫中山的股肱。曾為滬軍都督，時任上海討袁軍總司令。

上海討袁戰略佈署，一開始就計畫對據守在江南製造局的北洋軍立刻採取行動。攻打江南製造局的計畫，是蔣介石提出的，他向陳其美建言：「佔領製造局，是上海討袁之戰的成敗關鍵」，因為是中國少數的大兵工廠之一。江南製造局是李鴻章於一八六五年創建，為當時清廷強國強軍仿效洋務下的產物，專門製造洋槍洋砲。

一九一三年七月二十三日，蔣介石展開第一波對江南製造局的攻勢，該地既為兵家重

022

地，袁世凱當然派重兵把守，討袁軍久攻不克，退下陣來。

隨後，蔣介石為招兵源，隻身赴龍華北洋軍營，策反陸軍九十三團，該團正是蔣曾經帶過的滬軍第五團，於是全團起義，蔣遂率舊部第二次進攻製造局，這時陳其美等討袁軍也發動攻擊，頓時江南製造局陷入槍林彈雨之中，雙方激戰兩日，最終蔣、陳因兵力不足，寡不敵眾，只得再度撤兵。軍隊退到吳淞、寶山。

激烈的戰事讓上海商界備感驚恐，於是聯合組織了「上海保衛團」，希望維持當地治安和平、弭止戰禍。上海總商會特致函雙方，反對兩軍把上海當戰場，函中說：「上海係中國商場，既非戰地；製造局係民國公共之產，無南北爭持之必要。無論何方先啟釁端，是與人民為敵，人民即視為敵黨。」

這封反戰公函，反映了社會群眾的態度，如果進攻製造局，則視為公敵；客觀環境對陳其美的討袁軍事行動，極為不利。

二十四日，上海討袁軍司令部遷入閘北；而商務印書館總部及編譯所、工廠、宿舍都集中在閘北的寶山路一帶，一旦戰事爆發，該印書館難逃兵火之災。

夏瑞芳十分擔心自己和夥伴們辛勤創建的基業，因為軍閥的鬥爭，而毀於烽火之中，

在他心中，堅定地的相信：商務印書館可以為自己的民族國家作出更多、更大的貢獻，於是他毅然的與吳小敬等十七名商界領袖開會決議，要求租界「工部局」保護大家的生命財產，請租界的萬國商團到閘北出入口佈防。

「工部局」是什麼機構？它創始於一八五四年，時英美租界合併為「公共租界」（International Settlement）。七月十一日，英駐上海領事主持召開租地者會議（Land Renters' Meeting），決議成立管理租界公共事務的機構，稱為「工部局」，可以說是公共租界最高行政機構，下轄道路、碼頭和警務委員會（Roads、Jetties and Police Sub Committee），設置巡捕房（Police Station）。

果真，工部局就加強了閘北地面秩序的維護。反袁的部隊不能到閘北，這無疑給陳其美多上了一條緊箍咒。

英租界當局為什麼暗中阻擋革命軍討袁？原因很簡單，野心之所致也！利之所趨也！袁世凱當上大總統之後，就開始向列國大量借錢，英、法、德、美、日、俄對清朝的鯨吞掠奪之後，又對急需政府大量開支的初建民國更是食髓知味了，他們利用銀行給予北京政府巨額貸款，接著就可獅子大開口的要脅這個新政府。

而其中的英國有一個信念：統一的中央集權的中國，會在貿易上迎合英國的需要，並能保護在中國的利益。因此，在華的英國外交官、銀行家以及英租界都傾向支持袁世凱。

也因此，在廣袤中國土地上的小小上海租界區一隅，衍生出夏瑞芳與革命軍的恩怨情仇！

同月二十七日清晨，租界工部局接受中國商民要求保護的請求，對外以：「中國商民夏瑞芳等人要求保護生命財產」為由展開行動，根據上海地方誌記載：

「七月二十七日晨，工部局派遣公共租界的英國籍總巡捕卜羅斯帶馬隊三十餘人、美國商團兵馬一百五十人，攜帶機關炮六尊，開入閘北，驅散討袁軍士兵二○七名，並至市政廳駐防。」

陳其美當時在吳淞，駐守「南海會館」司令部的是蔣介石，其所率團部二○七人均遭英巡捕繳械驅逐。當時租界的巡捕是代表租界國的警務人員，不但具有執行警政公務合法性，而且絕對有強大公權力的威懾性！這就是反袁軍雖然武力裝備更強大，卻不願與之衝突，默默退出閘北的重要原因。

跡。

二十八日，工部局再派中西巡捕到閘北各區偵緝，直到證實其境內沒有討袁軍的蹤跡。

二十九日又派公共巡捕房數名印度阿三駐守寶山路商務印刷所。

由此可見，夏瑞芳與「租界當局」的關係，並非一般。

夏瑞芳之所以成為陳其美的眼中釘、欲去之而後快，顯然是有跡可尋的。

另有蔣介石刺殺陳其美政敵陶成章的歷史公案在前，準此，不難梳理出一些頭緒，窺得夏瑞芳之冤死，實與當時肆無忌憚的鐵血暗殺風氣有著千絲萬縷的糾葛；對夏招禍疑雲的爬梳探究，此上述論應該是比較接近真實的答案。

一九一六年五月十八日，陳其美則被袁世凱派人暗殺。世事無常若此，是天理因果循環？還是歷史輪迴的弔詭？

那是什麼樣的時代？讓人想到，文豪狄更斯以法國大革命背景所寫《雙城記》的卷首語：

「那是最好的時代，也是最壞的時代；是智慧的時代，也是愚蠢的時代；是光明的季

026

節，也是黑暗的季節；是充滿希望的春天，也是令人絕望的冬天；我們的前途擁有一切，我們的前途一無所有；我們正走向天堂，我們也走向地獄⋯⋯」

夏瑞芳在民國初年，政治鬥爭最黑暗的局勢下，一介文化商人也難逃暗殺厄運，風華正茂的生命，遽然辭世，艱困而輝煌的一生，有如天際飛過的流星，璀璨而短暫！

或許，因他逝世太早，同時沒有政治後台，既非國民黨也不是共產黨，乃至，中國近代史對商務的記載，台灣百姓只知王雲五、大陸官方則僅識張元濟；夏瑞芳顯然被忽視，甚至被遺忘了！

外一章

二十一世紀賈伯斯與十九世紀夏瑞芳

「賈伯斯唯一正式授權傳記──《賈伯斯傳》 *Steve Jobs: A Biography* 現已有售。締造蘋果傳奇的靈魂人物賈伯斯（Steve Jobs），於二〇一一年十月五日因病逝世，享年五十六歲。

賈伯斯生於一九五五年的美國舊金山，其後就讀俄勒岡州波特蘭的里德學院，但一個學期便退學。二十歲時與友人在車庫裡製造了首台個人電腦 Apple 1，一年後更成立蘋果公司，業務迅速拓展。一九八四年，首台麥金塔（Macintosh）電腦正式推出。一九八五年，賈伯斯因高層角力而被迫離開蘋果，後自立門戶，成立 NeXT 公司。

一九九七年，蘋果收購 NeXT，他回到蘋果接任執行長，並決心改革蘋果電腦，陸續推

出各種改變世界的產品——iTunes、iPod、iPhone、iPad 等。二〇〇四年，賈伯斯被診斷出

患胰臟癌，二〇一一年八月宣佈辭去蘋果執行長職務，同年十月五日去世。」

以上，是一則推介新書的廣告文字，是二〇一二年初，在「商務網上書店」新書推薦

的網頁內容。這則廣告的主角賈伯斯，是當代全球最受矚目的人物，他的貢獻改變了一個

時代。

「商務網上書店」，就字面上看來，似乎是一個商業服務，利用電子媒體推銷書刊的

網站。實際上，這是香港「商務印書館」的網站。

在華人世界裡凡喜歡閱讀的人，沒有不認識「商務印書館」的，隨著電腦時代的來

臨，該書局也與時俱進的進入了網站世界。

Cp1897.com 就是商務印書館網上書店的網址，Cp即其英文名號「Commercial Press」

的縮寫，而一八九七標示該印書館於一八九七年在上海成立。

且讓我們來看看北京的 Cp1897.com 是如何自我介紹的⋯

商務印書館是中國歷史最悠久的現代出版機構，在近代中國文化教育出版史上具有深

遠的影響。商務印書館的創立，標誌著中國現代出版事業的肇始。今天，走過一百二十一年歷史的商務印書館，秉承與時俱進的傳統，致力於資訊時代的文化教育事業，建設基於紙質和數碼媒介的新型出版，日新無已，正步入多元化發展的新境地。

台灣的商務印書館網站上，是這樣說明的：

華文出版砥柱，再現百年風華，萬種優質好書，盡在臺灣商務。臺灣商務印書館為台灣出版界重要的老字號出版社之一，業已出版萬種好書，並陸續推出新系列叢書。

重慶南路為臺北最知名、歷史最悠久的書街，而成立於一九四七年的臺灣商務印書館，更是許多老讀者的共同回憶。走過一甲子，至今已出版超過萬種書籍，隨手翻閱都是有口皆碑的經典之作。

香港商務印書館網站則如此自述：

商務印書館（香港）有限公司是一家新形態的綜合性出版企業，致力於文化教育事業發展，因應資訊時代發展的新路向，傳統的出版、發行、門市業務與多媒體載體、國際

網絡日益融合，並藉電腦技術的開發利用，形成跨地域、跨承載媒體的出版營銷的多元形態。

從以上兩岸三地「商務印書館」的自述，可以看到「商務印書館」是中國第一家現代出版機構，是近代中國文化傳播重鎮。它灌溉了中國一個世紀的文明，滋養、影響了跨世紀的文化發展。

「蘋果」帶給二十一世紀人類生活新境界，「商務印書館」則照亮了二十世紀初華人的生命，其文明光芒至今仍閃耀著，超過一個世紀的歷史。

夏瑞芳──本書的主角，正是給予「商務印書館」生命的人！

夏瑞芳在「商務」的角色，相當於今日的 CEO；他從學徒出身，創業後被推任為總經理，以今天企業界領導層觀之，「商務」的這位大掌櫃，其負責的業務，除財務盈虧、品質管控，還有市場調查、產品推廣、營運決策等等，無異於今日企業單位的首席執行官（Chief Executive Officer, CEO）的職務：對企業負有重大決策的反應和執行力。

他的一生雖短暫，但璀璨輝煌！

且讓我們走進清末民初的時光隧道，探尋這位一代ＣＥＯ的傳奇。

外一章

第一章 寂寂無聞的文化推手

夏瑞芳（一八七一—一九一四），這個名字在中國近代史上可說是默默無聞的，但他對我們民族、國家的現代化發展，卻是一位偉大的幕後推手；他創辦了中國第一個現代印刷廠「商務印書館」，他不但具有經營之才，更難得的是胸懷濟世之大志，他與編輯團隊張元濟等共同立下「吾輩當以扶助教育為己任」為商務出版方針，抱持「從教育著手，改變中國，變法圖強」的壯闊胸懷。

「商務」致力出版教課書、英文學習課本，開創新學廣為傳播的先例，同時為改進品質，引進最新印刷機具和技術。

「商務」印刷的不是死板板的文字，而是中國數萬萬百姓性靈饑渴需求的知識！「商務」出版的不是硬梆梆的書冊，而是衰老腐敗民族脫胎換骨時吸吮的新文明！在當時清末民初，百廢待舉的時代，夏瑞芳等人有如此高瞻遠矚的觀念，實屬橫空出

世的經緯俊傑。

話說從頭故事開始

這是上海的一所教會學校，名叫「清心書院」，從名稱上看，很有中國氣息，然而卻是一位美國長老會牧師所創辦的。

時值滿清王朝末年，也正是西方勢力東漸最熾烈的年代，一向被滿清王朝輕視的西夷番邦，居然從千萬里之外，耀武揚威的帶給中國人除了洋槍洋砲威嚇、掠奪的恥辱之外，也帶來了西方的文明和教化，對衰敗的東方古國人民的震撼，不只是肉體與精神上的痛楚刺激，還有更深的心靈上的自卑與新奇。

與此同時，因為宗教的傳佈，這些陌生的國度也送來許多神父和牧師。

「清心書院」有一學生名叫夏瑞芳，是個從鄉下來的苦孩子。

在一個西方教學方式的教會學校裡所見所聞，對一個十多歲、從上海郊區青浦來的窮人家小孩來說，或許談不上有「震驚」或「震撼」的強烈感受，但他深深被西洋人的知識、文明所吸引，尤其是學堂上用的課書本子，不但紙張白白的，「刻」的字也清清楚楚

的，驚奇的是，聽說這些課書本子是從外國漂洋過海運來的。在夏瑞芳稚嫩純樸的小心靈裡，驚嘆著這種無遠弗屆的教學課本，是怎麼「做」出來的，他百思不得其解！

小囝偷偷過江　上海灘尋母

夏瑞芳是一八七一年出生在青浦縣沈巷鄉南庫村的一個貧苦人家，父親是挑糖擔子的小販，只能賺一點小孩兒們的零碎錢，根本養活不了一個家；不得已的情況下，母親離開他們，到上海給人幫傭，賺錢養家。

瑞芳的家鄉青浦，位於上海西郊的一個村鎮，地處長江三角洲太湖平原東側，東與上海縣為鄰。因東北邊有青龍鎮，東有五浦（趙屯、大盈、顧會、盤龍、崧子）匯於吳崧江，故名青浦。當地氣候溫和，土地肥沃，民風純樸。

夏家世代務農，到了瑞芳父親這一代，因為戰亂凋敝，加上年成不好，種田的人家，很多放棄耕作，另謀其他營生餬口，其父原先挑擔賣糖，後來也離開家鄉到上海董家渡開了一家小店，買賣一些雜貨。

父母都出外打工，小瑞芳留在青浦老家，無依無靠，就寄養大伯家，年紀小又沒甚麼

氣力，他只能幫著放牛。

日子一長，孩子想母親了，他暗暗下定決心，要到上海找媽媽。

十一歲那年，一八八二年夏天的一個中午，日頭正炙熱的曬在田野上，瑞芳穿了條短褲，帶個斗笠，兩手空空，瞞著伯父，打算偷偷過江到上海灘尋親。

南庫村村後，是個小河口，村民叫那兒是河港，港口有個婦人撐船擺渡。

那天，瑞芳氣喘吁吁的奔到河口，看到擺渡的婦人，要求載他過江，擺渡婦見一小囝，沒大人跟著，心裡不踏實，就沒答應；沒料到，小瑞芳人小氣壯，居然下到河裡，嚷嚷著「你不渡阿拉，阿拉就游水過去！」

小囝想游水過河，可是很危險的，搖櫓的婦人趕緊喝止：「會淹死人的喲！儂弗要嚇煞吾啦！快上船來，吾送儂渡河去！」鄉下人心地是質樸善良的。

河對岸就是水陸交通要衝的朱家角，這個鎮埠地處江、浙、滬交界，是青浦、昆山、松江、吳江、嘉善等地的中心，水運四通八達，橫有澱浦河，縱有朱泖河直通黃浦江。小瑞芳就在這個人潮熙攘的大碼頭上，混在人群中登上一艘班船；初始他還以為會跟搭擺渡一樣，眨眼功夫可到彼岸，殊不知，天高水長，此船要在江上航行兩天才能到上海灘。那

個年代的小輪船，動力有限，航行速度其實是很緩慢的。

離家出走，第一次坐上這麼大的輪船，看到一望無際的大江大海，瑞芳心裡的激盪多於驚恐，雖然童稚的心靈只是單純一念去找媽媽，但他也意識到，他不會再回去做牧牛娃了。

兩手空空，身無分文，躲在船上一隅的小瑞芳獨自坐著，沒吃沒喝、不聲不響。旁邊的乘客覺得有異，有人反應給船上工作人員；船員過來向他問話，他怯怯懦懦的一五一十都照實說了。

「原來是夏家的小囝，你姆媽每次回鄉下看儂，都坐我們的船，算是常客啦！」船家的好心相認，不但給他吃的喝的，到岸下船，還找人帶他去媽媽幫傭的地方。

小瑞芳終於和母親團聚了，媽媽緊緊的抱著他，母子二人相擁而泣，久久不能自已！

夏阿孃抱著從鄉下投奔來的囝囝，母子相會哭成一團的景象，感動了這家主人范約翰牧師（John Marshall Willoughby Farnham, 1823-1917）。這位范牧師，改變了夏瑞芳的一生！

後來，媽媽和瑞芳都認為，這都是耶穌基督的保佑，否則，在車水馬龍、繁華擁擠的

偌大上海灘市面上，他一個十一歲的囝囝早就被吞沒掉了！

那年，清光緒八年時候的上海已經開始洋化了。

街面上，來來往往，可以看到許多穿著西服，剪著短髮的洋紳士，也有穿著圓蓬蓬長裙子、金髮碧眼的西方女士，他們之所以堂而皇之、趾高氣昂的出現在上海灘上，是因為「南京條約」簽定讓西方國家可以自由使用中國的五個港口，上海就是其中之一，這即是歷史上的「鴉片戰爭」的結果。

當時的清朝，國力衰微、政府昏庸，英國在中國公然大肆販賣鴉片，老百姓大受其害，一八三九年，道光十九年欽差大臣林則徐在廣東虎門銷毀鴉片煙，引發「鴉片戰爭」，一八四二年八月清廷戰敗，簽署了「南京條約」，這是近代中國的第一個不平等條約。

根據中、英簽定的條約，滿清政府將五個沿海城市──廣州、廈門、福州、寧波和上海關為通商口岸。在英國之後美國、法國等也見獵心喜，跟著強迫清廷，訂立「望廈條約」和「黃埔條約」，奪取同樣的權利。賠款外還割讓土地，香港就是那時候割讓給英國的。

上海就是受五口通商之賜，社會、人文、風尚各方面，都漸趨西化。

太平天國戰亂　誕生清心書院

范約翰（John Marshall Willoughby Farnham）是長老會派到中國的傳教士，他的家鄉在美國緬因州。一八六〇年，清咸豐十年的初春三月，約翰和妻子瑪利（Mary Jane）到達上海；可惜初到中國，他們沒有看到「百般紅紫鬥芳菲」的早春繁華，卻見「春風寂寞搖空枝」的凋零淒清，因當時正逢太平天國戰亂。

洪秀全在江南搞革命，佔有長江中下游數省，清廷以曾國藩、李鴻章為帥，組湘軍、淮軍征討，自一八五一年洪秀全金田起義至一八六四年太平天國首都天京陷落，兵災戰禍長達十四年。

一八六〇那年，太平天國戰亂鬧得正兇，由江南逃出來的難民，很多湧入了上海；剛從美國來的范約翰看到這種情況，於是發揮神愛世人的基督精神，就在大南門外陸家浜（今陸家浜路五九七號）創辦學校，收容這些流離失學的難民小孩，命名為「清心學堂」（Lowrie School）。一八八〇年更名為「清心書院」。

范約翰原先於清咸豐十年（一八六〇年）成立「上海長老會第一會堂」，開辦書院後，該堂做禮拜就在書院內。

當時，清心書院的師生都在那兒做禮拜，不論求知學習或宗教修行都需「清淨其心」，所以該書院和教堂都取名曰「清心」。

一九一九年教堂從學校遷出，在附近的大佛廠街（今大昌街三十號）另造一所「清心堂」。

至今當年的清心書院，現在的上海市市南中學內，還有那棟上海第一長老會教堂。這所學校培養出來的名人，先後有夏瑞芳、黃楚九、郭秉文、董顯光、李政道等。

「清心學堂」創辦第二年，因收容學生越來越多，於是進而分備女子學堂。一八六一年，范約翰的妻子瑪莉就創辦了「清心女塾」（the Mary Farnham Girls' School），這是中國教育史上最早的女校之一。一九一八年易名「清心女子中學」，一九五三年改為上海「市第八女中」，一九六九年起兼收男生，遂又更名「市第八中學」。

當時的清心堂，由范約翰兼任堂牧和書院院長。堂牧不忍拆散這對母子，他收留了這鄉下囝。

在當時的社會風氣，一般不准傭人攜帶孩子同住在僱主家中的，范約翰是主耶穌的侍從，本著神愛世人的精神，他打破了一般民間的舊習，同時收容了傭人母子；因此，可以說夏瑞芳是非常幸運的，他隨著母親在上海住了下來，母子二人相依為命。

小瑞芳在鄉下本就養成太陽露頭就起床幹活的習慣，在范牧師家，他一樣早早起床，甚至比媽媽還起得早；他往往自己會找活幹，經常把宅中院子灑掃乾淨、為牧師娘養的花木澆澆水。

「這男孩挺機靈的，老做些雜役，會不會埋沒了？」牧師娘對約翰說。

「孩子年齡該上學了，讓他進咱們的學堂吧！」約翰牧師做的決定，進一步改變了夏瑞芳的命運！

鮑氏家族關係　姻親影響一生

五光十色、洋場十里的大上海，在那兒上演的不僅是「大世界」裡的歌聲舞影，市面上活躍的也不都是追逐紅塵俗媚的白相人，老上海深層純樸堅實的底蘊下，還有許多像夏瑞芳一樣孜孜矻矻勤懇奮鬥向上的年輕人。

「清心書院」裡，夏瑞芳跟著遠從西方來的老師，學習到新的洋知識，不但學會英文，而且開闊了世界性的視野和心胸。

年少的學子，少不了結交一些談得來的同窗好友，夏瑞芳就有幾個好同伴，其中鮑咸恩、咸昌兄弟和高鳳池等人特別投緣，他們的結交，爾後，卻為中國的印刷出版事業，創建了一個開天闢地的宏大局面。

這幾人後來就是「商務印書館」的創業者，都是出自清心書院，也可以說都是受過洋學教育的基督教徒，而且這個組成與中國傳統的家族事業一樣，同樣有著世交、兄弟、姻親等千絲萬縷的關係。

夏瑞芳和鮑咸恩昆仲不但是好友，後來又娶了他們的妹妹翠玉，關係更是深厚密切了。

鮑氏，當時在江浙沿海一帶接受洋教的華人圈中，算得上是個大家族；他們的大家長是鮑哲才，字華甫，浙江寧波觀縣人，清朝道光十三年（一八三三）生，家中排行老大，有三個弟弟。

寧波和上海同是南京條約中，清廷開放外國五口通商的五口之一；一八四四年開埠，

隨之歐美許多國家的宗教團體開始進入，其中有美國長老教會也在當地開展傳教版圖，建

了教堂、醫院，並成立學校「崇信義塾」（Ningpo Boy's Boarding School），該所學校稱

為「義塾」，顧名思義，凡進入該校的學生，書本、膳食、住宿費用全免，他們靠著美國

的富裕經費支持，吸引華人子弟到校就讀，藉此傳播、教育其宗教思想。

鮑哲才那時剛十多歲，很自然的就成為「崇信義塾」的早期學生，畢業後也很自然的

選擇了牧師作為職業，乃種下日後到上海清心堂當牧師的因緣。

長老會於一八四四年曾在澳門開設一家小印刷廠，專門印製翻譯成中文的聖經，名稱

「花華聖經書房」（Chinese and American Holy Book Establishment），是取花旗與華文

聖經印刷房的簡稱。後來，因寧波開了口岸，長老會就把這家印刷廠搬到這個內地城市。

一八五八年，鮑哲才自「崇信」畢業後，就到這個廠子做排字工人。那時印刷廠廠長

是來自紐約專業印聖經的牧師威廉甘伯（William Gamble）。

一八六二年威廉甘伯帶著鮑哲才等幾名技工將書館搬到上海，並建了廠房，且將「花

華聖經書房」改名為「美華書館」（American Presbyterian Mission Press）。這所「美華

書館」後來成為「商務印書館」的搖籃。

第一章　寂寂無聞的文化推手

鮑哲才，這位鮑氏家長，可以說是商務一族中接觸印刷出版事務的第一人。似乎，這一切，冥冥之中老天早有安排，後來他的兒子咸恩、咸昌和女婿夏瑞芳，也受他影響，和他走了相同的事業道路。

傳教士的禮物　上海灘新式印書房

十九世紀晚期上海灘上，除了「美華書館」之外，前前後後，類似的印刷廠，如雨後春筍般紛紛冒出。據美國傳教士辦的「中國文庫」（Chinese Repository）雜誌記載，一八三二年，一位來自英國倫敦會傳教士麥都思（W.H. Medhurst）在廣州設立了「石印所」，開風氣之先，引進石版印刷術在中國境內印刷中文書籍。

根據記載：石版印刷是以石板為版材，將圖畫文字轉印於石版之上，進行印刷的工藝技術，在當時中國印刷術是使用傳統的鉛活字版，石版印刷較之鉛字雕版印刷有著明顯的優勢：這種早期的石印技術由西方傳教士於一八三二年間帶入中國，開始在中國印刷佈道小冊子或其它簡單印件。

一八四三年，麥都思又在上海開設了近代印刷史上著名的「墨海書館」，採用石版印

刷術印刷了《耶穌降世傳》、《馬太傳福音注》等書籍。書館座落在江海北關附近的麥家圈（今天福州路和廣東路之間的山東中路西側）的倫敦會總部。這是上海最早的一個現代出版社，為上海最早採用西式漢文鉛印活字印刷術的印刷機構。

當時鉛印印刷機是鐵製的，沒有電力或其他能源，就以中國傳統動力，用牛車在室外運轉，傳動帶通過牆縫延伸到機房，推動印刷機。

一八七六年（光緒二年），徐家匯出現一家「土山灣印刷所」，採用石版印刷書籍，專門印刷天主教宣教品。

一八七七年，英國商人美查又開設「點石齋印書局」，購進了手搖石印機，印刷《聖論詳解》、《康熙字典》等書籍。

這些傳教士經營的印刷廠，原先主要是出版一些為輔助傳教的書本冊子，然而間接又扮演了引介西學和漢學文化交流的角色，並且還是中文印刷從傳統木刻轉變成西式活字過程中的重要機構。

清朝時期，上海的出版機構大致有：掃葉山房、墨海書館、美華書館、土山灣印書館、點石齋書局、江南製造局翻譯館、同文書局、千頃堂書局、圖書集成局、廣學會、商

務印書館、南洋公學譯書院、廣智書局、廣益書局、神州國光社、文明書局、小說林社等。

在這個中國從傳統古老的時代邁進現代化的時間點上，鮑哲才正巧走在印刷術變革的巨輪之上，因緣際會的為後來的「商務印書館」奠下了基石。

鮑哲才一八九五年一月二十七日病逝，終年六十二歲，離他的子婿創立商務僅兩年。鮑氏育有三子三女，都在清心書院就讀。三個兒子畢業後也都進入他曾經參與建立的「美華書館」，長子咸恩（Yee Ung Bau 1861-1910）學刻字，次子咸昌（Yee Chong Bau 1864-1929）學排字，三子咸亨（Y.H. Bau 1867-????）學印刷。

由於「美華」是當時中國最大最先進的印刷機構，鮑氏兄弟在清心、美華半工讀學印刷，的確吸收到紮紮實實的專業知識，這對爾後創建「商務印書館」有很大的影響。

清心書院學生學習印刷工作，是有歷史背景因素的。一八六一年美國南北戰爭爆發，歷時四年，此期間美國大陸的長老會自顧不暇，遠在東方的上海清心書院必須自立更生，於是改成半工讀以維持，男生須參與種植園藝或印刷工作，女生則學刺繡針織。

在洋報打工　造創業契機

上海灘一如今日，是當個時代最大的試金平台，每天每時吸引各地叱吒風雲的人物湧入這座城市，多少英雄好漢還沒來得及施展拳腳，便悄無聲息的沉入茫茫人海，一圈兒漣漪也不曾激起。年輕的青浦縣鄉下夏家孩子，卻開始一步一足印的紮下穩健成長的腳跟。

夏瑞芳在清心書院用功勤學，一八八九年他遭喪父之痛，那時已十八歲，是個大小夥子了，也懂得事體了，想到自己在書院讀書，家境越來越貧困，因此便輟學找工作養家。

當時清心校長是薛思培（John Alfred Silsby），他不忍看這孩子工作無著，就介紹他到同仁醫院做學徒。同仁醫院也是基督教開設的慈善事業，當年規模不大，對入院工作者，也不太要求專業訓練，夏瑞芳在醫院做打雜、當助手，幹了一年，這個已經見過世面的孩子，很快地發覺，自己根本沒有醫學方面的根底，將來不可能有什麼出息。

夏瑞芳因在清心書院學過印刷工，因此帶藝投到「文匯西報」（The Shanghai Mercury）做英文排字工；後來又從「文匯西報」轉到「字林西報」（North China Daily News）。

「字林西報」初創時僅為對開四版一張，後擴大到十八─三十二版，根據《上海市地方誌》記載，這份報紙是英國商號「字林洋行」於同治三年，一八六四年創辦的英文報。

「字林西報」後來有代表在華特殊商務利益的「英國官報」之稱。起初其內容以刊載通訊報導、時事新聞和有關中國軍事新聞為主，另還有公佈上海租界當局政治、法律、商業等方面的法令通告，大量篇幅刊登商業廣告、船期資訊和市價行情。其中，我們看到了西方資本主義的本質和特色，充分反映在傳播媒體的廣告營利之上，當然，二十一世紀的今日，全球各國、各地方的媒體，廣告早已是這個行業追求的主要目標中的犖犖大者。這與當時中國的報紙，不論型式或內容皆大異其趣。

夏瑞芳成長的年代，中國只有一份報紙，是北京報房發行的報紙，稱為「京報」，京報初始發行時期，可推斷大約為清雍正年間（一七二三─一七三五）。

「京報」的內容，頭版為宮門鈔，如宮廷消息、人事升沈任免等，次版為上諭，也就是皇帝敕令或公告，再次為奏摺，即大臣的奏議或報告。版面按這個次序排列，沒有新聞標題，一如政府通告，由內閣每日抄發。

「京報」每日黃昏或晚上發行，猶如今日之晚報。京報改用鉛字排印，省時又省事。

京報出版至何時停刊，無法確查，而洋報盛行之際，京報仍在流行，光緒二十六年三月十六日（一九〇〇年四月十五日）曾有禁止義和拳之上諭，公佈於京報，可見京報至二十世紀初仍在出刊。

又據《津門雜記》載有：一八八三年（光緒九年）九月：「恭錄邸報，言李鴻章片⋯事。」此處又出現「邸報」的名稱。

「邸報」一般公認為中國最早的報紙；古代地方政府駐京辦事處謂之「邸」，對本地方政府的「京都新聞報告」就稱之「邸報」。

根據中國新聞史，「邸報」始於漢代。當時這份報的消息，大部分來自宮廷的記錄，而以「起居注」、「日曆」和「月曆」一類資料為主。由內廷摘要通傳，然後各蕃邸據以抄錄。後來的唐、宋、元、明各朝一直沿襲發展，由原來毛筆傳抄，至雕版、活版印刷術的發明，乃大量刊印，發生進步的傳播功能。

雍正之後，因異族統治，實行中央集權，遂以京報代替了邸報，並嚴禁邸報發行。

從「邸報」至「京報」發展軌跡中，除了看到中國傳統報紙與西方報紙的截然不同，我們同時可以清晰看到，印刷技術的研發和提升，是促進報紙傳播活動便捷、擴大的重要

推力。

夏瑞芳工作的「字林西報」，原為英國商人奚安門於一八五○年八月三日在上海創刊的「北華捷報」；一八五六年又增「航運日報」和「航運與商業日報」副報。一八六四年「航運與商業日報」改名「字林西報」，獨立發行。該報在中國建立了龐大的新聞通訊網路，免費寄送給教會傳教士，換取各地教會傳教士提供的通訊稿和情報。該報還經常就中英關係、清廷政局以及其他時勢發表議論；如要求清廷實行門戶開放、反對太平軍起義，目的在換取滿清朝廷給英國更多在華特權。因此當時負責洋務的清朝官吏，都要看這份洋報，包括李鴻章在內。

一八九六年李鴻章以「大清欽差頭等出使大臣」頭銜率團訪問美國；當載著大清外交使團的「聖路易士」號郵輪於八月二十八日上午九時抵達紐約港時，他受到的禮遇接待，為當時美國歷史上空前的盛大規格。

「紐約時報」當時的新聞報導如此記載：「人們爭相一睹清國總理大臣的風采，因為此人治理的人口比全歐洲君王們所統治的人口總和還要多。」

九月二日上午，李鴻章在華爾道夫飯店接受十二家媒體記者的採訪。李鴻章接受「紐

約時報」採訪時，被問到是否贊成把歐美的報紙引進到中國，李鴻章的回答是：「清國辦有報紙，但遺憾的是清國的編輯們不願將真相告訴讀者。他們不像你們的報紙講真話，清國的編輯們在講真話的時候十分吝嗇，他們只講部分的真實。由於不能誠實地說明真相，我們的報紙就失去了新聞本身的高貴價值，也就未能成為廣泛傳播文明的方式了。」

由以上這段「新聞報導」，可以印證，李鴻章以降諸清廷臣工，的確是關注「字林西報」等講真話洋文傳媒的。

李鴻章訪美時，上海已有好幾家中文報，其中最主要的有「上海新報」和「申報」。

一八六一年創刊的「上海新報」，可以算是當地首份華文報紙，其實後台老闆是洋人，由字林洋行出資、美國傳教士伍德擔任主編，一直佔據上海的中文報業。

一八七二年開辦了十多年的「上海新報」被「申報」擊垮宣佈停刊，「申報」在當年四月，由英國商人創辦，為了凸顯本土化，報紙名稱用「申」字，是上海的簡稱。該報發行策略首創僱報童方式進行推廣營銷。由於申報竭力推行本土化經營使得報紙銷量直線上升。半年後成為了本埠唯一的華文商業報紙。

除了「字林西報」，還有以梁啟超為主筆的上海「時務報」於一八九六年創辦；

一八九七年以嚴復為主筆的「國聞報」在天津創辦，兩報成了維新派的南北兩個重要輿論平臺。這兩大改革陣營，為了加強西方的資訊，乃借助翻譯外文報紙上的文章和最新消息。因此需要英文、法文、日文三種翻譯人才，在報紙的推波助瀾之下，加速了西學的興起，傳播媒體也開風氣之先，促進了中國人學習外語的熱潮。

「字林西報」歷經推翻滿清建立民國、軍閥割據、北伐，乃至抗日戰爭、國共內戰，直到一九五一年才停刊，結束了近百年的發行歷史。這份報紙是記錄上海和研究上海歷史最重要的資料之一。

該報矗立於外灘十七號（中山東一路十七號）的大樓被中華人民共和國上海市政府接管，一九九八年為美國友邦保險公司上海分公司租用，現被人們稱為「友邦大廈」，是一處極為時尚的觀光景點。

第二章 商務印書館的發軔

城隍廟邊湖心亭　盍各言爾志

當夏瑞芳在「字林西報」做到了排字部主任職位，他的收入已可以養家自足，於是想娶妻成家了，或許是近水樓臺吧，他娶了好友鮑咸昌、咸恩的妹妹翠玉；不幸，久病的老母親在他成婚的前一天，竟撒手西歸了，這對孝順的瑞芳而言，可是極大的遺憾。

夏瑞芳和翠玉結婚之後，與妻舅鮑氏昆仲的感情更加親切，他們仁和好友高鳳池一向無所不談。有時下了班之後，這幾個「親朋好友」會一起下下小館、喝喝茶、吹吹牛。

他們幾乎每個週日，到清心堂做禮拜之後，就一塊兒到城隍廟邊的湖心亭喝茶或到旁邊的小館打牙祭。正值意氣風發的年齡，免不了高談闊論、各言其志，談的最多、最深、最有興頭的，就是他們共同的未來志向──開印刷廠。

彼時，華人在洋人機構工作，是滿受氣的，他們在報館裡，就會經常遭到洋人的頤指氣使，並動輒喝斥；以今天維權的語言來說，夏、鮑等人是受到種族歧視的。這幾個年輕人，哪裡受得了這種窩囊氣，因此更堅定了自己開印刷廠的意志！他們志趣相投，存創業雄心，於是，更加省吃儉用、奮力工作，開始儲蓄資金。

與此同時，他們還試著伸出探測自己能力的觸角，「學習洋務是當代趨勢，印刷技術和業務，也應該從洋人處著手。」這是他們起步的教戰守則。

由於他們都出身西洋教會學校，英文都還能對付，幸運的，他們很快地接攬了一些洋文印務，這對夏瑞芳幾個人來說，真如吃了定心丸，證實了他們的計畫和策略是正確的，幾乎可以看到未來的潛力和前景，因此他們辦印刷廠的籌設腳步也隨之加快了。

一八九六年四月十五日，夏瑞芳約了妻舅鮑氏兄弟、高鳳池等幾個志同道合的好友，在他們經常光顧的三洋涇橋畔小茶館裡碰面，夏瑞芳在鮑咸昌的支持下，倡議著手籌資，正式開始準備辦印刷廠，當天到場的人都表示贊同，於是簽了一份簡單的契約，確定認股資金四千元，股東八人，一股五百元。

上海灘依然不斷開展著萬紫千紅的風采的繁華，而一場中華民族印刷出版業石破天驚

的變局，正悄悄綻放它的榮耀和喧嘩。

「商務印書館」名稱　先有英文

三洋浜橋畔小茶館會議後第二年，光緒二十三年，一八九七年二月十一日，夏瑞芳等人在上海江西路德昌裡租了兩間屋子，置了三部小印刷機。儘管還未傳出轟隆轟隆的開機聲，而他們年輕旺盛的心卻加速跳動著，因為這個只能稱為「作坊」的印刷廠，正等待他們胼手胝足實踐夢想呢！那年，夏瑞芳二十六歲。

「實踐夢想」的本錢，集資結果沒有超過四千元，準確的數字應該是三千七百五十元，每股五百元，夏瑞芳和鮑氏昆仲一人一股，各五百元，大股是沈伯芳，他跟夏、鮑不同，不是長老會的，但也是洋教徒，信天主教，其父為蘇滬地方官府的法文翻譯，不但為官面上人物，還是個洋幫辦，因此家道比夏、鮑兩家富裕，他一人占兩股一千元。餘下的兩股由徐桂生占一股，高鳳池（翰卿）、張桂華（蟾芬）、郁厚坤等各半股。

至於夏瑞芳和鮑氏昆仲他們湊齊的三千七百五十元，是哪一種錢幣？

鴉片戰爭後，隨著「五口通商」，洋人的銀元嘩啦嘩啦流進各大口岸，最多的是西班

牙的本洋，還有墨西哥的鷹洋。西洋銀圓鑄製的十分精巧，使用也方便，比起大清傳統用

秤稱的白銀既輕便又簡單，於是各地遂有仿造。光緒十六年（一八九○），張之洞在廣州

創辦的「廣東官錢局」鑄成銀幣系列，正面以滿漢兩種文字鑄「光緒元寶」，背面是龍蟠

花紋，因此稱之為「龍洋」，開始與洋銀一起使用。

接著，到了清光緒二十三年，也就是夏瑞芳等人開創「商務」的那年，清政府在上海

設立了中國通商銀行，發行紙幣（兌換券）。

從這些貨幣史的記載中，可見到當時使用貨幣的多元與紊亂，而夏瑞芳等人的資金，

應該是龍洋。

當時，夏瑞芳雖然領頭創業，但他在這幾個人當中卻是手頭最緊的，據說，賢妻鮑翠

玉為了讓丈夫得遂生平之志，還向一個女校的同學借貸幫他湊股金。

夏、鮑、高這幾個年輕人，都剛廿歲出頭，沒有一個是財主，都是辛苦做工賺辛苦錢

的小夥子，也沒有什麼官場背景，有的只是一股濃郁的團結精神和彼此信賴的友誼。而這

些精神和友誼則建立在他們相同的生長背景。

瑞芳被推舉擔任總經理，主持大局，咸恩、咸昌輔佐印務，鳳池留在「華夏書房」，

學習更新的印刷技術。

幾個人挽起袖子，展開雙臂，雄心勃勃的迎接嶄新的未來。

印刷廠說著就要開張了，可是還沒公司名字呢！中國人傳統上是講究「名正言順」的。

「我們印刷廠該有塊招牌呀？大家動動腦筋想個商號名稱。」夏瑞芳先發話了。

「得取個吉祥如意的，好讓生意順風順水！」有人應和。

一般商號取名，都希望沾些富裕榮華意味兒的，往往少不了鴻、昌、吉、盛、發之類的字眼，而且還要找算命先生算算筆畫，看五行、合陰陽、趨吉避凶，總要取個草木逢春、枝葉沾露大吉大利的名字，以助買賣百事亨通、順利興隆。

然而，夏瑞芳這幾個人偏偏是洋學堂出身，說ＡＢＣＤ要比之乎者也順溜得多，真要他們想出個名利雙收、逢凶化吉的中國名字，可是比登天還難。

正巧，這天鮑氏昆仲邀了大姊和姊夫一起到印刷廠參與共商工廠命名大計，鮑大姊人稱鮑大姑，也是清心書院畢業的，正當幾個大男人急得抓耳撓腮之際，一旁閑著翻看他們剛剛印出來幾件印刷品的大姑，自言自語又似乎有意的，悠悠的說：「你們印的這些簿記

和廣告宣傳單，都是Commercial檔呀！」

「Commercial……Commercial……」靈光乍現，就叫「Commercial Press」吧！

幾個人就先給公司取了個英文名字，隨後再翻譯成中文，命名「商務印書館」。

誰也沒料到，這個風雲際會、大業成就的名號，從此橫跨時空響亮至今！

工業革命與慈禧　「商務」的發展機緣

回首當年，深入審視「商務印書館」發軔時代的歷史背景，藉以進一層瞭解夏瑞芳辦廠子的社會文化環境，和他經營事業的謀略及眼光是如何醞釀成就的。

先從客觀的世界大環境來看：

清朝末年，十九世紀末正逢全世界各國思想文化、科學研發隨「工業革命」之後，進入另一個高點的時期；「工業革命」狹義的說，就是人類生產方式從手工業轉向機器大工業的階段。換言之，工業革命就是以機器取代人力，以大規模工廠化生產取代個體手工生產的一次生產與科技的革命。十八世紀中葉英國人瓦特改良蒸汽機之後，由一系列技術革命引起了從手工業轉向機器生產，這個重大飛躍，是後來一般所稱的「工業革命」之始。

英國因資本主義化與工業革命的成功，成為十八世紀中葉後最進步的國家，得以大肆開拓殖民地與市場，因而導致其他的歐洲國家紛紛依循英國的模式進行工業化，隨後，十九世紀才傳播到北美洲。從那時起，西方國家開始藉其強大的經濟和武力控制全世界。

「工業革命」的形成是諸多條件同時匯集的結果，包括：資本主義、農業革命、地理大發現帶來的新航路與海外殖民地、列國制度的形成、新教徒的精神、重商主義的興起、科學與人文思想的突破等等。

夏瑞芳正逢這個變局萬千的大時代，當時西方武力大舉侵略中國，大肆瓜分我領土作為殖民地，與此同時，也捲來了工業革命浪潮和宗教文化的移植，卻正給未來的「商務印書館」製造了中國歷史上空前未有的機運。

再回頭，從中國自己本身的主觀環境來看。「商務印書館」開創的那一年，一八九七年，當時朝廷當家作主的是慈禧太后。

這位太后，在近代史上是全球大名鼎鼎的人物：慈禧（一八三五—一九〇八），是咸豐帝的妃子那拉氏，祖居葉赫，故稱葉赫那拉，為滿洲鑲藍旗人。

一八六一年底，大清改元同治，實行「垂簾聽政」，慈禧掌握實權。同治、光緒兩

朝，慈禧獨攬朝政，為實際最高統治者。

一八八六年，中法戰爭期間，太后挪用辦海軍的預算修葺清漪園（後改名為頤和園），將大清國推向垂危敗亡的深淵。

「春帆樓」之恥　從甲午戰敗談起

年代再拉近點兒，從甲午之敗談起，那是一八九五年，也是夏瑞芳等人開辦商務印書館的前兩年……

一八九五年三月十四日晨，光緒二十一年二月十八日，李鴻章一行乘坐德國商船掛黃龍旗，由天津啟錨，十九日清晨抵下關，日方選定下關著名的旅館「春帆樓」為議和地點。

被尊稱為中堂大人的李鴻章去議什麼和？跟日本有甚麼關係？

就在這前一年，一八九四年（光緒二十年）九月十七日，日本艦隊在黃海突襲北洋艦隊，兩國海軍展開一場激戰。北洋海軍提督丁汝昌受傷，定遠艦管帶劉步蟾代替丁汝昌督戰；另一艘致遠艦管帶鄧世昌在彈藥用完之後，下令開足馬力衝向日艦吉野號，不幸被魚

雷擊中，全艦官兵犧牲。經遠艦管帶林永升也率領將士戰到最後一刻。海戰歷時五、六個

小時，北洋損失致遠艦等艦隻，此後中國遭到日軍海陸兩路的夾攻。

最後的威海衛戰役中，提督丁汝昌自殺殉國。威海衛陷落後，清政府無力再戰，只得

求和，於是派李鴻章為全權大臣，赴日議和。

「春帆樓」是日相伊藤博文享受河豚料理的「割烹旅館」；李中堂到此可不是為了大

快朵頤，走到春帆樓的窗臺前，遠眺關門（下關—門司）海峽，萬頃碧波上雖不見兵船炮

艇，然而心中翻騰的是自己辛苦經營三十年的洋務運動，就這樣在日本軍艦的大炮和魚雷

轟擊中灰飛煙滅，老中堂不禁搖頭感嘆：「我國之事，囿於習俗，未能如願以償。今轉瞬

十年，依然如故。本大臣自慚心有餘力不足⋯⋯此戰大敗，證明大清的洋務運動遠沒有日

本的明治維新成功。而此次戰敗，將使國人徹底醒悟⋯⋯」

春帆樓頭，李鴻章和伊藤所率領的中日兩國官員，唇槍舌劍，談判僵持不下。

三月二十四日下午四點十五分，結束了第三次毫無交集的會議後，憂心忡忡的李鴻章

搭轎返回行館「引接寺」，轎子快到達驛館時，突然間，一名日本青年自人群中竄出，對

著李鴻章開了兩槍，其中一槍正中他左臉頰，現場頓時大亂，路人四處逃竄，七十三歲的

李鴻章昏厥送醫，險些送命。此案一時躍登全球頭條新聞。

中堂大人甦醒過來後，想到自己遇刺，血灑東洋，老邁而無力的李鴻章不禁悲嘆：

「此血可以報國矣！」

養傷兩週後，四月十日李鴻章再度親赴會談，過七日，雙方終於簽訂了「馬關條約」。

「馬關條約」的內容是：承認割讓遼東半島、台灣和澎湖列島，賠償軍費白銀二億兩，允許日本在中國開設工廠，開闢沙市、重慶、蘇州、杭州等地為商埠。這是割地賠款、喪權辱國的不平等條約。

一九一一年，梁啟超遊下關春帆樓時，感慨萬千，於是賦詩記愁，題為「馬關夜泊」：

「明知此是傷心地，亦到維舟首重回，十七年中多少事，春帆樓下晚濤哀。」

甲午之敗讓老百姓都覺悟到，滿清政府的腐敗無能，尤其海軍軍費被慈禧挪用修建頤和園，以致一八八九年之後，海軍未添新艦，未置新炮，連彈藥也多是過期、不合格的廢

品；如此艦隊焉能不敗？

甲午之敗也使社會形成亡國大禍已經來臨的共識，促成中華民族的覺醒，民族主義因之崛起、民主精神的高漲和革命觀念的逐步深入人心，更催動人們探尋新的救國之路。以致有後來康有為、梁啟超的「維新變法」和孫中山的革命運動。

夏瑞芳的好友，也是「商務」創辦人之一的高鳳池，在《本館創業史》中這樣寫道：

「甲午失敗後，痛定思痛，變法自強，廢科舉、興學校，差不多是朝野一致的主張。正是維新時代，小印書坊設的也很多，機會極好，所以說商務的成功半由人事半由機會。」

一生在商務工作達四十年之久，歷任商務印書館總經理、臺灣商務印書館董事長的王雲五，在他的〈商務印書館與新教育年譜〉文中這樣記載：

「時在甲午對日首次戰爭挫敗後三年，戊戌維新前一年，中國在創深病巨之際，醞釀革新運動。此一運動以辦理新學堂，從事新教育為中心。新學堂之最早開辦者為設於北京

之同文館（時在西元一八六二年，清同治元年，壬戌），次則為設於上海之廣方言館（時在西元一八六三年，清同治二年，癸亥），皆以教授外國文為主。

隨後各省先後開辦各種學堂，如福建之船政學堂，上海之正蒙書院，天津之電報學堂，天津之水師學堂，上海之電報學堂……。凡此或為專業，或為普通，皆按需要而設，初無整個系統。

……然猶待六年後之西元一九○二年張百熙奏進學堂章程，新學堂系統方具體化。商務印書館則於此六年間之第二年應運而起，期以新式印刷業贊助此革新運動。然此新式印刷業之興起，實亦有賴於初步出版事業予以支持。」

王雲五先生，本名日祥，號岫盧，祖籍廣東香山（中山）縣，清光緒十四年（一八八八）生於上海，一九七九年卒於台北，享年九十二歲。他是二十世紀中國最聲名卓著的學者、教育家、出版家、圖書館事業家和政壇人物之一。

王只曾受五年私塾教育，其父將他送到五金店當學徒，晚上學習英語。十七歲時進入同文館學英語，在校內圖書館廣泛閱讀西方著作。十八歲後，在上海各校任教英文、史地

等。

民國元年，孫中山就任中華民國臨時大總統，特聘王雲五擔任總統府秘書，並任職教育部。一九二一年，經胡適推薦，王雲五出任商務印書館編譯所長，後任總經理。從此以後，他與商務印書館結下不解之緣，主理商務期間，出版多種詞典、百科全書及叢書，以「教育普及」和「學術獨立」為方針，對中國的知識傳播有舉足作用。

第三章 從印刷走向出版

上海稱美國人為「花旗人」

商務印書館開辦伊始，夏瑞芳和合夥人商量，以手上可用資金，只能購置兩部手搖式小印刷機、三部腳踏圓盤機和三部手動壓印機，還雇用了十來個工人。這些機具人力，已然足夠應付他們承印的商業帳冊、廣告之類的文件；因此，可以說他們最早的業務是以印刷起家的。

夏瑞芳是個勤奮的人，除了是總經理外，他對外還兼接活、採辦、收帳，在內兼接待、校對等工作，經常忙到深更半夜，回到家，妻子難免會勸他：「別忙壞了身子」，他總也回同樣一句話：「自己的事業，自己不帶頭幹，誰幫你呀？」

他是個天生的ＣＥＯ人才，因為他領頭苦幹，公司業務蒸蒸日上，雖然有了盈利，他

引著大家不拿紅利，轉投作股本並招新股，一九〇一年已將原先四千元的股金升值到五萬元。

天生的ＣＥＯ不會因此滿足的，他還用盡心思，要開闢更多、更廣的業務，於是商務走向「出版」的新領域。除此，他還不斷培訓出版人才，組織國外考察，引進先進印刷技術；在商務建立之初，夏瑞芳就親赴日本考察，訂購印刷設備和器材。

「商務」開辦之初，上海的社會風氣，可以說是僅次於廣州的「洋化」，這種洋化，也與「維新」潮流有著緊密關聯，相對的，也影響著「商務」總經理夏瑞芳的經營決策。

有本筆記小說《清稗類鈔》，集了一萬三千五百多條清末上海的掌故遺聞，是晚清遺老徐珂（一八六九年—一九二八年）所編撰。徐珂是光緒年間舉人，曾任袁世凱幕僚，還做過商務印書館編輯。其書中可以找到一些當時夏瑞芳所處的社會文化風氣，如書中寫道：

「清末上海人稱英人曰「大英人」，稱法人則曰「法蘭西人」（間有音訛作拔蘭西者，與洋文原音相去更遠矣），稱美人則曰「花旗人」，稱德人則曰「迦門人」（迦門係

070

日爾曼之省音）。**此種稱謂，稍一移易（如直稱德人、美人）中下層社會即不知所對。**」這部三百多萬字的巨著，商務印書館於一九一六年出版。

可見那時候整個社會已然瀰漫著「崇洋」、「媚洋」又「畏洋」的氣氛。

夏瑞芳英文姓　特改為HOW

一八九二年二月四日的「紐約時報」有一篇報導，這樣寫道：「中國上海（一八九一年）十二月二十八日訊：今年二十歲的清國皇帝陛下，目前正由兩個受過英美教育的北京國子監學生負責教授英語，而這件事是由光緒皇帝頒布詔書通告全國的。」文中還說，大清國開始發生該國歷史上最大的變化。

毫無疑問，這個變化在整個滿清帝國產生巨大影響，當時上海的夏瑞芳這年正好二十歲，已自清心書院輟學，轉入英商「文匯西報」當排字工，他應該也知道連皇帝都學英文了。

年輕的夏瑞芳內心不免澎湃，他看到，若想在上海生存，必須與洋人打交道、學洋

文，他慶幸自己學了英文，他暗自想著社會上有太多人想學英文，如果印些教人們學習英文的書，肯定會受歡迎。

當時的上海灘，通洋文不但時尚而且能賺大錢，一八九六年十二月二十九日上海「申報」一篇〈論習西學當以工藝為急務〉的文章中這樣寫道：「通洋文始能為洋行買辦，始能赴洋行寫貨。與西人交易，每歲所入，或數萬、或數千數百，以視中國為商則奚啻天壤，此人之所以欲習西國之語言文字也。」懂洋文的學生，找工作容易而且高高在上，其薪金待遇就「少則十餘圓，多則數十圓。當世之鮮衣華服、乘輿策馬者，無不從洋務中來，其在官場，則翻譯焉、隨員焉。」

這種風氣可比今日中國白領在外企單位工作一樣。

又，一八九八年十一月十日，英國駐上海總領事館在「中外日報」上登載「聘請上等英文翻譯」的一則廣告內容：「今有英人三位，由上海至雲南，計應行半年有餘，取道四川成都，仍回上海，願請能說官話之翻譯一位，偕同前往。諸君樂偕行者，乞於日內移至上海大英國總領事署面商一切。」

這些老資料，在在證明上海、廣州等通商口岸，尤其外國租界地區，當洋行買辦或替

外人服務，是當時致富之道。

或許因為這種形勢迫人，夏瑞芳自己便將英文姓氏題為ＨＯＷ以減少「中國味」，目的是方便跟外國人談生意。而「ＨＯＷ」很接近上海人唸「夏」的發音。

「華英初階」 洛陽紙貴

一八九八年，商務印書館創立的第二年，他們出版了第一本書──《華英初階》，就是英文教材，果然非常暢銷，一時洛陽紙貴！

初始，「商務」只承印一些洋商、洋行的文件，根本無法滿足夏總經理的雄心，他早年就已埋下的印英文教科書的種子，此時已然冒芽露頭。

雖有心，可是到哪兒找可用的課本材料呢？靈機一動，何不就近取材？他想到自己在「清心」所讀的英文課本；那是英國人給印度小學生編的「primer」──初學讀本，印度自一八五八年始受大英帝國的殖民統治。（一直到二戰爆發，於一九四七年印度才獨立。）

這些課本是從印度運到上海的，以他們的人力物力，根本不可能飄洋過海到印度或

英國取經，那個年代也沒有甚麼「版權」、「智慧財產權」的觀念，於是，他們就把這本 primer 依樣畫葫蘆，照原樣翻印出來。

原書只有英文，若沒有老師教導，一般讀者不太容易自學，夏瑞芳腦筋一動，趕緊找來蘇州博習書院（後來改蘇州大學、東吳大學）助教謝洪賚，此人與他也是姻親關係，把課文翻譯成中文，以中英文對照排版，中文書名叫《華英初階》，第一版印了二千冊，夏瑞芳親力親為，向各學校四處推銷，不到二十天就銷售一空。

「五四」新文化運動先驅之一，曾發現培養和舉薦過巴金、丁玲、戴望舒等的近代語文教育家葉聖陶就說過：幼年初學英文，讀的就是《華英初階》，在梅溪學堂讀書的少年胡適，讀的英文教材也是《華英初階》。大學問家梁漱溟說在北京上中西小學堂，學的就是《華英初階》、《華英進階》。此書之盛行及影響之廣泛，由此可見一斑。

「再版！我們再加印！」夏瑞芳和鮑咸昌兄弟，歡喜地喊著，他們不斷再版，書一直旺銷，風靡一時！這也印證了當年夏瑞芳對「印些學英文的書，肯定會受歡迎」的想法。

夏瑞芳再接再勵，請謝洪賚繼續註譯比「初階」更高一級的課本，名稱《華英進

夥伴們和同行們，不得不佩服夏總經理的獨到生意經了。

階》，幾經增修共出版六冊。如此一淺一深兩種課本，一直被學習者選用，在市場上流行十多年，印刷達六十三版。

一九○○年六月十九日《申報》的一則『重印《華英進階》』廣告，是這樣介紹的：

是書華英文字並列，句讀明顯、釋解詳盡、久已風行字內。凡中外之書院學堂皆藉以教授生徒，均稱受益。並稱各報讚揚，不煩贅述。茲將《華英初階》和《進階》初、二、三、四、五集合訂成一大本。書面用英國頂上藍色全布，飾以真金字，精緻異常。每大本賣洋二元二角半。敝館編輯《華英讀本》諸書，早經遐邇流售，成為有功後進。計《初階》五分、《進階》初集一角、二集二角半、三集四角、四集五角半、五集七角半。

從這段廣告詞中，可以看到當時夏總是如何運用簡明又吸睛的字句，廣告他的產品，足見他對大眾傳播媒體的運用手法十分嫻熟。

扮演一個成功的領軍人物，除了專業也須全面。

因為《華英初階》和《進階》的暢銷全國，奠定了「商務」成為出版教課書方面領袖群倫的的基礎。

香蕉（banana）就唸「白奶奶」

上海坊間開始「跟風」出版學英文的冊子，一九○六年一本《新增繪圖幼學故事瓊林》，可用來檢視當時「山寨」版的英文單詞教材是怎樣的水準，如：「香蕉（banana）」注讀為「白奶奶」、「汗衫（sweater）」注讀為「史為脫」、「襯衫（shirt）」注讀為「休脫」、「咳嗽（cough）」注讀為「哭夫」等，不一而足。雖然今天看起來讓人啼笑皆非，但這本書反映當時英語已被認為是重要的社交語言。與今日北京、上海等大城市中人人口邊掛著English為時尚，並無兩樣。

順便一提，當時上海流行一種「洋涇浜英語」，曾一直被使用到二十世紀中期；「洋涇浜」原是黃浦江的一條支流，也是上海英法租界的界河，有許多商業機構出現在小河兩岸；洋涇浜因此成為當地對外貿易的集中地，也是華洋雜處的地界，當時中外商人語言交流不便，於是應運而生了「洋涇浜英語」，這是一種英語、上海話、寧波話的混合語言，由於教育還不普及，因此為上海灘眾洋行買辦廣泛使用。

洋涇浜英語也有教材，用漢字注音，但須用寧波方言念才接近英文發音，茲舉幾個常

用的例子：

「來是康姆（come）去是穀（go）、是叫也司（yes）勿叫諾（no）、打屁股叫班蒲曲（bamboo chop）、混帳王八蛋風爐（daffy low）、那摩溫（number one）先生是阿大，跑街先生殺老夫（shroff）、麥克（mark）麥克鈔票多、畢的生司（empty cents）當票多、紅頭阿三開潑度（keep door），自家兄弟勃拉茶（brother）、爺要發茶（father）娘賣茶（mother），丈人阿伯發音落（father-in-law）。」

「我在租界不怕清廷」

　　時勢造就英雄，英雄必然也會開創時勢。隨著業務發展、資本額的增加，夏瑞芳也掌握機會不斷擴大廠房規模，然而開館第二年，一八九八年，正是印行《華英初階》忙得如火如荼之際，江西路德昌裡的廠房因工人大意引發火災，原有的機具和材料付之一炬，這個損失可不得了，幸運的是，當初這幾個觀念新派的年輕人，給廠房保了險，因此他們意外的獲得一筆保險賠償金。

「我們不能延誤印務和出版大計，必須盡快恢復印務工作！」幾個股東一致決議，責成夏瑞芳盡快重新復業。

總經理夏瑞芳展現出擴大事業的雄心壯志，決定趁此機會另遷更大的位址，重新建廠房，購置更多更先進的印刷機器。

很快的，他向股東們報告：「我找到北京路順廣裡的一處房產，面積夠大，我看可隔成十二個廠房和辦公間。」

還留在「華夏書房」學習新印刷技術的高鳳池，尤其關心添置的新機器：「老舊又費人力的機器，該汰換了吧？」

「對！我看好用煤油發動機拖帶的機器，可以節省人力，印刷速度又快，你們認為如何？」

所獲答案，當然是「同意」！

有了新廠房，夏瑞芳的底氣更足，「商務」陸續出版《華英字典》、編譯《華英國學文編》擴充了新機器，他們在市場上佔有率，節節上升。

除此，夏瑞芳還繼續到各教會承攬印製「聖經」的業務，這是極大宗的「買賣」，當

時聖經的需要量，隨著基督教會、天主教堂在中國各地的擴張可以說是無限的。

這些都是一八九八年「商務」承接的業務，換言之，這是他們開張後第二年，如此短短時間內，能創造出如此成績，對任何一個新公司而言，都屬驚人和傲人的！

一九〇〇年，光緒二十六年他又收購了日本人在上海的一家「修文印刷局」，利用它較為完備的設備率先在國內用紙型印書。

到了一九〇六年，北京城的朝廷批准的一〇二種小學教科書中，就有五十四種出自遠在上海的「商務印書館」。

他們開業之初，還代印「昌言報」、「格致新報」。單看這兩份報名即可望文生義，顯見都是在改革中國的浪潮下，以廣開言路、救亡圖強為宗旨的報刊，其中不乏康梁等人的身影，這些刊物也堪稱是推動中國進步的推手之一。

承印這些報刊，在兵荒馬亂、專制極權的時代，無庸置疑的是要擔掉腦袋的風險，夏瑞芳並未因此而退縮，不但接受這兩份報刊的印刷風險，此外，據說，戊戌六君子之一譚嗣同被慈禧砍頭之後，其遺作《仁學》，維新人士想要印行發散傳播，有人找到商務印書館，夏瑞芳慨然承擔。

譚嗣同，維新運動的激進派人物，一八九八年戊戌變法失敗，九月二十八日在北京宣武門外的菜市口遭斬首之刑，臨刑前他還仰頭高呼：「有心殺賊，無力回天。死得其所，快哉快哉！」

譚嗣同出身官宦人家，父譚繼洵曾任湖北巡撫，嗣同本人時任四品卿銜軍機章京，與林旭、楊銳等人參與新政，時號「軍機四卿」。他卻視一己之榮華富貴如敝屣，為了民族國家的救亡圖存，譚嗣同選擇了「廢除君主專制，還政於民」的坎坷悲壯之路。

至今仍被傳頌的「望門投止思張儉，忍死須臾待杜根。我自橫刀向天笑，去留肝膽兩崑崙」是譚嗣同在獄中寫的絕筆詩。

當時一同遭戮受害的維新人士還有林旭、楊深秀、劉光第、楊銳、康廣仁，他們被後世稱「戊戌六君子」。

《仁學》一書，認為「仁」是萬物之源，它「以通為第一義」。書中指斥二千年來封建專制制度為「大盜」之政，專制君主是「獨夫民賊」，一切罪惡的淵藪。宣傳「君末民本」的民權說。

如此內容，此書毫無疑問在當時為政府查抄的「禁書」，若以今日俗稱的「白色恐

怖」來看，偷印此書，極可能會被綁到「菜市口」去。

梁啟超為譚嗣同作傳，文末這樣寫著：

「故孔子言不憂不惑不懼，佛言大無畏，蓋即仁即智即勇焉。通乎此者，則遊行自在，可以出生，可以入死，可以仁，可以救眾生。」

短短數言，道出了為拯民族、救蒼生，不惜肝腦塗地的仁者之勇；而以生死相酬，印行《仁學》的夏瑞芳，應也是抱持這般大仁大勇之忱！

正因如此，夏瑞芳在接受承印《仁學》之時，對請託之來人說：「沒有關係，我在租界，不怕清廷。」

顯然，夏瑞芳這種支持圖強救國、致力言論自由改革的雄偉襟懷，孕育了日後商務印書館「從教育著手，改變中國，變法圖強」的大業方針。

第四章　廣納賢才　昌明教育

十九世紀「軟實力」的培養

今日，常聽聞國際間以「軟實力」較勁。

「軟實力」的相對詞是「硬實力」，中外歷史上可看到國與國的戰爭或鬥爭，多以比「實力」誰「硬」，然而，戰爭兵器再硬也硬不過大刀、長槍、箭矢，乃至於飛機、機關槍、導彈；的確，人類一直是依賴武力來保護自己、消滅敵人。在今日的和平年代，開始以傳播方式，透過文化、思想、文學、藝術來穿透對方的防範，改變對方的觀念、思維，促彼此思想、利益趨於統一，這便是「軟實力」，其力道，並不亞於坦克車、飛彈。

「軟實力」這個名詞，是二十一世紀才流行起來的，而在十九世紀末，夏瑞芳就開始以這種溫和的硬理念，在中國大地上以開發民智、提高國人文化素質的「軟實力」致力播

種和耕耘。

商務對大眾社會的貢獻，很重要的一點是，在清末民初一度引起閱讀風潮，對知識界產生巨大影響。在張元濟等精英文人的支持與輔助下，總經理夏瑞芳勠力經營下，他們為中國近代的知識、文化傳播，開創了空前的局面，除了先前談到的教科書幫助普及了基礎教育外，他們還出版了嚴復翻譯的《原富》、《天演論》等現代重要學術文獻。

《原富》就是英國經濟學家亞當史密斯（Adam Smith）的經濟學專著《國富論》（The Wealth of Nations），全名為《國家康富的性質和原因的研究》（An Inquiry into the Nature and Causes of the Wealth of Nations）。它被視為西方經濟學的「聖經」、經濟學的百科全書、影響世界歷史的十大著作之一，被譽為「第一部系統的偉大的經濟學著作」；《原富》則是影響中國近代社會的經典譯作。

《天演論》，全名為《進化論與倫理學》（Evolution and Ethics and other Essays）是英國生物學家湯馬斯·亨利·赫胥黎（Thomas Henry Huxley）的論文集。重點是演譯達爾文生物進化論，書的前半部講進化論，後半部講倫理學，此乃首次向國人介紹了達爾文生物進化論，物競天擇的思想觀念。

嚴復在此書的導言開頭便說：

　　譯事三難：信、達、雅。求其信已大難矣，顧信矣不達，雖譯猶不譯也，則達尚焉。

因此嚴復翻譯此書時，沒有完全依原文，而是有選擇地意譯。

序中還道：

　　此在譯者將全文神理，融會於心，則下筆抒詞，自然互備。至原文詞理本深，難於共喻，則當前後引襯，以顯其意。凡此經營，皆以為達，為達即所以為信也。

這「信、達、雅」便成為後來者做翻譯時奉行的圭臬。

嚴復（一八五四年—一九二一年），乳名體乾，初名傳初，改名宗光，字又陵，後名復，字幾道，福建侯官（後併入閩縣，稱為閩侯，今福州市）人。光緒三年（一八七七年）被選為滿清政府第一批派遣到英法留學的學員。在英國格林威治海軍學院（即今日皇家海軍學院）學習，成績優異。

光緒六年，李鴻章在天津創辦北洋水師學堂，在英兩年學成歸國的嚴復被任該學堂總

教習，後又升任總辦（校長）。甲午戰敗，國家危亡懸於旦夕，嚴復發表多篇針砭時政論述文章，疾呼變法，曾為之撰寫〈原強〉、〈辟韓〉、〈救亡決論〉、〈上光緒皇帝萬言書〉等文章。

民國成立後，一九一二年京師大學堂更名為北京大學校，嚴復任首任校長；十月辭去校長職務。

他系統地將西方的社會學、政治學、政治經濟學、哲學和自然科學介紹到中國，是中國近代啟蒙思想家、翻譯家。曾翻譯了《天演論》、《原富》、《群學肄言》、《群己權界論》、《社會通詮》、《法意》、《名學淺說》、《穆勒名學》等著作。這些譯著在當時影響巨大，是中國二十世紀最重要啟蒙譯著。

商務印書館在那封建閉鎖的年代，有遠見的將西方的新觀念、新思潮引介到中國來，打開了中國知識份子的視野，把一個陌生而廣袤的新世界展現國人眼前，無疑的，商務印書館的「產品」對近代文化產生了澎湃激盪的推動力。

另方面，對中國固有文化寶藏的開發與傳揚，「商務」並未因引進西學而稍有怠忽，諸如《辭源》、《四部叢刊》、「萬有文庫」、《叢書集成》、《百衲本二十四史》等，

他們沒有落下！

從今日客觀的角度看，商務的社會功能，不可僅視為出版與發行的商業行為，實際上，夏瑞芳團隊在中國現代化建設「軟實力」的進程中，發揮了了不起的作用，扮演了奠基者的角色。

在那個朝野動盪、風雨如晦的年代，這群人能對社會責任、國人需要、自我奉獻，而且是在困頓客觀地環境裡，堅忍卓絕地實踐裡，有如此清晰認識。他們真是今日紛亂社會中，令人嚮往的人物！

「小翰林」張元濟　逃亡上海

清末民初知識分子中的有識之士，看到國事衰危而西洋諸國強權霸道，深深體會喚醒民眾、辦教育啟發民眾是民間可為、必為的當務之事，因此辦新聞、幹出版成為一種新興的社會教育方式，其實，這就是今日大家普遍知道的「大眾傳播」功能。

可是當時社會凋敝、經濟蕭條、文盲眾多，新聞、出版的教化功能大打折扣，同時需要大資本的投入，因此成功者很少。

上海的「商務」在那時候，因夏瑞芳的銳力經營，很快建立信譽和口碑，以致在各出版傳播行業中顯出鶴立雞群之勢；另一方面，由於讀書人只會搖筆桿著述論說，並無獨立經營之術，在此因緣聚合之下，「商務」就成為有志以文化救國的知識分子發揮所長、抒展抱負的理想所在。加上夏瑞芳深諳尊士禮賢，求才若渴，乃延聘了張元濟、蔡元培、高夢旦、蔣維喬、杜亞泉，乃至胡適之、王雲五等，不僅是人才濟濟，更可謂是集天下之英才。

一八九八那年，光緒皇帝看到國勢日微，有心圖強，於是開始實行「戊戌變法」。

在戊戌維新變法過程中，有一位小翰林名叫張元濟號菊生，浙江海鹽人，光緒壬辰年（一八九二）五月中進士。同科日後成了名人的還有：蔡元培、葉德輝、沈寶琛等二十四人。

張元濟被點翰林院庶吉士，戊戌之前進入「總理各國事務衙門」為章京，這個衙門在辛丑條約後，改為「外務部」，換言之，這就是中國最早的「外交部」。

章京是甚麼職位？原來「章京」一詞來自滿語「janggin」，是漢語「將軍」的轉音，原是清朝武官的一種，後來外四品文書官員也稱「章京」。

戊戌變法期間，光緒帝命康有為總理衙門章京，譚嗣同、楊銳、劉光第、林旭四人賞四品卿銜在軍機處章京上行走，參與新政事宜。

光緒皇帝維新心切，廣讀新書，吸納外界新知，張元濟就在總理衙門蒐集新書給皇上送去，每次進呈書籍都具名「總理各國事務章京張元濟」，因此光緒知道有個張元濟這個小官員。

以慈禧太后為首的頑固派反對變法，於九月二十一日發動政變，幽禁光緒帝於瀛台（位今日中南海內），廢除全部維新措施，捕殺維新派首領譚嗣同等六人。

一八九八年九月二十八日譚嗣同、楊銳、劉光第等六君子在北京宣武門外菜市口刑場，遭砍頭示眾；當時慈禧大抓維新份子，許多總理衙門和參與維新的士子，人人自危，命不保夕。

據說，有一天，慈禧太后下旨革職一批京官，光緒在旁趁機說「那麼張元濟也是小京官，應一起革職永不敘用。」

於是張就革職回家了，他明白，這是光緒皇帝有心保全他。

因他在戊戌事變中保全了性命，才有了日後與夏瑞芳的相遇、相識、相知，也才造就

出「商務」的新紀元。

且說這張元濟逃過刀下之劫，京城是待不住了，於是火速離京赴滬；由於當年曾與當朝大臣李鴻章有些交往；李鴻章為壯大自己的羽翼，特別攏絡一些傑出的維新份子，因此電告南洋公學主辦人盛宣懷在上海關照張元濟。

南洋公學，盛宣懷一八九六年創建於上海，隸屬於招商局和電報局。公學分為師範、外院（相當於附屬小學）、中院（中學）、上院（大學）四院，盛宣懷首任督辦。與北洋大學堂（設於天津）同為中國近代歷史上最早創辦的大學；當時中國海岸線的劃分，黃海、渤海稱為「北洋」，而長江口以南（東海在內）直到福建、廣東、台灣稱為「南洋」，因此盛宣懷在上海新辦的學堂稱為「南洋公學」。

南洋公學就是今日上海交通大學的前身，一九〇〇年庚子義和團事變，北洋大學堂的一些學生因避戰亂，從天津乘船來上海，轉入南洋公學就讀。該校又添鐵路班，多年後乃改組為「交通大學」。

盛宣懷就在他的南洋公學新設了一個譯書院，請張主持。

張元濟主持的譯書院翻譯了一些洋文書稿、編了一些課本，需要印刷廠印製，於是他

認識了印刷業的名人夏瑞芳。

一九○一年張元濟辦了一份「外交報」，內容以記載一些國際時事為主，也委託商務印刷；當時，商務也印了些外文翻譯新書，但銷售並不理想，虧本近萬元，這在當時不算是小數目，夏瑞芳認為茲事體大，於是拿著這些書稿去看張元濟，求教賢達，他開門見山的問：請問這些書問題出在哪裡？請你給把把脈。

張也開闊的說：把書稿留下，我給你看看！

過兩天，張把夏找來，直言無諱的說：書稿我看完了，問題出在翻譯欠佳。

其實夏也心知肚明，於是拜託說：請您幫忙補救補救啊！

張元濟果然把書稿帶回去，找書院學生重新修改。「商務」以新稿再出版，銷路果然不同。夏瑞芳認識到，經營出版事業，在未來的發展道路上，若自己沒有專業而優良的編譯部門是不行的。

夏瑞芳是個有雄才大略的人，他一方面致力事業的推廣發展，二方面用心尋找人才，希望找到更多、更有能力的夥伴，以壯大經營陣容。

聘前朝章京　做編譯所長

夏和張的結識，初始於商務印刷廠承印南洋公學的書稿；張元濟擔任南洋公學代總理的日子，其實過得並不舒坦，因為與美國學監福開森全盤西化的辦學理念不合，張曾經幾次向盛宣懷提出辭去代總理的職務，但都遭拒絕，就在這時張元濟結識了商務印書館的總經理夏瑞芳，兩人敞開胸懷，暢談印書市場的理想和實際運作，在充分交換意見之後，兩人不由升起惺惺相惜之情，夏瑞芳心裡篤定認為，這張元濟就是他要找的人才。而張元濟則肯定這個踏實肯幹的年輕人，讓他看到了普及教育的另一種道路。

還有一次，因為資金周轉問題，夏瑞芳遇到小困難，而士林望重的張元濟對夏有惺惺相惜之感，於是介紹一家錢莊為其借貸，並作擔保人。這顯示出他對夏非常的信任與器重，夏瑞芳當然心存感激，他也瞭解這位官場上並不得志的張元濟，絕非池中之物。

商務當時多承印些小商業廣告和一些宣傳單，這對雄心勃勃的夏瑞芳而言，自是不能滿足，他在給教會印書和給公學印書稿的經驗中，發現書的市場很大，因此暗下決心，要開闢印書的業務。

一九〇二年，商務增設編譯所，這個單位由誰來主持呢？夏瑞芳心裡有數，張元濟是不二人選，但他沒把握能不能請這高人出山。

那個時代，上海是個接受西方文化風氣極盛的大都市；因此，印書業很盛行，如點石齋、同文書局都屬大規模的印書局，他們都設有編校機構，負責文稿的校正、編輯工作，以提高印書內容的品質。

這些有規模的印書局，多是聘請翰林出身的文人主持編校機構。

翰林，是古代官名，也是有學問、有才能者的代稱。它的由來可追溯至唐朝。唐玄宗時，自文學侍從中選拔優秀人才，充任翰林；翰林學士掌皇帝直接交代的極機密文件，如任免宰相、宣佈戰爭的命令等。

到了夏瑞芳生長的年代，清代共有六千四百七十二人入翰林，形成了龐大的翰林群體，他們對清朝社會產生了巨大影響。到了清朝末期，西學東漸，翰林中也出現了主張改革教育制度，以救亡圖強的聲音。洋務運動的領導者曾國藩、張之洞、李鴻章、沈葆楨等都是翰林出身。清朝滅亡後，遺留下來的翰林群體依然活躍在政治、軍事、外交、文化、教育、經濟的舞臺上。中華民國建立之初，教育總長蔡元培、北洋總統徐世昌、武漢國民

政府主席譚延闓、代理國務總理顏惠慶都是翰林中人。

清末翰林的後代子孫，受到家學薰陶，成為大家的文士不在少數。清代首科狀元傅以漸後人傅斯年、翰林張佩綸的孫女張愛玲、庶吉士周福清之孫魯迅（周樹人）和周作人、嘉慶狀元趙文楷後人趙樸初、翰林毓隆之孫啟功等等，都是近代中國著名文學家、教育家。

夏瑞芳為了編譯所的主持者，真是百般思慮、苦心琢磨，這個人不但要有翰林之才，還要熟稔新學洋務才行，因此，張元濟就是夏心中獨一無二的理想人選。

可惜，張元濟在公學的工作才開展，要想「挖牆腳」，時機並不成熟。不久張元濟又代理南洋公學堂堂長。於是，夏只得把這個心思，暫時按下不表，他在等機會。

商務既設立了編譯所，主持大局的人不能空在那兒，於是張元濟就推薦了蔡元培（子民），蔡與他是同榜翰林出身，蔡也因印刷刊物與「商務」有些交往，他當時在上海搞革命活動，思想前進，具有時代感，主持一個「愛國學社」。

經過多次交換意見，蔡元培同意兼任商務編譯所所長，但他不離開「愛國學社」。

從這裡，也可以看到夏瑞芳，不但是個精明的經理人才，同時也是個與時俱進的思想

新潮人物，他並不因為蔡元培是搞革命的，而不敢引用這樣的人才。

「墨水瓶事件」　張菊生萌去意

一八九六年創辦的南洋公學，座落在上海徐家匯的原址，相信很多人都曾拜訪過，可能還有不少人在那受過春風化雨的教化與薰陶，那兒也就是現在的上海交通大學徐匯校區。

走在校園裡，仍可處處發現一些人文景觀、多幢老建築，讓人發思古之幽情，因為那都是百年老交大風雨歷程的見證。

一九〇二年，張元濟忍受不了陳腐的官僚體系，到底還是辭去了代總辦的職務，又回到譯書院；接替張元濟擔任總辦的是汪鳳藻，此人是個百分百的保守派。他在中日甲午戰爭時，曾為駐日公使，兩國開戰前，還站在第一線做外交折衝，搞得焦頭爛額，後奉召回京。

汪鳳藻接掌公學後，發生一樁學潮運動；那年張元濟離開南洋公學投入夏瑞芳的「商務」，顯然也受其影響。

這是中國近代教育史上第一次規模龐大的學生風潮，史稱「墨水瓶事件」，在那個封閉專制的社會，引發很大反響。當年十一月十六日，公學二百多名學生，抗議學校當局的不公而集體退學，南洋公學由《蒙學課本》培養起來的第一批外院學生，一九○二年已升入了中院，習慣了開放式教育的學生們對汪鳳藻保守的教學作風很不適應；其中有中文教習郭鎮瀛，作風更頑固守舊，他禁止學生閱讀一切新書報刊，就連國文還選用《大清會典》和《聖武記》等一些老舊教材，這讓學慣了《蒙學課本》的學生很不滿。

郭鎮瀛還反對中院五班同學在週末時聚會，研討西方自由平等；他以開除來威脅學生，不許他們聚會。

這年十一月五日，郭鎮瀛到中院五班上課時，發現老師座上有一支洗得乾乾淨淨的墨水瓶。

一支空墨水瓶能掀什麼波瀾？

空墨水瓶，肚內空空的、沒啥東西，影射「腹笥甚窘」？指肚子裡沒學問的意思，這是學生的侮辱還是挑釁？教習先生對號入座了！

郭鎮瀛在講臺上大發雷霆，「這是誰幹的？」

學生們回答：「不知。」

他責令同學嚴加追查，不得要領下，教習指著坐在前排的學生貝蠅伯、伍石卿，氣急敗壞的說：「限汝等三日內告發，否則嚴辦！」

始終找不到「元兇」，十三日，郭老師惱羞成怒，要開除三名學生，並以同學們隱匿不告，宣佈全班記大過一次，這下可引起五班學生的憤怒與不滿。激憤的學生找總辦汪鳳藻申辯、力爭，但汪袒護同僚郭鎮瀛，不改決定。

全班學生隨即決定分頭去其他各個班說明原因，表示反對這種專制壓迫，希望獲得同學們的支持，這一行動被新總辦汪鳳藻知道後，不但未深究情由，竟宣佈要開除五班全體學生，消息一傳出，全校大嘩，學生們當即推出代表，請求校方收回成命。

前面說過，汪鳳藻是個頑固保守派，他哪裡吃學生這一套，反而大發脾氣，堅決「以方專制武斷，最後決議全體退學表示嚴正抗議！

事態越鬧越僵，學生的反抗越發激烈，全校學生緊急開會，為捍衛學生公義、反對校儆效尤」。

這次學潮，二百多名學生全體走出學校，造成校內盡室皆空。總辦請人多方勸說，

有少數人返回學校，退出者仍有一百四十五人。當時社會輿論給予了支持和極高的評價。

「新民叢報」、「蘇報」等報等都以斗大標題並深入報導。一樁平地起風雷似的學潮，當時成了上海灘的焦點新聞。前總辦張元濟見到這個狀況，心中萌發去意。

在勸說學生回校繼續唸書的過程中，校方請出極受同學尊敬的先生蔡元培來調解。

看到這個情況，蔡元培是愛護同學的，雖心也不平，但還是先安撫同學，希望大家繼續回校上課，獲得學生代表承諾暫緩退學行動後，他隨即連夜去拜見公學督辦盛宣懷，而盛卻以「別有要事」避而不見。

十六日晨，仍無期待的結果。全體學生打好行裝，集體在大操場，等候最後的答覆。上午十時左右，未聞回音。全校學生以班級為序，一一走出了南洋公學。素有民主思想的蔡元培也憤而辭職，跟隨學生一起離校。

蔡先生把學生帶到「中國教育會」請求幫助。在教育會負責人章炳麟等的支持下，當即成立了「愛國學社」，使退學學生得以繼續學習。

這就是當初張元濟推薦蔡元培給夏瑞芳時，蔡無法全職在「商務」的前因後果。

現代化的新學啟蒙，讓中國無數懵懂的少年，變成了追逐民主自由的先行者。

幾年之後，從南洋公學走出來的蔡鍔、邵力子、黃炎培等人，在清末民初的政治舞臺上扮演了舉足輕重的角色。

此時，張元濟、蔡元培在商務印書館推出了一套體例完備的最新教科書，實現了他們普及新學的理想。

歷史的演進不但有優良的傳承，更可貴的還具有推動改革的啟後力量！夏、張、蔡等「商務人」寫下的近代中國文明教育改革史，無異給中國的現代化開啟了第一道閘門，激盪衝撞著舊時代枷鎖的巨潮，沛然莫之能禦！

元濟罷官　與粹翁訂交

張元濟不耐公學體制仍舊不脫衙門氣息。官方機構牽制繁複、人事勾心鬥角，讓他感覺像又回到北京詭譎險惡的官場，這個心理障礙，讓他興起不如歸去的念頭。

這個變化，對夏瑞芳而言，真是天賜良機，他知道，正式邀請這位人才進入商務的機緣成熟了。

一天，夏瑞芳邀張元濟吃小館，兩人寒暄過後，夏便單刀直入對張展開說項，他問

張，既然在譯書院不能展其所長，何不到商務來，大夥同心協力，共創理想未來？夏瑞芳一聽，心中大樂，因為在商場上的經驗告訴他，只要是錢能解決的，都不是問題，更何況，出多少高薪，對張元濟這個人才都是值得的。

夏瑞芳慨然提出張原先在南洋公學的月薪三倍多的數目，以示延攬人才的誠意。他的這片真心實意，張元濟深深的被打動了。

張元濟心動了，但為了測測夏的誠意，於是問，商務可請得起他這樣高薪的人？夏瑞芳一聽，心中大樂，因為在商場上的經驗告訴他，只要是錢能解決的，都不是問題，更何

這頓飯吃的賓主盡歡，自不待言。重要的是，兩人的商談，奠定了商務百年之基；張元濟經過一番痛苦的心理平衡和調整，他毅然選擇了民間創業，加入了商務印書館。張也略做投資，當時他兩袖清風，就讓夫人把一些首飾典賣了，作為資金。

佛家講的因果，或許就是這樣吧，水到渠成，還要靠因緣具足，清末民初的時勢，在推進民族整體的大改革之際，在某個因緣際會的角落裡，造就了夏老闆和張翰林的曠世結合；後來張元濟筆下有這樣的紀錄：

「昔年元濟罷官南歸，羈棲海上，獲與粹翁訂交，意氣相投，遂投身商務印書館。」

時為一九〇二年初，夏瑞芳主印務，張元濟掌編務，他們以「編教科書—編工具書—整理古籍—介紹西學」以啟民智，為國培元，因此成就了推展中國文化教育的輝煌大業。

張元濟先後任商務印書館編譯所所長、總經理、監理、董事、董事長等職，於一九五九年辭世。

張元濟加入商務印書館後，夏瑞芳勤與討教溝通，這個尊賢禮才的人格特性，也是他事業成功的一大因素。經過兩人的多次交流、討論，他們形成了業務發展以文化教育出版為主軸的共識，可以說對商務的方針走向作了改弦易轍的定調，此一變革，不但給商務帶來更多的盈利，而且大大增加了這個小小印書館的社會影響力。

社會影響力，是無形無狀的、但卻是雄渾巨大的，並非金錢可以購得，也不是靠政治力量可以攫取，必須根植於社會大眾的信賴和肯定，必須在民心裏樹立良好形象，此若非對社會群體有正面貢獻，則難以立碑。

《蘇報》案發生　蔡元培出逃

蔡元培雖然在商務編譯所時間不多，但他的理想實踐離不開「商務」。答應配合張

元濟策劃出版中小學教科書，但無法全職任事，因此他與管財務和印務的夏瑞芳總經理商量，採包辦制編寫新教科本，稿費是每兩課一元。

蔡制訂了這三種教科書的編輯體例和要求。這套課本中的修身教材、初小十冊和中學五冊由張元濟編寫，高小四冊由高夢旦編寫，另有蔣維喬、吳丹初負責史地，這套最新教科書融中西文化知識於一體，編纂者字斟句酌，苦心編修，開創了中國學校用書的新紀元。蔡元培曾明確指出，中國近代新式教科書的編撰「其創始者實為商務印書館」。

沒多久，由於受「蘇報案」牽連，蔡元培遠走青島避風頭，離開了「商務」，因此，張元濟只得自己接任所長之職。

《蘇報》原是一家日僑開辦的報紙，一八九六年六月創刊於上海。報刊內容多載市井瑣事。一九〇〇年由中國教育會成員陳範接辦，教育會和愛國學社的蔡元培、吳稚暉、章太炎等人，受陳範之邀由學社社員輪流為《蘇報》撰寫時評稿件。一九〇二年南洋公學發生退學風潮，《蘇報》首先報導，旋設「學界風潮」專欄，及時報導學潮消息，該報支援中國教育會和愛國學社的活動，聘章士釗為主筆。

一九〇三年夏天。鄒容、章太炎分別寫出轟動全國的〈革命軍〉和〈駁康有為論革命

書〉。並連續發表「讀〈革命軍〉」、「序〈革命軍〉」、「介紹〈革命軍〉」等文章，高呼革命為神聖「寶物」，要求建立「中華共和國」，推薦〈革命軍〉為國民必讀的第一教科書。一九〇三年六月，清政府照會上海租界工部局，以「勸動天下造反」、「大逆不道」罪名將章太炎等逮捕。鄒容激於義憤，自動投案。

《蘇報案》共審理三次，審訊地點在公共租界的會審公廨。會審公廨是中國政府設在公共租界的基層法庭，但在實際操作和運行，卻是依據西方的司法理念和程式審理案件，外國領事起主導作用。為此，當時慈禧老佛爺特別發話，一定要將「蘇報案」犯押到南京，凌遲處死。一九〇三年七月，《蘇報》被封。一九〇四年五月，章、鄒分別被判監禁三年、二年。一九〇五年，鄒容被折磨致死。

「蘇報案」終成歷史悲劇！有「晚清最後文字獄」之稱。

「商務」佚事　派歐洲特約撰述

蔡元培和商務有一段佚事，從其中可以看到雙方的傳奇關係，也顯示了中國傳統士子與儒商的氣度和人文精神。

那是一九〇六年，蔡元培三十八歲，已入中年的老翰林沒趕上「公派」出國留學的機會，於是向清廷駐德國公使孫寶琦提出申請，希望到德國半工半讀，並在使館兼「半職」，這個要求竟成功了。可是，蔡元培此時已是兒女成群，必須撫養妻兒一家四口，負擔可不輕。然而，孫寶琦答應每月只贊助白銀三十兩（合四十二銀元），而公使館只提供食宿，沒有職務和薪金。

海外生活大不易，蔡元培無計可施之下，想到在上海的同科老友張元濟，請他跟商務印書館打商量，能幫忙資助一些，張元濟找總經理夏瑞芳商量，夏尊重蔡是人才，於是破格資助，兩人就幫蔡安了一個歐洲特約撰述和編譯的名義，翻譯文稿以每千字三銀元計，撰述文稿則以每千字五銀元支付稿酬。除了部分匯到德國給蔡元培供生活費之外，並且將另一部分送到蔡家，作為妻兒家用。

據資料，這筆稿費每月可達一百銀元，比駐德國公使孫寶琦給的多了一倍有餘。因此蔡元培得以安心在歐洲學習，因靠「爬格子」半工半讀，乃至著述極豐。如〈世界觀與人生觀〉、〈文明之消化〉等論文，寄給商務印行的《東方雜誌》、《教育雜誌》發表，後來陸續還根據在德、法進修得到的新知識，結合中國文化編著了《哲學大綱》、

《倫理學原理》、《中國倫理學史》、《中學修身》等，也都由商務印書館出版。

今日，開車從上海延安路高架轉至G50滬渝高速，在青浦城區出口下，出收費站右轉至外青松公路，便能看到「上海人文紀念公園」的路標，順著指示，即可到達匯聚百位海上名人珍貴遺物的這座紀念館，在園內「意返苑」裡，一組精巧傳神的人物雕塑，必然會引起讀者的注視。

這組雕像塑造的正是蔡元培和張元濟。

兩人長達四十八年的交往中，為傳播新知、開啟民智真誠合作，不愧為近代中國文化發展史上劃時代的人物。

蔡元培被毛澤東讚為「學界泰斗，人世楷模」，張元濟被冰心稱作是「傳播知識的大師」。

二〇〇四年三月六日這組雕像落成。張元濟的長孫張人鳳表示，兩位老前輩身體力行，為二十世紀中國的文化教育事業做出了巨大的貢獻，在提倡科教興國的今天，學習兩位老前輩的思想和精神有很大的意義。蔡元培的女兒蔡晬盎在雕像前端詳時說：這尊雕像非常神似，很好地表現了兩位前輩的精神。看到中國社會翻天覆地的變化和文化教育事業

的進步，兩位前輩在天之靈也會含笑。

相隔「商務」意氣風發、引領教化風騷的年華，已跨過新的世紀、距離清末民初的「商務」印刷作坊只有幾個小時車程的「意遐苑」，後人看到的雖只是一座雕塑，但，那堅硬青銅凝固的是傳播新學、開啟民智的永恆功業；賢者交談的優雅，傳遞出的是志氣相投、惺惺相惜的千秋佳話。

哪天，當您有機會站在兩位賢者雕塑之前，抬頭仰望之際，或許還將引起幾聲緬懷的喟嘆吧？

第五章　為近代教育改革奠定基石

中國近代的教育改革，是晚清以來各項改革運動中最有成效的；而促進這項改革最有力的，是各種新式教科書的編製和普及；當時全中國編印教科書貢獻最大的，就是「商務印書館」。

清末民初，國事蜩螗之際，一家民營且無鉅資支撐的小印刷廠，能有如此成就，其傲人處，不單單只是這些「第一」，其深層意義乃在這個網站上標示的「昌明教育、開啟民智」，這是為民族播種、為社會立命的偉大貢獻，或許當初夏瑞芳並無此「功在千秋」的政治用心，但其結果則立下了近代中國的文明基石。

中國的近代基礎教育起步很晚；戊戌時，一八九六年，梁啟超的〈變法通議〉倡議變法維新，其中有學校總論、論科舉、論學會、論師範、論女學、論幼學。可以說這是近代中國倡導西化教育的開端，「學校總論」中指出：

「自強於今日，以開民智為第一義。」

他力主民智開於學，興學立於教，強調教育是繫乎國家興亡的大事！

梁啟超在〈幼學通議〉中進一步提出：

「西人每歲創新法，製新器者，以十萬計；著新書，得新理者，以萬計。而中國無一焉。西人每百人中，識字者自八十人至九十七八人，而中國不逮三十人。頂同圓也，趾同方也，官同五也，肢同四也，而懸絕若此。嗚呼！殆天之降才爾殊哉！」

這裡痛陳了清朝和西方國家在印製「新書」上的天壤之別。

晚清自強變法　革興新學

到了一九○○年，二十世紀的第一年，逢庚子年，因慈禧縱容義和團在北京「扶清滅洋」，圍攻使館、殺教士，英、美、法、德、日、意、俄、奧八國遂組成聯軍，攻陷大沽口，繼犯天津，直迫北京。八月十四日凌晨，八國聯軍對北京發動總攻。俄軍攻東直門，

日軍攻朝陽門，美軍攻東便門。上午十一時東便門被攻破，部分美軍最先攻入外城。英軍中午始達北京，打廣渠門，至午後二時許攻入。晚九時，俄、日軍各自由東直、朝陽破門而入。

慈禧見大勢已去，於是挾光緒倉皇逃到西安，隨即義和團兵敗，北京淪陷，聯軍大肆屠殺居民，搶掠財物，焚燒宮殿園林，頤和園珍寶也被掠奪一空。不得已，慈禧只好派李鴻章與奕劻為代表向列強求和，簽訂了遺臭萬年的「辛丑條約」，八國聯軍退兵，這次事件史稱「庚子之變」。這個辛丑條約有「九七國恥」之稱。

「辛丑條約」，中國要負擔鉅大的賠款，共付各國戰爭賠償四億五千萬兩銀，分三十九年付清，每年利息為四厘。此外，外國獲准在中國首都和一些要塞地方駐軍，使得國家幾無國防可言，自此中國人的民族自尊和自信心受到嚴重創傷。這場動亂也使中國百姓看清了清政府的腐敗無能，因而紛紛支持反清的革命運動。

「庚子之變」，對慈禧這位不可一世、掌控清末政局的皇太后打擊是巨大的。

一九〇一年元月二十九日，在回鑾之前，慈禧以前所未有的決心發佈「預約變法」上諭，隨後，湖廣總督張之洞和兩江總督劉坤一聯銜上了「江楚會奏三疏」，揭開了清末新

政的序幕。

「江楚會奏三疏」上奏後，慈禧頗有感觸，於是下詔，詔書中說：

「爾中外臣工，須知國勢至此，斷非且補苴所能挽回厄運，唯有變法自強，為國家安危之命脈，亦即中國民生之轉機。予與皇帝為宗廟計，為臣民計，捨此更無他策。」

慈禧認為「事多可行」，詔曰：「劉坤一、張之洞會奏整頓中法以行西法各條，其中可行者，即著按照所練，隨時設法，擇要舉辦。各省疆吏，亦應一律通籌，切實舉行。」

這個「江楚會奏三疏」在第一疏中就提到教育制度改革的問題，核心是倡新學、廢科舉。

看來，這一次慈禧頗有些痛下決心的味道。

朝廷上下一致共識，認為科舉要廢，可以慢慢來，但新學要興，刻不容緩。

光緒皇帝變革圖強的雄心更堅強了，一九〇一年夏，趁陪著老佛爺回鑾前後，接二連三發佈聖旨，督促各地督撫興辦新式學堂，訓稱：

「作育人才，端在修明學術，除京師已設大學堂應行切實整頓外，各省所有書院於省城均改設大學堂，各府廳直隸州均設中學堂，各州縣均設小學堂，並多設蒙養學堂」。

逢近代教育伊始　逐鹿新式課本天下

在這段變革時期，新式學校數量並不多，而且其課程多偏重語言、技藝訓練。

在興新學的同時，慈禧還根據張之洞、袁世凱等人的意見，鼓勵中國學生赴國外留學。因為歷史和地域原因，大清留學生赴日留學人數在一九○一年之後驟增，一萬兩千人為其頂點。

一九○五年，光緒三十一年，清廷終於廢除了科舉制度。這個走過了數千年時光、歷經無數朝代更迭的科舉考試制度，是由隋代開始實施的。廢科舉後，各種師範、實業、法政、軍事等專門學校設立，私人興學才開始蔚為風氣。

由於新式學堂普遍設立與出國留學興起，社會風氣和文化氛圍也跟著改變，凡受新式教育的讀書人，被稱為「新知識分子」，人數越來越多，他們漸漸取代傳統士大夫，成為社會主流。

這個千古大轉變，正好讓「商務印書館」趕上了！當時，朝野有志之士，開始推動改革教育目的的活動。

蔡元培認為，面對西學東漸趨勢，改革教育為救國之本，而新型出版業則是不可或缺的推動力量；對此，他曾這樣論述：

「我國印刷工業，始於五代，歷宋元明以迄於清，積漸發展。顧其所注意者，率在四部巨帙，供成學治國聞者之涉覽，間或稗版，以餉舉子，至於村塾課本，大多數兒童之所誦習，則大抵粗率不求精也。清之季世，師歐美各國及日本之制，廢科舉，立學校，始有教科書之名，為教習者，以授課之暇編纂之，限於日力，不能遷密。書肆絀於資而亟於利，以廉值購稿而印之，慰情勝無而已。近二十年，始有資本較富之書肆，特設印刷所，延熱心教育之士，專任其事，於是印刷工業，始影響於普通之教育……」

夏瑞芳和張元濟、蔡元培等「商務印書館」夥伴都看到中國必會有翻天覆地的改變，而傳統的科舉制度必將廢止，新式學堂會因應而起，必然普遍設立，於是他們共同商定著手編輯整個中國亟需而又欠缺的「新式教科書」。

戊戌後朝野上下對啟蒙教育，急著要從「三、百、千」的傳統教材中找出一條新路。

所謂的「三、百、千」，指的是三字經、百家姓、千字文；這些課本已經在中國這片土地上，被沿用了數千年，這段難以數計的日月裡，居然一直沒有任何改變、也無人試圖改變它，究其原因，有人將之歸咎為科舉考試制度的遺害之一。

在夏瑞芳、鮑咸昌等人創立「商務」的同年，一八九七年，盛宣懷的南洋公學又設外院（附屬小學堂），分國文、算學、輿地（地理）、史學（歷史）、體育五科；招生一百二十名，年齡在十一～十八歲之間。

就在這公學外院裏誕生了一套《蒙學教課書》，這套書是該公學師範院的師範生陳樊治、杜嗣程、沈權達等人所編纂，共三編，這是中國現代教科書的萌芽之作，光緒二十七年（一九〇一）年，由南洋公學印行。

在此之前的數千年，學生們的語文教育都來自於經史子集和聖賢書。而在此之後，他們有了真正的語文課本。但是，其內容多仿外國課本，而用字遣辭則不脫古文窠臼，如第一編第一課：燕、雀、雞、鵝之屬曰禽。牛、羊、犬、豕之屬曰獸。禽善飛，獸善走。禽有兩翼，故善飛。獸有四足，故善走。

第二課：人能言，禽獸不能言。鸚鵡雖能言，然不能知言之意。若讀書而不能知書之意，與鸚鵡無異矣。

在中國教育發展史上，《蒙學教課書》第一次較完整地表現出近代學科意識，推動了價值觀念和知識體系的更新，促進了近代中國人常識體系的轉型。

一九○三年，光緒二十九年開始廣設蒙養院，這「蒙養」兩字緣自中國傳統的說法「蒙以養正」，意思是說幼兒開蒙之際，要施予端正之教導，開發其更高的智慧，幫助孩童成為棟樑之材。換言之，蒙養院即為中國幼兒學校之始，是中國學前教育萌芽的開始，以現代語言來說，蒙養院就是幼稚園、幼兒園以至小學三年級。

光緒皇帝頒下多設蒙養學堂的上諭後，全中國各地老師有著共同煩惱──找不到合乎需要的好教科書，教學者也有一共同的希望──及早看到好課本的出現，蒙學課本的出版前景看好。

當時許多印刷廠都躍躍欲試，上海就有好幾種新課本。商務印書館當然不會缺席。

商務總經理夏瑞芳敏銳的嗅出這是個嶄新的無限商機。他立刻召開股東會，爭取股東同意多籌些資金，作為編印教科書之用，他慷慨陳辭：「這是個千載不遇的機會，我們非

但要掌握住，而且要爭取時間搶在前頭，時機不等人的。」

很快的夏瑞芳籌集了相當資本，劍及履及的開始朝著這個大目標邁步前進；但是，有了資本並不代表即可成事，他也明白自己的學歷程度，絕無法開展更大的局面，為此，他開始積極尋找人才加盟。此後，就有了張元濟、蔡元培、高夢旦、蔣維喬，乃至他逝世後的胡適、王雲五等文化巨人的加入。

「最新教科書」如何誕生？

一百多年了，是誰奠定了中國現代化教育的張本？是誰開啟這扇厚重的大門？又是哪些人在這漫漫長路上默默開拓前行？讓我們探尋的腳步就從這裡再深入一些。

趨前走近十九世紀初的「商務」，好更清楚的看看「最新教科書」是如何誕生的。

總經理夏瑞芳就找負責編務大計的張元濟商量，請他尋覓高手編輯新學課本，終於他們聘請到在紹興中西學堂任教職的杜亞泉加盟「商務」。

張元濟將編譯所分成國文、英文、理化三部，這種分類排組，很類似今日中學課程的安排。三部負責人分別是：國文高夢旦、英文鄺富灼、理化杜亞泉；這三位飽學之士之

間，卻留下一段有趣的軼聞：儘管他們才富五車、學有專精，但由於高、鄺、杜三人來自三個不同省份，依序分別是福建、廣東、紹興，出奇的是他們各講各的方言，雖南腔南調卻不同語，三人雞同鴨講無法溝通，只好勞動「翻譯」即席轉述，有時或者用筆談。此一趣聞佳話，至今還在「商務」的歷史回音中傳頌不已。

編印小學教科書的計畫是一項巨大的投資，夏瑞芳、張元濟等人肩頭壓力同樣是巨大的，他們知道自己必須全心全力投入，在延請到杜亞泉後，他們一步一步，謹慎而仔細的開創新工程。

一九〇二年（光緒二十八年）初，經過數月規劃編寫，於當年夏季第一冊脫稿付印，它開創了沿用至今的楷體字排文，而且每課都在一個新頁面上，並附有美麗的插圖。因此名為《繪圖文學初階》，共六冊，供蒙學堂每半年讀一冊，正好讀三年。出版後風行一時，不斷重印，和《華英初階》一樣暢銷，造成風行！

這是中國最早的一套精寫細編的國文教科書之一。蔡元培讚嘆為觀止的說，「這本書的認真，改變了整個出版業編書草率的風氣。」

如此的讚嘆，對任何一家印刷廠、出版商而言，都是非常重大的歷史定位。

「繪圖文學初階」 穿越至二十一世紀

《繪圖文學初階》，出版一百一十年後，二〇一二年，一個古籍收藏拍賣網站貼出《清代課本文學初階》的資料，供有興趣購買者瀏覽，轉載主要內容如下：

品種：古籍／善本其他古籍

屬性：年代不詳，普本線裝活字本八開頁碼不詳

簡介：帶圖卷全三

最高出價：一百二十元（人民幣）

成交時間：二〇一二─一─十五十七：十三：四十二

讓我們再進一步看看這本「年代不詳的善本古籍」內容，其實這是《文學初階》第三卷，其課文內容適宜小學初級班教讀。

　　第一課　花之色

園中有桃，其花之色紅。庭中有梅，其花之色白。盆中有菊，其花之色黃。

第二課　美人

此人之貌可謂美矣，此人之貌亦美乎，

此人之貌豈不美哉。

第八課　同行

兄弟同行，兄偕弟而行，弟隨兄而行，兄先行而弟隨其後，兄弟同行，兄先而弟後。

第十三課　玻璃

以玻璃為窗，則可以透光，以玻璃為燈，則可以避風，以玻璃為鏡，則可以照面。

同年同一時期，另一個拍賣網，貼出《文學初階》第六卷，其課文適宜小學高年級用，茲摘錄兩段課文，看看當時高小學生的程度是怎樣的。

第一課　孔子

春秋時有孔丘魯人也，生之於魯之昌平鄉，身長九尺六寸，年少好禮長仕於魯，官至司空，已而去魯適齊，齊人沮之，適宋衛，宋衛人逐之，適陳蔡，陳蔡人困之，於是反魯，時魯君失政，國事大亂，孔子知道終不行，遂不復仕，退修詩書禮樂，教授弟子，弟

子自遠而至，多至三千人，年七十三而卒，弟子皆心喪三年而去。

第四十六課　女學

女子猶是人也，而今人視女子，若以其賦稟懸殊不堪造就，僅能任針黹烹飪之事，而讀書識字者，百人中不得其一，豈知有賢女而後有賢婦，有賢婦而後有賢子孫，蓋丈夫之於子女若婦人之親故，幼童之得母教者為多，母賢而子孫無不賢也，母不賢而子孫難望其賢也，如是，則女學之重，顯見乎。

從這兩篇課文，可以明顯看到，「商務」編印之用心，承先啟後兼顧古今新舊觀念。

一九〇四年杜亞泉又編寫了《最新格致教科書》三冊、《最新筆算教科書》六冊。廣為各學校長期採用。近代有人讚譽商務這幾本小學用的格致、筆算課本，是「中國五千年文化史上開天闢地第一本」。

時至今日學術界的研究，對夏瑞芳經營的「商務印書館」的貢獻，多所肯定，如北京師範大學學報研究論文〈商務印書館近代教科書出版探略〉中，作者史春風於摘要中，開宗明義指出：

「商務印書館出版的教科書曾影響了幾代國人，潛移默化直至今日。商務教科書所創立的出版原則、出版思想，包括教科書的內容選擇，對我們今天的教科書編輯與出版都有相當的借鑑意義。而在屢遭劫難的近代中國，商務印書館以民營出版家們的艱辛奮鬥，努力為國人提供精神滋養，這樣的精神也將對後人產生長期的影響。」

第六章 民國第一CEO展現實力

在杜亞泉《繪圖文學初階》出版同一年（一九○二年）清政府頒布「欽定學堂章程」。且說光緒二十七年（一九○一）十二月，清政府任張百熙為京師大學堂管學大臣，命他制定一套新式學堂章程。第二年（一九○二）七月十二日，張百熙果然不負聖恩進呈了這套「欽定學堂章程」，因當年為壬寅年，故亦稱「壬寅學制」。這可以說是中國近代由國家頒布的第一個規定學制系統的檔，包括《欽定蒙學堂章程》、《欽定小學堂章程》、《欽定中學堂章程》、《欽定高等學堂章程》、《欽定京師大學堂章程》及《考選入學章程》等六件。規定各級各類學堂的目標、性質、年限、入學條件、課程設置及相互銜接關系。分學堂為三級七段。從蒙學堂、小學堂、中學堂、高等學堂（大學預科）、大學堂、大學院。從六歲入蒙學堂乃進小學堂至大學堂共二十年。

小學堂授以道德知識及一切有益身體事，中學堂增加科目，四年畢業，升入高等學堂

或大學預科，分政、藝兩科。政科為入政治、文學、商務三科的預備；藝科為入格致、農業、工業、醫術四科的預備。修業三年。大學堂以端正趨向，造就通才為宗旨，分政治、文學、格致、農業、工藝、商務、醫術七科。

可是這套「壬寅學制」並未實施，但是，它卻吹響了中國新式教育的衝鋒號。於是全國上下開始為迎接新教育時代動員了起來；其中站在最前沿、最重要的一環，就是編印新式教科書。

編輯出版一套適用國情、符合潮流的教科書，乃是當時民族興衰的關鍵。

這是一個歷史性的機遇，能否抓得住？端看主事者的眼光和魄力！

站在當時中國翻天覆地巨大改變的時刻，時勢把夏瑞芳推上了風口浪尖，他若無法在歷史巨浪中把好舵、掌好槳，「商務」也將被歷史吞噬。

「最新教科書」　開啟新紀元

編輯小學教科書的困難，主因是沒有經驗，無例可循；夏瑞芳不禁搖頭了，「這完全沒有章程可循呀！就算幾位先生學富五車，作首詩、寫篇賦還輕而易舉，但要給小學童編

寫一本實用的讀本，那可真難死人！」他暗自思索、暗自焦急。

當時「商務」的外資夥伴，正是日本著名的金港堂書籍株式會社，在明治維新運動發展近代義務教育時，該株式會社曾致力開發新式教科書，因此是富有歷史經驗傳承的出版社。

主持編寫教科書的張元濟腦筋一動，何不就近取材？透過總經理夏瑞芳延請有編制教科書的經驗的日資夥伴長尾慎太郎、加藤駒二、小穀重等當顧問，他們分享了很好的經驗和提出很多建議，以日本明治維新的教科書為藍本，去蕪存菁、配合國情重新編寫，並聘早稻田大學學成歸國的劉崇傑做翻譯。由張元濟、高夢旦、蔣維喬、莊俞四人共同編著，從一九〇三到一九〇四年之間，開過十五次動腦會，幾乎每個月都開會。

「商務」就在這樣不厭其煩的開會討論之下，擬定了一套跨越時代的編輯方針，以教材必須符合兒童心理，與兒童智力發展程度一致為大前提，一切以方便學生學習為最高原則。

這套編撰方針的制訂，由當時參加編輯工作的張、高、蔣、莊開圓桌會議共同腦力激盪，他們用很民主的方式進行，不管誰提出一個原則構想，大家詳加討論，有時過程激烈

如辯論，常常為一個構想，幾個人討論到深更半夜，幾乎廢寢忘食，也因此，這些原則越辯越周延，乃至於有些形式成為後來編寫教科書者的典範。

從編撰者之一蔣維喬回憶錄中，看到這樣記載：

「首先發明之原則，即為第一冊教科書中，採用之字，限定筆畫。⋯第一冊採用之字，筆畫宜少；且規定五課以前，限定六畫；十課以前，限定九畫；以後漸加至十五畫為止。」；此外，「選定教科書採用之字，限於通常日用者，不取生僻字。」；還有其他的原則：「第一冊每課之生字，五課以前，每課不得超過十字。」就連全書各冊的課文字數，他們也訂了規則：「第一冊每課從八字到四十字；第二冊每課從四十字到六十字；第三冊以下，不為嚴格限制，聽行文之便，⋯」

為求一定程度的高水準，他們每編一課必須經過四人一致點頭，才能定稿。這也就是前述夏瑞芳、張元濟等人採用「三個臭皮匠勝過一個諸葛亮」的集思廣益的編輯策略。

「往往一課之題，數人各試為之，而擇其較善者，又經數人之檢閱及訂正，審為無遺

憾焉，而後寫定」。

這些都是蔡元培在夏瑞芳遭刺殞命後所寫的哀悼文「商務印書館總經理夏君傳」中的記載。

凡此種種，真是思維周詳、鉅細靡遺，「商務」編印此書所下之苦心，了然可見！

蔣維喬當年親身參與編寫教科書，根據他的回憶，提供了第一手的現場印象。「教科書之形式，內容漸臻完善者，當推商務印書館之『最新教科書』。非作者身與其役，竟敢以此自誇，乃有客觀之事實可以證明。」

除了在編寫課文上精益求精，夏瑞芳是印刷業的行家，他不止一次的思考著：已然有了好的內容，該如何用好的印刷把它體現出來？

教科書是給學童讀的，如果用一般印廣告或聖經的紙張，雖色白但反光，很可能會傷到幼童的目力；因此，「商務」乃採用毛邊紙印刷，他們又增加一項基本原則：「但求結實耐用、不事外觀之美」。

《最新國文教科書》第一冊，終於在光緒三十年二月廿三日（一九〇四年四月八日）

出版了。蔣維喬在日記中寫著：

他還舉出的證明有：一、此書一出，無人能與其爭鋒！其他書局出版的相類讀本，漸漸不再發行。二、「最新教科書」領風氣之先，與後來的白話文讀本提前接軌，在文言當道的年代，不但許多民間經營書局、甚至學部國訂的教科書都仿效商務「最新」書例體裁。字裡行間，可以看到蔣先生很自豪。至一九〇六年，該套全書十冊出齊。

一百多年之後，再看到商務印行的這本教科書，仿佛墜入時光隧道，可惜不能見到夏瑞芳、張元濟、蔣維喬幾位先生的身影！這本書封面正中是書名《最新國文教科書》，「最新」二字做橫寫，字體較小，餘為大字直書，十分醒目，這種編排方式至今仍被運用。封面右印有四位校訂者的「抬頭」和姓名：日本前文部省圖書審查官小穀重、日本前高等師範學校教授長尾慎太郎、福建長樂高鳳謙、浙江海鹽張元濟。分四行並排列印。左列為編纂者：江蘇武進蔣維喬、陽湖莊俞、陽湖楊瑜統（陽湖、武進都屬江蘇境）；其下方為「上海商務印書館印行」字樣；其中「江蘇」、「上海」兩地名是橫排，字體也略

126

小，使得視覺上感到左列文字，上下兩節錯落有致，其編輯設計已有現代的「美工」概念了！

有心人可能會發現，五位中國先生未用其頭銜而以籍貫代之，從這一個小細節，可以看到中國人對其祖籍是非常重視的，時至二十一世紀，我們仍可見許多字畫作品落款處，還是有「武進」某某某、「汝南」某某某、「杭州」某某某等的字樣。溯其寓意，標示中國人心存祖上、不忘本的傳統美德也。

該書封底印的是英譯書名：*Commercial Press's New Primary School Text Books*

CHINESE NATIOAL READERS, WITH ILLUSTRATIONS.

接著是「編輯初等高等小學堂國文教科書緣起」，直指「萃海內外人士，以數人之力，費月餘之時，僅成此區區一小冊」，以說明編輯之謹慎、辛苦。

第一冊的「編輯大意」有如下說明：

授課進度，「每星期教授三課，每課二節，每天一節教授半課」。關於生字，「第一課至第六課，限定六畫；第七課至第十五課，限定十畫；全冊限定十二畫」，「每課字

數，自八字遞加至四十字，每課文字，必取其類似而相連貫者，雖純用文言，而語義必極淺明，且皆兒童之所習知者。」

選材上德智體群並重，如：「德育之事，注重家庭倫理，使兒童易於實行」，「智育之事，只言眼前事務，不涉機巧變詐，以鑿兒童之天性」，「體育之事，以振尚武精神」，「群育方面，多及學堂事，使兒童知讀書之要、多及遊戲事，使兒童易有興會。」

版面編排和印刷設計上，重視插圖：「插圖至九十七幅，並附彩色圖三幅。使教授時易於講解，且多趣味」；版面安排：「每半課中，其文字圖畫，必在一開之內。俾省翻閱之勞，以便兒童誦讀」、「以空格斷句。每句必在一行之內。誦習時，可免錯誤句讀」；字體級數以「初號大字印刷，俾兒童不費目力」；更難能可貴的是，夏瑞芳等認為「潔白有光之紙，易傷兒童目力。因此其用紙，「只求結實耐用，不事外觀之美」。

由之可見，諸位飽學之士和夏總經理，為了《最新國文教科書》的問世，幾乎經歷了一場「千錘百鍊」的編印煎熬。他們從擬定題目、集思廣益、彙整大綱、分工成編，接著又要經過分別審閱校對的關卡，人人都得聚精會神、不敢怠懈。如果有不符標準的，或者

128

出差錯的，即使已然費神費時完工，也要捨棄，絕不貪奢所花的時間和金錢。蔡元培也曾為此註解：「緣是而需靡者巨，不敢吝也！」。

如此精益求精的要求，正是「商務」成功的王道吧！

就《最新國文教科書》第一冊來印證，其主要功能是識字，一至五課為「單字」，筆畫少，且是兒童日常接觸到的事與物。第一課要學的是八個大字「天地日月、山水土木」，第二課是：「父母子女、井戶田宅」。第四課為「上下左右、大小多少」。第六課起才以兩字相連成詞，如第十課課文為：「父子、母女、兄弟、朋友，山下、地上、城市、村舍」。

第四十四課以四字連句：「姊執我手，降階看花，我欲採花，姊急搖手。」

自這些編排中，看到編輯們由淺入深、字字斟酌、句句推敲的用心，顯示了他們對學童學習心理和學習興趣的關心和細心。這套書學科齊備、內容優良、容量合理、選材周詳，超過了同時代的學堂教科書，成為一時之選。

編輯之一莊俞曾說：

「只有我館的《最新教科書》是依照學部所頒布的學堂章程各科俱有的，所以獨步一

又說這種按學期制度編輯的方法，「實開中國學校用書之新紀錄」。

「時。」

此後，另外的高級班教科書編寫完成，書名均標以「最新」字樣，如《最新初高小學國文教科書》，後陸續編印十冊，各科配套，同時又出版了《最新中學教科書》，銷數仍佔全國第一。

根據商務資深專家汪家熔先生研究，指出這套教科書「僅初、高小就有十一門三十二種一百五十六冊，是當時我國小學教科書課目最完備的一套課本，從一九〇四年一直發行到一九一一年底，發行量佔全國課本份額的百分之八十」，並強調：「這是我國第一套完整的中小學教科書。」

商務版《最新教科書》除初小國文外，還有筆算、修身、歷史等科目用書。

事實證明，夏瑞芳等幾位把舵人成功的將「商務」帶向時代的主流，並且長久以來一直是引領風騷前行者，至今已進入第三個世紀！

助教育改革　西方世界關注

鴉片戰爭後，在不平等條約保護下，基督教傳教士大量湧入中國。傳教士同時也開辦了教會學校。當時教會學校雖然有一定數量，但都零星分散在中國的各個地方，規模很小，缺乏系統性。直到一八七七年（清光緒三年），在華基督教宣教士在上海舉行第一屆全國宣教會議，在會議中一位名為狄考文（Calvin Wilson Mateer）的傳教士發表了一篇關於中國教育的演說，被認為是宣教史上的里程碑。

大會組成「益智書會」，專門負責教科書，包括數學，天文，測量，地質，化學，動植物，歷史，地理，語文，音樂等科目，直接影響了近代中國教科書。後改稱「中國教育會」，該組織有一個機關報──「中國報導」，顧名思義，是西方國家對中國事務的觀察站，一九〇四年該報特以一個專欄，報導「商務印書館的教科書」。文中對商務編輯出版的「最新教科書」（Primary School Textbooks）稱之為「拳頭產品」，他們非常關注這套教科書價所帶起的影響，竟然視作「拳頭」一般的強而有力！

該文更深入的分析，認為這些教科書：

「非常有助於新教育改革，而這新教育變革對中國的學校又將起到革命性作用」。

一九〇七年又有一篇報導，指出商務印書館教科書的出版，是「過去幾年裡最重要的事件之一」，並稱那是：

「標誌著中國的兒童從傳統經典的束縛下解放了出來，進入到充滿趣味與知識的新的文學作品中」。

文章中認為中國在經受了許多外國人或腐敗的異族政府帶來的苦難之後，產生了一種「日本式的愛國主義」，尤其指出「愛國主義與革命的邊界已經非常模糊」，從而覺察到了中國已經醞釀著革命的思潮。

它的「最新教科書」以超群出眾的影響力開啟了中國學生的「教科書時代」。應該說，它「最新教科書」成為西方世界觀察中國的重要視窗，因此有學者認為：商務印書館和是塑造現代中國人的重要起點。

這位狄考文（CalvinWilsonMateer）是美國北長老會牧師，一八三六年出生，一八六二年神學院畢業，第二年，一八六四年來到中國，在山東登州（今蓬萊）開始傳教。不久在城裡一個人稱「觀音堂」的小廟裡辦起免費義塾，招收家庭貧困的子

弟。一八七二年取「以文會友」的意思，學堂正名為「文會館」，全名「登州文會館（TengchowCollege）」，是中國境內第一所現代高等教育機構，其規模不斷擴大，以致後來成為「齊魯大學」的前身。狄考文直到一九〇八年在青島去世，他一生在中國傳教幾達半世紀。

齊魯大學於二十世紀三〇年代是其全盛時期，老舍、錢穆、顧頡剛、馬彥祥等學術名家先後在該校執教。孔祥熙曾任該校董事長兼名譽校長。齊魯大學曾號稱「華北第一學府」，和燕京大學並稱「南齊北燕」。

在大量出版新式教科書之外，商務也很重視傳統古籍，例如《辭源》、《四部叢刊》、《萬有文庫》、《叢書集成》、《百衲本二十四史》、《漢譯世界學術名著叢書》等等。

夏瑞芳的「野心」並不滿足於這種種讀物，商務還創辦了《外交報》、《東方雜誌》、《教育雜誌》、《小說月報》、《少年雜誌》等，更多面向的、多角度的為讀者開啟廣闊的閱讀視野，同時也為中國社會開闢了多元的文教、文化、文學出版傳播領域，用響亮、震撼的印刷滾筒機器，在灰暗的、陳腐的古老民族史頁上，鋪墊出色彩絢麗、內涵

壯闊、形象嶄新的全民知識化的大道。

現代出版史上　眾多「第一」

商務印書館是中國第一家現代出版機構，在中國出版史乃至文化史上創造了諸多第

一。

擇要列之如下：

* 出版第一部語法學學術專著──《馬氏文通》（一八九八）；

* 出版第一部中英文對照排版印刷的英語教科書──《華英初階》（一八九八）；

* 出版第一部英漢字典──《商務書館華英字典》（一八九九）；

* 第一個使用紙型印書（一九○○）；

* 第一個系統地介紹西方學術論著（一九○二）；

* 第一個使用著作權印花（一九○三）；

* 第一個作為文化企業引進外資（一九○三）；

* 第一個作為民間企業聘請外國專家和技師（一九○三）；

* 第一個系統地編印出版「最新教科書」等近現代中小學教科書（一九○四）；
* 第一個創辦《東方雜誌》等一系列現代意義的雜誌（一九○四）；
* 第一個採用珂羅版印刷（一九○七）；
* 出版第一部由中國學者自己編纂的雙語辭典《英華大辭典》（一九○八）；
* 第一個採用電鍍銅版印刷（一九一二）；
* 第一個使用自動鑄字機（一九一三）；

以上，是Cp.com.cn（商務印書館中國網）刊載該館創造的中國現代出版史上的「第一」，其中發生於一九一四年之前的「第一」；一九一四年之後還有許多了不起的「第一」，因本書主角夏瑞芳當年遇刺身亡，其後諸項在此暫不列舉。

民國第一CEO　創意管理特質

夏瑞芳從學徒出身，創業後被推任為總經理，在十九世紀的中國，「總經理」一詞，應該是很新鮮、很新潮的。當時的買賣行號負責人或稱大掌櫃、或叫老闆。以今天企業界領導層觀之，夏瑞芳在「商務」大掌櫃這個位置，他所負責的除財務盈虧、品質管控、市

場調查、產品推廣、營運決策等等，無異於首席執行官（Chief Executive Officer, CEO）的職務。對企業負有重大決策的反應和執行力。

夏掌櫃懂得人才對公司發展的重要，他求才若渴、廣納天下高手，禮賢尊士敬重有加，他對編譯所的先生們，一聲一句「老夫子」，還讓印書館工人稱先生們「師爺」。他對有能力、有貢獻的人，不惜高薪侍奉，而且善解人意的給予體貼照應，編譯所的「老夫子」們，不但享有高薪水，夏總經理還供給膳宿、茶葉和水煙。如此待遇之下，若其他公司想從「商務」挖牆腳，那真是難上加難！

一個成功的大掌櫃或總經理，在二十一世紀行政領導的理論中，有所謂的特質與行為。領導者之所以獲致成功，這是因為領導者個人具有某些人格特質，例如雄心或者是野心。

近代心理學家多年來一直在探討一個問題：「能夠創新的領導者有哪些特質？」夏瑞芳那個時候可能連領導人的概念都不存在。

本書外一章中，以二十世紀電子革命中的傳奇人物賈伯斯做引子，以比喻夏瑞芳對中國近代文化傳播的貢獻，同樣是傳奇人物；如果進一步做比較，也可看到這兩位距離幾乎

一百年的「CEO」，他們有哪些相似的領導特質？

哈佛大學研究人員花了六年時間，訪談三百多位高階主管，對創新的領導者有哪些特質？做了非常深入的研究。假設他們直接去問夏瑞芳或賈伯斯，會否得到同樣的答案？

根據這項研究，創新者與一般無創造力者相比，前者擁有最重要的獨特能力：「連結」（associating），也就是將看似不相關的問題、或者不同領域的思維結合起來。這篇發表在二〇〇九年十二月號《哈佛商業評論》的論文〈創新者的DNA〉（The Innovator's DNA）中，有這樣的論述：

「若詢問富於創造力的人是如何做到的，這個答案很尷尬，因為他們並不是用「做」的，而是「看到」的。富於創造力的人具先天特質，很機敏的可看出端倪。原因在於他們能夠機靈的連結自己的各種經驗，即時產生新的點子。可惜的是，這種特質並不常見。」

夏瑞芳於一九〇一至一九〇二年，三顧茅廬找到張元濟作編譯所所長，開拓洋文書籍市場，以及後來占領新教科書市場等等，他的創造性可以說是他敏捷的「連結」了政治時勢與社會氣候，他先「看到」了而後也「做到」了。

二〇一一年八月三十一日一篇報導：蘋果公司的雙i產品（iPhone、iPad）風靡全球，靈魂人物賈伯斯閃辭執行長，世人為之震撼。當期美國「新聞週刊」以賈伯斯為封面人物，介紹他的人生故事和帶領蘋果邁向巔峰的過程，並分析歸納賈伯斯出類拔萃的創意管理十大準則，戲稱為「十誡」。

讓我們來檢視其所歸納的賈伯斯創意管理「十誡」：1.追求完美，2.指定專家，3.冷酷無情（賈伯斯對腰斬的產品一樣引以為榮。），4.拒絕民調（賈伯斯說過，「人們唯有在看到東西時，才知道自己要什麼」，所以他自己就是「焦點團體」，親自測試產品達數月。），5.處處留心，6.化繁為簡，7.保密防諜（蘋果內部每個人的所知都僅限於分內須知的部分，高度保密讓賈伯斯能夠盡情發展出驚天動地的商品，且不怕消息走漏。），8.短小精悍（麥金塔電腦的原始團隊正好一百人，如果增聘一人，表示有人要走路。），9.恩威並重，10.極致樣品。

如果硬把這「十誡」套在夏瑞芳的身上，確實不太恰當也不公平，因為時代環境不同、競爭對象不同、產品性質不同，「大掌櫃」的做法也會不同；然而，若再仔細歸納夏

瑞芳的經營手法和策略，我們還是可以找到符合這「十誡」的特質，例如：「專注」、「留心」、「極致」、「完美主義」、「菁英主義」等等。

特別是「商務」在夏瑞芳的擘畫與領導之下，樹立了延攬菁英、追求完美的優良傳承；他不僅用高薪聘才，而且真心尊重人才，除張元濟、蔡元培、高夢旦、蔣維喬，還有後來的葉聖陶、胡愈之、胡適之、鄭振鐸、王雲五等大學問家。

因著這些人才寶庫，夏瑞芳等人的審時度勢，在大時代的變革中，掌握先機，加上處處留心、極致成品的經營優勢，商務才能歷經烽火與動盪，走過一百多個春秋，依然屹立不搖，成為文化、出版界的泰山北斗！

雄心與氣魄　創最早中外合資企業

晚清民初的文化出版重鎮不在北京而在上海，除了拜五口通商之賜，很大程度上受惠於商業利益與文化傳播的衝激與結合。口岸都會從當年就是思想變革「瘟疫」的溫床也是其傳播的搖籃。上海是通商口岸文化最典型的代表，街頭巷尾處處洋溢著西式思想和生活方式，順勢也散播著時髦的消費形式。

商務印書館在如此氛圍下，除了不遺餘力的引介西方的思想文化，在古老國家土地上傳布現代化的文本和思維，他們同時也吸收了資本企業經營的嶄新理念。

夏瑞芳銳意經營下，「商務」已然超越「印書館」的規模和型態，以今日的標準來看，當年的商務可說是中國最早的現代化企業。

事實上，商務也是中國第一個收納外資的企業。

一九〇三年十月商務與日本極具聲譽的「金港堂」出版會社簽訂中日合資經營合同。雙方決定將「商務」改為股份有限公司，資本額為二十萬元，雙方各出十萬元。總經理由夏瑞芳擔任。

商務擴大了資金，遂即在上海閘北寶山路購置地皮建造新廠房，添置新機器、引進國外技術，率先在中國採用彩色石印、照相銅版和珂羅版（collotype）印刷技術，這是一種最早的照像平版印刷，因多用厚玻璃作為版基，所以又叫「玻璃印刷」。

在經營管理方面，商務也逐步從一個家族企業走上了現代企業制度運作的道路。這個決策的拍板人就是「CEO」夏瑞芳。

「金港堂」是日本明治維新時代日本四大教科書出版社中最大的一家。它起到的關鍵

作用，是商務近水樓台引入日本編製新式教科書的模式、理念，並得到「金港堂」專業人士提供經驗，致使商務教科書在競爭激烈的當時，能夠市場勝出、領袖群倫。

而其中一套十冊的《最新國文教科書》，風行長達十年之久，發行至千萬冊，影響之大，難以估計。可以說，這是「商務」爾後雄踞中國出版業龍頭、成為第一文化傳播機構的基礎。

因此，「中外合資」的歷程應是「商務」成功的重要因素之一。

辛亥革命後，日本侵華野心暴露，侵略行徑日益強橫，引發全國性的反日情緒，商務與日本人合資受到社會的側目，商務負責人非常重視這個問題，幾經會議討論，決定不計一切代價收回日股。

這個重任還是落在夏瑞芳肩上，他不計奔波之苦和溝通之艱困，多次往返上海和日本之間與日本股東交涉，最後以多支付股金作為補償，才讓日本商人退讓股權。

張元濟公子張樹年撰寫的〈紀念夏公粹芳〉文中，對這件事的敘述和評價是這樣的：

「夏公在商務與日本金港堂的十年成功合作問題上，所表現出的深謀遠慮，令人欽

佩。一九○三年，日本金港堂主想在上海辦出版公司，按其印刷技術的優勢，商務難與四敵。夏公採取與其聯營的辦法，利用日方的資金、技術和人才，發展中國民族出版業。在聯營中，夏公堅持由中方承擔日常經營、人事、行政權，日方只在董事會中派員行監察之職。這在列強侵華、國勢頹危之際，恐怕是絕無僅有的、堅持主權利益的一次中外合資吧。

一九一三年，夏公親赴日本，商務印書館與金港堂簽訂日方退股協議。翌年一月十日在《申報》刊登商務印書館廣告，宣佈公司為完全由國人集資營業的公司，已將外國人股份全數購回。這又全靠夏公堅韌不拔的毅力。

一九一四年一月十日，《申報》刊登了商務印書館的一則廣告，宣佈：

「公司為完全由國人集資營業的公司，已將外國人股份全數購回。」

這天，坐在辦公室裏的夏瑞芳看著《申報》上的這則廣告，深深地鬆了口氣，肩頭感覺輕了許多。

這天，當他下班走出位於河南路的發行所，準備登車回家；竟遭暗殺，子彈正中要害，夏瑞芳沒有留下一句遺言，便與世長辭。

同年一月三十一日，，夏瑞芳被刺殞逝後二十一天，商務印書館召開股東大會，針對收回日股權作報告說：

「本公司創業於光緒二十三年，資本甚微。至光緒二十九年，有日商糾合資本來申開設書肆。本公司彼時編輯經驗、印刷技術均甚幼稚，恐不能與外人相競，乃與之合辦。資本各居半數，即各得十萬。並訂明用人行政一歸華人主持，所有日本股東均須遵守中國商律。資本既增，規模漸擴，利益與共，辦事益力。自是以來，吾華人經驗漸富，技術漸精，嗣後增加股份亦華人多而日人少。至民國二年底，華人股份已居四分之三，日人股份僅得四分之一，即三千七百八十一股。日本股東對於公司毫無干涉，遇事亦無不協同維持。

……但同業競爭甚烈，恆以本公司外股為藉口，詆排甚力，公司因大受障礙。即如前清學部編成中學書，發商承印，獨不與本公司，謂其有日本股之故。近來競爭愈烈，如

江西則登載廣告，明肆攻擊；湖南則有多數學界介紹華商自辦某公司之圖書，湖北審查會以本館有日本股，故扣其書不付審查。如此等事不一而足，此不過舉其大概。每逢一次之抨擊，辦事人必費無數之疏通周旋，於精神上之苦痛不堪言喻。故由董事會議決，將日股收回。此事關係重大，本應召集股東會籌議辦法。只因商機宜密宜速，故由董事會擔負責任，先行議決。此事應請股東原諒。

……此項收回日股均係夏總經理苦心經營，乃得達此目的。不意大功告成，本公司可免去同業傾軋最為有力之一題目，朝登廣告而夏總經理即於是夕在公司門首遇害。此誠公司最不幸事，想眾股東聞之亦必惻然者也。」

末一章　子女有成　夏瑞芳精神長存

夏瑞芳遇刺後，商務印書館董事會本計畫於外灘立銅像紀念這位開創老闆，此議被他的遺孀鮑翠玉婉拒了，她相信，丈夫的心念是幫助更多的年輕人有書可讀，因此，最後決定在夏瑞芳貧困的家鄉青浦興建一所學校，也就是「夏氏小學」。

鮑翠玉，一八七三—一九三八，為瑞芳生有一子八女；時年翠玉四十一歲，長子夏鵬十七歲，最小的女兒只有二歲，丈夫的遽然去世，對一向依賴深重的愛妻與子女而言，不啻天崩地裂、頂樑柱傾頹，感情上、精神上和生活上的依託頓失，但篤信基督的她堅強地毅然將撫養、教育九個子女的責任一肩扛起。

為了支持子女們出國留洋，翠玉把寶山路有十二個房間的巨宅出租並抵押，換取現金供給子女海外學費和生活支用。

夏鵬字筱芳，或小芳（一八九七—一九七六），是英美子繼承父名的叫法，有junior

瑞芳的意思，他是夏家獨子，也是長子，上海聖約翰大學畢業後負笈美國深造，一九二〇年畢業於賓州Wharton商學院，攻讀工商管理碩士。

夏鵬婚禮　宋美齡女儐相

夏鵬娶的媳婦是香港的世家小姐吳思卿（Rose Ng-Quinn），他們的婚禮當然是十分洋化的海派形式，而在多位美麗時髦的女儐相中，有一位後來在中國歷史上非常顯赫的人物，那就是宋美齡，當天的新郎倌一定不會想到他們的這位女儐相後來嫁給了蔣介石！歷史的足跡風雲流轉、無常變幻，也充滿啼笑皆非的無奈與荒謬。

一九二二年他學成歸國，為了能為商務做更多的貢獻，他又渡重洋到英、德考察印刷實業。等他進入商務工作時，先在進口部當值、隨後調任工廠部秘書兼營業部主任的秘書，一九二五年當選董事、一九二七年升任經理。

一九三二年日本侵華發動「一‧二八」事變，日軍向閘北一帶進攻，駐守上海的國軍十九軍奮勇抵抗。據統計，事件中中國金錢損失約為十四億元。閘北華界的商號被毀達四千二百零四家，房屋被毀一點九七萬戶，損失慘重。

位於閘北的商務印書館大樓等建築均遭轟炸，當時夏鵬負起重建商務大樓的重任，同年八月一日商務在戰火廢墟中復業，與此同時，中國大地上有千千萬萬的商家行號重新站立起來，他們見證了中國人堅強與勇毅的民族特性。

夏鵬在商務復業後出任發行所所長，爾後轉換事業跑道，在三〇年代中期任職上海商業儲蓄銀行，主掌新成立的保險業務。夏鵬在三〇年代末期偕其夫人及女兒離華赴美定居。其後，直到五〇、六〇年代他在紐約仍負責上海銀行在美業務，一九七一年他移居香港，仍獲邀出任香港上海銀行和臺北上海銀行的董事。

夏鵬於一九七六年去世，享年七十八歲，由於父親過世得早，長兄如父，他對妹妹們還有外甥輩，都很悉心照顧。

夏鵬給他們夏家留下唯一親骨血夏連蔭（Julie Lien-Ying How, 1926-1982），是哥倫比亞大學的高材生，尤其對中國當代史很有研究，曾和美國學者韋慕庭（Clarence Martin Wilbur）哥倫比亞大學教授合編《關於共產主義、民族主義及在華蘇聯顧問文件，一九一八—一九二七年》（哥倫比亞大學出版社，一九五六年出版），此書成為中國共產黨和美國研究中國近代史的重要文獻。

在史學家唐德剛一篇「談《顧維鈞回憶錄》」文章中有一段提到夏連蔭：

　　五〇年代初，中國共產黨革命成功，國民黨中的大批要人紛紛移居美國，其中包括胡適之、李宗仁、孔祥熙、陳立夫等。於是，哥倫比亞大學便擬就了一個中國口述歷史的計畫，並組建了一個研究室。然而，全室的人員僅僅才兩名，一名是我，一名是夏連蔭小姐。夏小姐是哥倫比亞大學的一名碩士，她的英文很好，但中文差一些（事實上連蔭會講流利的上海話、粵語和國語、法語。作者按）。起初，校方指派她去訪問孔祥熙，採訪工作結束後，她又去訪問陳立夫。而我最初訪問的是胡適之博士，工作完畢之後，我又去採訪李宗仁先生。

　　顧維鈞先生在中國政治舞臺上的時間很長，在許多重大的歷史事件中，他都是一位很有資格的歷史見證人。……當時顧維鈞正在海牙國際法庭裡做大法官，每年在紐約的家中僅有三個多月的休假時間。於是，哥大就與我們商量，希望我們能抽空在顧維鈞回到紐約度假的時候訪問他，當顧維鈞假滿返回海牙之後，採訪工作就告暫停。那時，我正忙於訪問李宗仁先生，實在擠不出時間，因而最初訪問顧維鈞的是那位夏連蔭小姐。

特別的是，夏連蔭訪問過的陳立夫，正是涉嫌槍殺夏瑞芳的幕後主使人陳其美的姪子。據指出，連蔭曾在訪問過程中，詢及此一歷史懸案，而陳立夫顧左右而言他，未正面回答此尖銳問題。

夏連蔭因為做口頭歷史訪問，結識很多國民黨風雲人物，例如與宋子文一家就成為好友，宋的長女宋瓊頤結婚時，她是伴娘之一。可見她們的親暱關係了。

夏連蔭夫婿華仲厚一九一八年出生在無錫蕩口。父親華繹之先生曾是清政府候補道台，是無錫近代著名的實業家、教育家、收藏家和慈善家。於一九四一年獲麻省理工學院內燃發動機工程的碩士學位。華仲厚一九九八年退休後，返回故鄉修惠山腳下的華孝子祠，族人特別為文記載，其中介紹了他們的婚姻：

華先生有過傳奇的婚姻，年輕時他在美國，正值二次大戰。當時，他不能回國，卻又不想在美國成家，從而耽擱了青春年華，回國時已是而立之年。以後局勢動盪，顛沛流連，他沒有過多地考慮自己的婚姻大事，直到五十三歲時（一九七一年）愛神光顧，華先生與認識多年的夏連蔭小姐在美國結婚。夏小姐天生麗質，從小在美國長大。祖父是上海

商務印書館的創辦人，父親是上海商業儲蓄銀行的董事，曾與華先生同在紐約的環球貿易公司工作，擔任副經理職務。

夏連蔭是個才女，具有驚人的記憶力，能過目不忘。她在美國凡賽（Vassar College）大學畢業後即去法國留學，後在美國哥倫比亞大學讀碩士，從事中國歷史的研究，對陳獨秀思想和中共黨史頗有研究，是著名的中國問題專家。會說流利的上海話、廣東話、英語和法語。華先生和夏小姐結婚後十分恩愛，周遊列國，遍閱各地風情歷史，生活無憂無慮。然而天有不測風雲，婚後幾年夏小姐就得了癌症，一九八二年不幸病逝，年僅五十六歲。

夏家八千金　人生際遇美滿

夏瑞芳的八千金全部在上海中西女子中學畢業，而且多數也都出國深造。

長女瑪莉（Mary Mo-Li How, 1900-1957）在波士頓Simmons學院進修，未完成學業即返國，隨後下嫁上海商業儲蓄銀行任經理的黃漢樑（Han Liang Huang），兩人未能白頭偕老，以離婚結束關係。

次女璐德（Ruth Loo-Tuh How, 1901-2005）畢業於新英格蘭音樂學院（New England Conservatory），返國後任音樂老師，她的婚姻有些傳奇，因為她嫁給了與姨媽離婚的男人，也就是前姨父郭秉文（Ping-Wen Kuo, 1880-1969）。

郭秉文，字鴻聲，南京江浦人，一八九六年畢業於清心書院。此後十年間，除在清心書院任教一年外，曾在海關、郵務及浙東鎣金局等處工作。一九〇八年入美國俄亥俄州的伍斯特學院（Wooster College）深造，宣統三年，一九一一年獲理學士學位。民國元年，獲美國哥倫比亞大學師範學院碩士學位，兩年後，一九一四年獲教育學博士學位，為中國獲得哥大師院博士學位之第一人。同年八月回國，被商務印書館聘為韋氏大字典總編輯。

一九一五年任南京高等師範學校教務主任並參加學校籌建工作。一九一九年任南高師校長，又積極策劃在南高師基礎上，建立中國第二所國立大學——東南大學，於一九二一——一九二五年出任國立東南大學首任校長。

中國的高等學校，「五四」之前除教會大學外大都僅招男生而不招女生。教育史上稱此現象為「女禁」。一九二〇年四月七日，南高決定自一九二〇年暑期正式招收女生，郭秉文與蔡元培、蔣夢麟和胡適等人商定，南北一致行動，共同開放「女禁」，此後中國的

大學開始招收女生。

女婿郭秉文　安排梅蘭芳登百老匯

郭秉文在促進中美文化、學術交流方面，藉著留學美國的人脈，開啟了前所未有的局面，一九二六年二月，杜威、孟祿等倡議，以庚子賠款來源，三年為限，常年補助二點五萬美元設立「華美協進社」。

一九二六年五月，哥大教授保羅曼洛（Paul Monroe）與胡適等，在紐約創立「華美協進社」（China Institute），郭秉文任首任社長。該機構以「促進中美文化交流」為宗旨，邀請國內名流到美講學或表演，宣傳中國教育與文化。

郭秉文擔任社長期間有兩件特殊事蹟值得記述：1.一九二六年費城博覽會中，郭秉文以華美協進社為基礎負責籌備中國館的展覽。郭秉文環繞著「東西方文化史比較」、「最近我國新學制一覽」、「中國教育制度之進化」三個大項目組成「Five Thousand Years of Education of China（五千年之中國教育）」展覽主題，用英文形式向參觀者展示了中國教育的歷史、現代教育的迅速發展以及在西方影響下的新的中國文明的發生。展品中重要的

圖表和教育物品有：中國教育史之發展觀、孔子與中國之教育、中國大學教育之一斑、實業教育與中國之經濟改造、中國之平民教育運動以及商務印書館所出品之各種教科書與雜誌、清華學校之校景模型等。

2. 一九三〇年二月十六日晚，中國著名京劇藝術家梅蘭芳在郭秉文精心安排下登上紐約百老匯第四十九街劇院，首次向西方觀眾展現中國國粹之魅力，西洋觀眾為之傾倒，造成空前轟動，這可說是首開中西方戲曲文化交流之先河。

華美協進社成為了民國初年以來，中美文化交流的重要平臺，先後邀請眾多中美兩國名人前往相互往來、演講與討論。例如中國新文化運動的領袖人物胡適和燕京大學神學院院長劉廷芳前往美國講學，另一方面，也邀請了美國多位大學校長赴華演講、介紹美國文化。

近百年來華美協進社，除了上述梅蘭芳外，還有馮友蘭、趙元任、吳貽芳、賽珍珠、老舍、林語堂等著名人士來拜訪，儼然成為來自中國的學者在美國舉行演講、座談的重要舞臺。

華美協進社一直走進二十一世紀，一直默默扮演中美文化交流的推行者的角色，不但

未曾間斷，而且日益活躍生動，為了繼承和傳播中華文化，促進中國學者與社區的交流，發揚學者之家的傳統，也是西方人士學習中國文化、藝術、語言、乃至建立商業關係的重要橋樑。

華美協進社於二○○三年成立「人文學會」，由何勇、汪班擔任共同主席，在紐約向美國主流社會搭建了推廣中華文化的廣闊平臺，舉辦各項文學、戲曲、書畫等演說、演出活動，諸如夏志清、白先勇、余秋雨、鄭愁予、王安憶、張充和、舒乙等兩岸名家專題演講，精緻文化精采紛呈，受到中美文化界的肯定與讚譽。

郭秉文一九三一年受孔祥熙之邀再次回國出任國際貿易局局長，並加入銀行金融界。

一九四五年抗戰勝利，出任聯合國救濟總署副署長兼秘書長。

一九六九年八月二十九日郭在美國逝世，此後，璐德繼續在華府郵局工作，一直到退休。郭秉文過世後，夫人璐德仍然致力於郭氏創辦的位於華盛頓的中美文化協會工作，同時與友人合創「美華婦女會」，宗旨在提高美國社會對中國婦女的認識。夏氏家族凡有活動聚會，璐德總是中心人物，她對待所有子侄輩以寬厚與慈愛，此外她與首都華盛頓附近的華人音樂家過往熱誠而頻繁。晚年她還承繼先夫的教育理念，曾在台灣的大學及紐約

華美協進社設立郭秉文獎學金，並在八〇年代末期，中國文化大革命結束後，為紀念父母（夏瑞芳先生及夫人），慷慨資助青浦的夏氏小學復校。

三女名璐懿（Louise Loo-Yee How. 1903-1983），留學俄亥俄州的歐柏林音樂學院（Oberlin Conservatory of Music），她嫁的夫家是上海灘台灣首富，板橋林家花園的少東林勤（Frank Ling），生有一子林京（Bobby Ling, 1937-1962）。林家是台灣數一數二的望族，座落於板橋占地面積約六千零五十四坪的「林家花園」是他們家族興旺的見證，據說該林園是根據曹雪芹《紅樓夢》中描繪的大觀園形式興建的，歷經戰火摧殘和風雨滄桑，一度失修破敗，而今經重新修葺，恢復部分建物，可說是台灣先輩留下的珍貴遺產，也是一座體現台灣歷史與傳統建築的寶庫，現為台灣著名觀光景點。

四女璐梅（Loo-Mei How, 1904-2001）是Julliard音樂學院的高材生；話說當年夏瑞芳夫人很懂音律，經常在清心堂彈風琴、唱聖詩，在她的薰陶下，八位千金都有相當音樂造詣。

璐梅在美國時經表姐介紹得識康乃爾大學土木工程系畢業的江元仁（Nelson Y Chiang），回國後就結婚，生有二子：江成賢（Louis Chiang, 1931-）和江齊賢（Paul

Chiang, 1934-）。此君隨國府遷台，改行經營旅遊業，在蔣經國任退輔會主委開闢橫貫公路時，參與上海儲蓄商業銀行所屬中國旅行社於天祥山麓興建「天祥招待所」，亦即「太魯閣晶英酒店」前身。

史濟良祖父　曾任紐約總領事

五女璐雅（Rhoda Loo-Ya How, 1905-2006）畢業於上海滬江大學，一九三二年與史久榮（Albert K.Y. Suez）結縭，生下獨子史濟良（Julian Suez, 1933-），也就是促成本書完成的主要人物，他的祖父史悠明（Iuming Suez）為民初外交官，曾任紐約總領事。

史濟良對其英文姓氏何以是Suez，而非一般通用的拼音（台灣是Shi、大陸也是Shi、香港是Sze），他表示：我祖父號『藹士』，他做外交官駐節外邦時，發現西洋人對『史』的發音有困難，於是靈機一動，乾脆把『史藹士』做為英文的last name，因此他家的姓就拼成了Suez。

史濟良的父親史久榮可算是中國汽車工業發展的拓荒者，他長期在雲南昆明汽車廠擔任廠長，因工作與事業難以兼顧，一九四八年終於與長期分離兩地的妻子璐雅仳離；他們

的獨子濟良自小是跟著母親長大的，後來在麻省理工學院學成，一九六二年進入IBM紐約
州工作，曾在香港及北京分公司任職，於一九九三年退休，但他退而不休，仍然為老東家
IBM做中國客戶到美國的接待、幫IBM到中國接洽業務等。他現寓居紐約。

六女璐韻（Loo Yuin How, 1906-1972）在上海滬江大學畢業後，也進入紐約茱麗亞
音樂學院深造，在美與從事貿易的應和春（Paul Huo Chin Yin）結婚，生有二子一女：應
國瑞（Robert K. Yin, 1941-），應樂美（Theresa Yin, 1947-），應國民（George K. Yin,
1949-）。

他們的次子應國民是University of Virginia 法學教授。二〇〇三—二〇〇五年曾任美
國國會稅務聯合委員會幕僚長（Chief of Staff, Joint Committee on Taxation）。史濟良認
為這位表弟，是其家族同輩中在政界最有成就的，而且也是年紀最輕的。

七女夫家叔王正廷　駐美首用「雙橡園」

七女璐瑛（Lydia Loo-Ing How, 1909-1968）則是聖公會寧波最早的華人牧師王有光
的孫媳婦，民國初年大外交官王正廷是王有光的第三子，璐瑛丈夫王恭芳的父親王正康是

正廷的二哥。

王正廷一九一九年為中國出席巴黎和會全權代表之一，北洋政府代理內閣總理。南京政府長期擔任外交部部長、駐美大使等，一九三八年胡適接替他的大使職務，其駐美時租用的「雙橡園」（Twin Oaks）官邸，後來成為中華民國駐美大使館，至今仍為駐美臺北經濟文化代表處所在。王正廷並為中國第一位國際奧會委員，被後人稱「中國奧運之父」。

么女的公公黃佐庭命案　震驚美國

么女璐敏（Loo-Ming How, 1911-1999），夏瑞芳逝世時她只有兩足歲。及長下嫁黃宣平（Wilfred S. B. Wong）生有一子：黃翊民（Wilfred Wong Jr., 1935-2013）和一女：黃安琪（Winifred Wong, 1938-）。宣平也是黃家的老么，巧合的是，他的父親黃佐庭（Theodore Tso-ting Wong）也是在盛年（四十三歲）時遭人殺害辭世。

一九〇八年，美國政府將當時清朝政府賠償給美國的庚子賠款中超出美方實際損失部

份的一筆錢款作為獎勵中國優秀學生赴美留學全額獎學金，中美雙方協定創辦中國學生留美預備學堂「清華學堂」，一九○九年由清華學堂負責從全國招考庚款留美官費學生。趙元任在被錄取的七十二人中名列第二，胡適名列第五五。

這「庚款」即是庚子賠款。前面第五章〈晚清自強變法迎革興新學〉一節中曾提到庚子那年，八國聯軍侵華，打進北京，後逼著清政府簽訂喪權辱國的「辛丑合約」。僅「賠款」一項，就按當時中國人口總數每人白銀一兩，計上四億五千萬兩。後來，英、美等國宣佈將賠款中尚未付給的部分「退還」，用作在中國興辦學校、圖書館，及設立各種學術獎金，或派遣留學生的經費。美國於宣統元年（一九○九）開始退還庚款，當年就選派了第一批留美官費生。趙元任、胡適這一年考的是第二批。

而黃佐庭當時受清華學堂委派出任「中國留美學生監督」，「衙門」設在華盛頓特區，他的工作主要是管理留美中國學生的生活、學習。他在一九一一年升任中國留美學生華盛頓分校校長。在黃佐庭任留美學生監督十年中有數百名優秀中國留學生學成歸國，其中有梅貽琦、趙元任、胡適、竺可楨等。

趙元任在他寫的〈從家鄉到美國〉中有這樣一筆記述：

「我第一次到哥倫比亞特區的華盛頓市，和清華學生監督黃佐庭以及後來在一九二〇年代任清華大學秘書的李岡發生接觸。」

一九一九年冬，某日，黃佐庭辦公室遭兩槍手打劫，是兩名中國留學生，他倆向黃佐庭「借用」公款，遭黃佐庭拒絕，兇手開槍殺害了黃佐庭及他的兩個聞聲趕來的男秘書吳炳新、助手謝昌熙。

三屍命案新聞曝光，震驚全美，華盛頓郵報、紐約時報等主要大媒體，連日以頭條新聞處理。

這件謀殺案很快就被美國當局偵破了，二個兇嫌被判了有期徒刑二十五年。但過了幾年，美國有某宗教團體前去探監時，訪問了這兩人，他倆都表露出真心悔過的樣子，該慈善團體向司法部門提出要為他們減刑，所以不久這兩人竟被假釋出獄。

黃佐庭因保護公款而遭歹徒殺害，當局給他家屬頒發了一筆撫恤金，並用美國的銅棺材將他的遺體運回上海，安葬在當時的外國人公墓「靜安公墓」內（即現在的靜安公園）。

黃家家世與西方基督教關係密切，是上海聖約翰大學早期奠基者，黃佐庭的姊夫便是

上海聖約翰書院（大學前身）創辦者卜方濟（Francis Lister Hawks Pott）。

後記　外孫給的定位　史濟良心中的外公

傳承尊重文化、重視教育偉大精神

不求聞達於世，全心力澤於萬萬代

史濟良（Julian Suez），夏瑞芳的外孫，是夏氏第五女璐雅的兒子。

他的記憶中，初始，外公只是一張泛黃的遺照，自打記事起，這照片不論昏晨一直矗立在外婆大客廳的木櫃之上。濟良幼年與母親、兩位姨母、以及江氏表兄弟姐妹，在外祖母一九三八年去世前，同住在外祖母家。濟良對當時外祖母家如何簡樸，如何特別注重教育，篤信基督教以及熱愛音樂的種種家教，至今記憶猶新。濟良記得外祖母曾告訴孩子們當年外祖父生活樸素，就是在商務印書館業務發展，經濟日進後，還是僅僅擁有一套會客裝，每天晚上要洗乾淨，第二天才能穿著了去上班。

對外祖父的印象是模糊的、就像那張泛黃的老照片，有關外公的回憶也是片片斷斷的。

「還不到十歲的時候吧，我聽大人們談到外公，隱隱約約感到有些神秘與畏懼，因為大人們用極輕而又謹慎膽怯的語音迷說外公是被壞人用槍打死的，而且最好少提這件事，免得招來更多不測。」

濟良又補充說：「我媽告訴我，外公逝世時，她只有八足歲，對自己父親的記憶也是有限。」但濟良記得母親對他說過的外祖父的二三事。

一件是：在二十世紀初，商務印書館業務蒸蒸日上時，在上海某一名戲園每天夜戲都訂有戲票數張，以供濟良的外祖父母觀賞，或供商務其他經理招待印書館特別貴賓或主顧觀賞。但他們本家孩子們都不准用這些戲票看戲，有多餘戲票，孩子們也不能用。所幸當時濟良以及其他本家孩子們都自幼受鼓勵欣賞西方音樂，對傳統中國戲曲一無興趣。

另一件是：當時無論外祖父工作到多晚，回家時必定攜帶水果幾籃給兒孫們吃。

濟良的外祖父這些生活上的事雖屬平常，然而也顯示出外祖父如何愛護並教育子女，並向他們介紹了西方文化。

甚麼動力讓史濟良興起為外祖父立傳記的念頭？

他表示從小到大，對外公的認識，一直是朦朦朧朧的。到了四十多歲在ＩＢＭ工作多年後，接觸到西方大企業的營運，一天突然想到外祖父當年在思想封閉的年代，他突破幾千年的傳統禁錮，率先引進日本的資金、先進的技術，而又掌控實際經營權，「這讓我不由得對他生出極高的肯定和敬仰之情。」

事實上，這位外孫對祖輩的認識與瞭解，的確極有限。「我不瞭解，這樣一個對中國近代文化、出版、教育等發展，做出這麼大貢獻的人，為什麼鮮為世人所知？連他自己的子孫後輩，都對他如此陌生。」

「我自覺有責任，把外祖父的事蹟做個完整的整理，在歷史的背後，將他發掘出來，重新面向陽光，讓世人知曉他，最起碼我們夏家後人，不可不知這位在近代中國貢獻卓著的先人。」

這就是深藏在史濟良內心深處最大的渴望和期盼。

「可惜我表姊夏連蔭早逝，她去世時年僅五十六歲。使得今日我們家族已無姓Ｈｏｗ的了！這可說是令人相當遺憾的。然而至今我們家族裡，雖沒有真正夏姓子孫，但在我們

這些與夏氏有關的表兄弟姐妹的心底，都深深認為我們「就是」夏氏家族！我們也都心意一致地要我們的後代子孫們永永遠遠記得，我們的外祖父是怎樣的一位偉大不朽的文化實業家！

跳脫家族感情的因素，僅就歷史角度審視，史濟良覺得「夏瑞芳」這個人物雖陌生，但外祖父對國家、民族的貢獻，使他更感到敬佩，而且認為應該讓這位先人重新站在今人眼前，讓更多人認識他、肯定他。

史濟良心中如何給夏瑞芳作歷史定位？

「我外公並非學者型的人物，他未受過太多的教育，他也不是叱吒疆場或政壇的廟堂人物，他是一介布衣，充其量可躋身出版業的商人。要給他做歷史定位，的確不易。」史濟良有些遲疑。

「但，反過來看，一個未受過很高教育的人，卻能為民族復興與改革教科書作為事業大計，這種智慧和胸懷，何等了不起呀？他並非居廟堂之上運籌天下的人物，但他一生所做所勞，卻比爾虞我詐、兵戎廝殺，自認有豐功偉業者更有益於國族、人民。所以，我覺得，與其為他做歷史定位，不如做他個人生命的肯定；外祖父經營商務印書館，已然超脫

營利與出版的範疇，他和張元濟、蔡元培、王雲五等人傳承的是尊重文化、重視教育，這是放諸古今中外都仰之彌高的偉大精神；他們做到了，而且是默默地耕耘，不求聞達，但澤被萬萬代。」

外孫史濟良心中，夏瑞芳為中華民族奉獻的是經世偉業，所謂的「歷史定位」已然不足以彰顯他博大、無私、心懷千秋的胸襟和思維。

「夏瑞芳公，儘管他已逝世一百年，雖然很孤寂，但他長存我們心中，他值得後人敬重和懷念的，不是甚麼金銀財產、豐功偉業，而是讓人景仰欽敬的千秋胸懷！他老先生給人們留下了智慧，正直無邪的人格，以及一種至高的創新與企業精神！」

外孫史濟良深情有感，如是說。

尾聲　天道酬功　精神不孤

一代巨人的殞落，不但是夏氏家族的棟樑傾頹，也是一個民族社會的重大損失。

夏瑞芳的不幸遇難，雖結束了一代CEO的生命，但為商務印書館的千秋發展，奠定了永續經營的基礎。這也歸功其高瞻遠矚、魄力雄渾的特性。

商務印書館後來歷經抗日戰爭（國共內戰），受到炸彈、砲火轟炸，印書館大樓遭大火吞噬，機器遭毀壞，但，該館上下仍同心齊力，克服困境，共度難關，屹立不搖，為廣大讀者服務，在兩岸三地同創老字號盎然生機。

夏瑞芳是大時代的見證者，也是推動者，任何一個大時代都有破舊立新、衝擊歷史的巨大變革，而其中必有頂天立地或中流砥柱的重要人物；夏瑞芳在清末民初，中華民族最紊亂、最脆弱的時刻，以他短暫的生命，為民族的現代知識教育建立的基礎，淵遠流長影響至今；以他卓絕的意志，為中國印刷出版事業，鋪展了現代化的軌道，引領風騷垂範至

169

今。

　夏瑞芳遇刺辭世，倏忽百年矣！雖然兩岸史書疏於記載，使他默然沉寂，然而天道酬功，巨人其萎，貢獻不朽，斯人精神不孤也！

附錄

• 茲收錄蔡元培等三位先生給夏瑞芳寫的紀念文章，這也是百年來可尋及有關夏先生傳記的三篇專文。

商務印書館總經理夏君傳

蔡元培

我國印刷之業，始於五代，歷宋、元、明以迄於清，積漸發展。顧其所注意者，率在四部巨帙，供成學治國聞者之涉覽。間以餖飣稗販，以餌舉子。至於村塾課本，大多數兒童之所誦習，則大抵粗率不求精也。

清之季世，師歐美各國及日本之制，廢科舉，立學校，始有教科書之名。為教習者，以授課之暇編纂之，限於日力，不能邃密。書肆詘於資而亟於利，以廉值購稿而印之，慰情勝無而已。

近二十年，始有資本較富之書肆，特設編輯所，延熱心教育之士專任其事。於是印刷之業，始影響於普通之教育。其創始之者，實為商務印書館。

商務印書館者，青浦夏君之所建設，而以漸擴張之，且總經理之，以終其身者也。君諱瑞芳，字粹方。少孤貧，學於基督教長老會之清心堂，習排字于英人所設之《文匯報》館。歷在《字林西報》館、《捷報》館任事，積有資本，乃與妻兄鮑君咸恩，創設商務印書館。其始翻印印度英文讀本，而以華文譯注之，名曰《華英初階》，若《進階》，在當時初學英文者甚便之。

戊戌以後，有志維新者多游學日本，競譯日本書以求售，君亦數數購之，然不輕于付印，丐通人抉擇。其中太草率者襲諸簁，所費雖不貲，不惜也。

庚子以後，學校漸興，教授者苦不得適宜之教科書，君乃為商務印書館厚集資本，特立編譯所，延張君元濟主其事。亦常以重資購當代名士嚴復、伍光建、夏曾佑諸君之著作，且發行辭典、小說、雜誌之屬。而尤所聚精會神以從事者，實為小學教科書。其事在我國為至新，雖積學能文之士，非其所習，則未易中程式。往往一課之題，數人各試為之，而擇其較善者，又經數人之檢閱及訂正，審為無遺憾焉而後寫定。其預擬而為目，綜

合而成編，審慎周詳，無不如是。編輯者之目力，緣是而虛靡者頗巨，不敢吝也。

教科書以外，又有教授法參考書，非學生所需，售書遠遜，然亦盡心力以為之。以是

出版後，大受教育界之歡迎，而同業之有事於教科書者，度不能以粗筋之作與之競，則相

率而則效之。於是書肆之風氣為之一變，而教育界之受其影響者大矣。

民國三年，君年四十有三，追溯商務印書館之創設，既十有七年矣。一月十日，以有

於總發行所之門前狙擊君者，君負傷而歿。君對於印刷業之盡瘁，遂以是終。知君者無不

痛惜之！君娶於鮑，有子一，曰鵬。女八人。

蔡元培曰：君信仰基督教，內行甚修，接人甚和易，宜若可以盡其天年，而卒被暗

殺，倘所謂天道無知者邪？然君雖歿，而君所創設之事業，方興未艾，其於教育之影響，

則輾轉流布而不能窮其所屆，雖謂君永久不死可也。

夏君瑞芳事略 蔣維喬

夏君，名瑞芳，字粹方，江蘇青浦縣人，居南庫，先世業農，父母以貧故，鬻其田

宅，至上海設小肆于董家渡，而以君養於戚家，時年方九齡也。

君年十一,已有知識,會母因事旋裡,欲隨至上海,母不許,潛行,君逾時方覺,知母必取道珠家閣,尾追之,中途阻於河,不得渡,鄉人以小舟至,君求附載,鄉人以其幼也,勿之許。君乃大號曰:「若勿載我,我將投河死」。

鄉人憫之,乃移舟傍岸,遂得渡。行抵珠家閣,遇母於船埠,母憐其志,乃挈之至上海。是時,基督教長老會設清心堂于滬南,而分設小學於各鄉,凡小學生肄業二三年,成績較優者,得升入清心堂。其學科則語言文字之外,兼教工藝,概勿取學膳費。

君父母乃令君入小學肄業,三年,升入清心堂,復五年,父歿,君年十八矣。自念家益貧,不能久讀書,必習一業以自給,乃謀於清心堂監院某君,入同仁醫院習醫。同仁醫院者,亦基督教中所設立之慈善事業也。爾時院中規模尚小,凡入學者,無一定資格,亦無醫科科目,惟學為助手而已。君留院一年,自問不能出人頭地,乃棄之至文匯報館習英文排字。

後數年,入字林西報館,工資所入,足以自給,乃娶同事鮑君咸恩之妹為室,而母氏又於未娶前一日病歿矣。旋入捷報館,為排字領袖,所入益豐。乃與鮑君咸恩兄弟謀,合資自營印刷業,凡集資四千餘金,創立商務印書館於上海。時君年二十六歲,即民國紀元

前十五年丁酉正月也。

我國向無印刷事業，君乃親赴日本考察，有所得，歸而仿行之。於是印刷之術，煥然一新，營業亦日盛。至戊戌歲，變法議起，新書新報，風行一時，印刷事業，亦隨之發達。越三年，拳亂既定，清廷復行新政，廣設學校，君以為國民教育，宜先小學，而教科書尤亟，乃於印刷所外，兼設編譯所。君計畫宏遠，欲廣集資本，成一出版之大公司，謀諸人，無一應者。壬寅年冬，日本人原亮三郎、山本條太郎等，攜鉅資來上海，思營印刷及出版業。

君念我國之印刷術及編輯上之經驗，皆甚幼稚，非利用外資，兼取法其經驗不可，遂與訂約合資，改商務印書館為有限公司，華股日股各半，而用人行政權，悉歸本國人，並遵守我國商律。自是以來，編輯印刷，均大進步，營業亦益擴張，支店遍於全國，全傭者凡三千餘人，公司資本，屢有增益，計丁酉至去歲癸丑，閱十七年，由四千增至四五十萬，而是時日本人所占股額，亦僅四分之一矣。世人或以此巨大公司非完全華商自辦為惜，君乃親往日本，與諸有股者謀，卒盡數購回，轉而售諸國人。

民國三年一月六日，議定立約，至十日登報佈告股東，而君即於是夕，為暗殺黨狙擊

於公司總發行所之門前，傷重不能言語，送至仁濟醫院，遂歿，年四十三歲。

君豁達大度，性果斷，知人善任，喜冒險進取，百折不回，故能以微細資本，成極大之公司，於我國工商及教育事業，影響絕巨。君本基督教徒，其待人接物，和易寬厚，愛人如己，視敵如友，深合基督教義焉。

其弟瑞芬，幼孤，撫養之至成人，為之授室。瑞芬視君如父，而視嫂如母也。君居商界久，積有資望，被舉為總商會議董，凡商人因賬務受平成於商會者，多為君所區理，在職三年，人無閑言。君平生於公益，多所盡力，嘗獨立設一學校於其鄉，教里中子弟。以清心堂為所從受教也，則合同學為聯舊會，集資為擴充齋舍，改為清心中學校。其他如愛國女學校、尚公小學校、孤兒院，皆有所資助焉。葬之日，執紼者數千人，聞其事者，無知與不知，皆為淚下云。

紀念夏公粹芳

張樹年（張元濟之子）

商務印書館的成立，可謂「應運而生」反映了民族的覺醒，代表了國人的希望；這正是商務得以發展成今日這般規模的基礎。當然，回顧商務的百年歷程，初期一些主

事者篳路藍縷，艱苦奮鬥的業績，令人欽敬，難以忘卻。其中夏瑞芳先生（一八七一——一九一四）所表現的創業者氣魄和企業家眼光，尤為突出。

夏公名瑞芳號粹方，商務印書館創辦人之一。在他任職期間，商務從一家家庭作坊式的小印刷廠，發展成為當時我國最大的出版企業，夏公功不可沒。

我自幼就從父親菊生先生口中經常聽到夏公的名字和他的故事，至今留下深刻印象。

夏公出身于排字工人，熟悉印刷技術，他與鮑咸恩、鮑咸昌、高鳳池等創辦商務印書館，開始以承接印件為主。可是他不滿足於此，受維新圖強的時代潮流影響，夏公把精力轉向出版。要出書，就得有編譯力量。於是，商務設立了編譯所。夏公先後請蔡元培先生和我父親任編譯所所長，為嗣後商務數十年間執全國書業牛耳奠定了基礎。這在本世紀初是個了不起的舉動。開近代風氣之先的一些出版物先後問世。從商務出版嚴譯名著、林譯小說之後，知識階層風氣漸起變化，西方文化逐步傳播，影響及於全社會。因此，我說夏公瑞芳不僅是我國新式印刷事業的先驅者，更是一位思想開明、目光遠大、魄力恢宏的企業家。

我父親曾說過：「夏君招余入館任編譯，余與約，吾輩當以扶助教育為己任。夏君諾

之。」從系統編寫新式教科書，到出版「帝國叢書」、「歷史叢書」、「法政叢書」及各種辭書，商務印書館始終以開啟民智、發展教育為宗旨。父親與夏公的友誼正是建築於此基礎之上。

一九○六年，吳興陸心源宋樓擬出售全部藏書，夏公得知後向父親徵詢意見，願以八萬元購下，供編譯所諸君之用。父親十分感動。當時商務全部資產僅數十萬元。這是何等魄力！後來此事未能成功。宋樓藏書為日本財閥靜嘉堂文庫囊括而去。從此事可見夏公「扶助教育為己任」的至誠之心，和保存祖國文化典籍的愛國情懷。

夏公在商務與日本金港堂的十年成功合作問題上，所表現出的深謀遠慮，令人欽佩。

一九○三年，日本金港堂主想在上海辦出版公司，按其印刷技術的優勢，商務難與匹敵。夏公採取與其聯營的辦法，利用日方的資金、技術和人才，發展中國民族出版業。在聯營中，夏公堅持由中方承擔日常經營、人事、行政權，日方只在董事會中派員行監察之職。這在列強侵華、國勢頗危之際，恐怕是絕無僅有的、堅持主權利益的一次中外合資吧。

一九一三年，夏公親赴日本，商務印書館與金港堂簽訂日方退股協議。翌年一月十日在《申報》刊登商務印書館廣告，宣佈公司為完全由國人集資營業的公司，已將外國人

股份全數購回。這又全靠夏公堅韌不拔的毅力。可是就在這一天，夏瑞芳先生不幸遇刺身亡，享年僅四十又三。我清楚地記得，那天我正發高燒，睡在母親的床上，有人來報信，說夏先生被人暗害，中了槍彈。全家為之震驚。父親後來談起夏公，常常黯然神傷，其情其景，我至今記憶猶新。

蔡元培先生在《商務印書館總經理夏君傳》中說：「君雖歿，而君所創設之事業，方興未艾，其於教育之影響，則輾轉流布而不能窮其所屆，雖謂君永久不死可也。」

今天商務印書館已走過百年坎坷之路，正迎接新世紀的來臨，這是可以告慰夏公英靈的了。

夏瑞芳先生年表

一八七一　　生於上海青浦縣南庫村。

一八八二　　離開青浦，尋抵上海與在美籍牧師家中做傭人之母親相聚。

一八八四　　入美國教會主辦之清心書院學習，結識鮑咸恩、鮑咸昌兄弟及高鳳池等人。

一八八九　　父歿，離開清心書院，受僱於上海同仁醫院做勤雜工。

一八九〇　先後於上海英文「文匯西報」及「字林西報」任排字員。

一八九五　母歿，同年與鮑翠玉女士結褵。

一八九七　於上海創立商務印書館。

　　　　　子夏鵬出生。

一九〇〇　長女夏瑪莉出生。

一九〇一　結識並問策於張元濟（張氏於一九〇二年入商務）。

　　　　　次女夏璐德出生。

一九〇三　三女夏璐懿出生。

一九〇四　四女夏璐梅出生。

一九〇五　五女夏璐雅出生。

一九〇六　六女夏璐瑛出生。

一九〇九　七女夏璐韻出生。

一九一一　八女夏璐敏出生。

一九一四　　一月十日「申報」頭版報導商務印書館全為中國獨資。

一月十日晚六時半左右於上海河南路上的商務印書館前遇刺身亡。

夏瑞芳擔任總經理期間，商務印書館大事紀

一八九七年　　夏瑞芳、鮑咸恩、鮑咸昌、高鳳池在上海創立本館

一八九八年　　出版中國第一部融會中西文化的學術著作《馬氏文通》

　　　　　　　出版中國最早的英漢對照讀物《華英國學文編》

一九〇〇年　　中國首次用紙型印書

一九〇二年　　張元濟進館，設編譯所、印刷所、發行所，蔡元培任編譯所所長

一九〇三年　　在湖北漢口設立第一個分館，其後在海內外共設分館支館八十多家

　　　　　　　首次使用著作權印花

　　　　　　　首創新學制最新小學教科書

一九〇四年　　創刊《東方雜誌》，至一九四八年終刊，是中國出版發行時間最長的雜誌

典瑞流芳──民國大出版家夏瑞芳

一九〇五年　開設小學師範講習班，並設附屬小學

一九〇七年　創辦尚公小學

一九〇八年　出版《物理學語彙》《化學語彙》，是中國最早出版的審定術語彙編

一九〇九年　辦商業補習學校

一九一〇年　辦師範講習社，辦養真幼稚園。
　　　　　　創刊《小說月報》

一九一四年　香港分館開設

（節錄自「商務印書館（香港）」網站『大事紀』）

這是夏家唯一的全家福照，攝於1912-1913年冬。左起：夏璐梅，夏璐德，夏璐韻（前坐者），夏瑞芳夫人鮑翠玉，夏璐敏（八女），夏璐瑛（七女，前坐者），長子夏鵬（立者），夏瑞芳，夏瑪莉，夏璐雅（前立者），夏璐懿。

Left to right: Loo-Mei How; Ruth How; Loo-Yuin How (seated in front); Bau Tsui Nyoh (seated); Loo-Ming How (seated on table); Lydia How (seated in front); Bang How (Standing); How Zoen Fong (seated); Mary How; Rhoda How (standing in front of Mary); Louise How, circa 1912-1913.*

夏瑞芳像（約攝於1912-1913）。
How Zoen Fong, circa 1912-1913.

夏瑞芳夫人鮑翠玉（約攝於1933-1934年）。
Bau Tsui Nyoh, Mrs. How Zoen Fong, circa 1933-1934.

圖版

1
8
3

繪圖部（1910-1913年）。
Illustration / Drawing Department at the Commercial Press, circa 1910-1913.*

商務印書館攝影部（1910-1913年）。
Photograph Department at the Commercial Press, circa 1910-1913.*

閘北商務印書館大院裡的馬拉靈車。
Horse-drawn hearse at the Commercial Press compound, January 1914.*

閘北商務印書館大門
前的抬棺人，1914年1
月。
Pallbearers in front of the Commercial Press main entrance, January 1914.*

夏瑞芳靈堂，1914年1月。
Mourning hall, January 1914.*

馬拉白綾靈車。
Decorated horse-drawn hearse, January 1914.*

夏家九兄妹攝於大哥從美國留學歸來後（1922-1923年）。
左至右：璐韻，璐德，璐梅，璐敏，夏鵬，璐瑛，璐懿，瑪莉，
璐雅。
Left to right: Loo-Yuin How; (seated) Ruth How; Loo-Mei How; Loo-
Ming How; (seated) Bang How; Lydia How; Louise How; (seated)
Mary How; Rhoda How, circa 1922-1923.

攝於夏鵬與吳思卿小姐的婚禮上，1925年。後排（左至右）：璐瑛，
璐雅，璐韻，璐敏。前排（左至右）：璐懿，瑪莉，璐德，璐梅。
Back row (left to right): Lydia How; Rhoda How; Loo-Yuin How; Loo-
Ming How. Front row (left to right): Louise How; Mary How; Ruth
How; Loo-Mei How, 1925.

夏瑞芳九個兒女及家眷與夏夫人，攝於1933-34年冬，六女赴美之前。後排（左至右）：七女婿王恭芳，四女婿江元仁，夏璐敏，夏璐懿，夏璐韻，夏鵬，五女婿史久榮。

前排（左至右）夏璐瑛，夏璐梅，四女兒子江成賢，夏瑪莉，鮑翠玉，五女兒子史濟良（夏夫人膝上），兒媳吳思卿，長子女兒夏連蔭，夏璐德，夏璐雅。
Left to right: Wang Kungfong; Nelson Y. Chiang; Loo-Ming How; Louise How; Loo-Yuin How; Bang How; Albert K.Y. Suez. Seated (left to right): Lydia How; Loo-Mei How; Louis Chiang; Mary How; Bau Tsui Nyoh; Julian Suez (on Bau Tsui Nyoh's lap); Rose How; Julie How; Ruth How; Rhoda How, 1933-34 winter.

愚園路夏宅前，1934-35年冬，後排，左至右：四女婿江元仁，（抱著嬰兒江齊賢），三女婿林勤，璐懿，媳婦吳思卿，璐梅，璐雅，瑪莉，璐敏，八女婿黃宣平，璐德，五女婿史久榮，抱著史濟良，夏鵬。前排左至右：四女兒子江成賢，吳思卿侄女吳鴻碧，鮑翠玉（坐者），夏連蔭。
Back row, standing, left to right: Nelson Y. Chiang, holding infant Paul Chiang; Frank Ling; Louise How; Rose How; Loo-Mei How; Rhoda How; Mary How; Loo-Ming How; Wilfred S.B. Wong; Ruth How; Albert K.Y. Suez, seated and holding Julian Suez; Bang How. Front row, left to right: Louis Chiang; Rosie Ng-Quinn; Bau Tsui Nyoh (seated); Julie How, 1934-35.

夏璐敏的孫女、夏瑞
芳的外曾孫女黃珍
蕙，在指夏瑞芳1914
年1月10日遇刺的地
方，攝於2006年。
Genevieve Wong, a
great granddaughter
of How Zoen Fong,
pointed at the very site
where How Zoen Fong
was shot on January
10, 1914, taken in
2006.

江成賢（左）和史
濟良在上海愚園路
上外祖母的房子
前，攝於2009年。
他們20世紀30年代
後期曾在這裡住過
幾年。這裡現在
是同仁醫院的行政
樓。

Taken in 2009, Grandsons Louis Chiang (left) and Julian Suez at their
grandmother's house on Yu Yuan Road, Shanghai, where the two lived
for a few years in the late 1930s. At present, it is the administration
building of St. Luke's Hospital.

史濟良在外祖父夏
瑞芳和外祖母鮑翠
玉的墓前（1952
年）。
Julian Suez at the
grave site of his
grandparents, How
Zoen Fong and Bau
Tsui Nyoh, taken
in1952.

上海閘北商務印書館鳥瞰（1910-1920年）。
Birds-eye view of the Commercial Press Compound, circa 1910-1920.**

印刷車間
（1910年）。
Machine Shop in the Commercial Press plant, circa 1910.**

插圖印刷車間（1910年）。
Letterpress Shop in the Commercial Press plant, circa 1910.**

閘北商務印書館大院內的編輯大樓（1910年）。
Editorial Building at the Commercial Press compound, circa 1910.**

行政大樓，
（1910-1920）。
Administration Building
at the Commercial
Press compound, circa
1910-1920.**

上海河南路上的營銷大樓
（1906年）。
Sales Office Building on Henan
Road, Shanghai, circa 1906.**

清心堂大門，攝於2013。
The new main entrance to
Pure Heart Church, taken in
2013.

清心堂翻修過的大門，攝
於2013年。
The renovated entrance to the
old Pure Heart Church, taken
in 2013.

建於1923年的清心堂門外
的這塊區是1994年掛上
的。夏瑞芳1880年代在此
教堂度過不少時光。
The plaque was affixed in
1994 to the old Pure Heart
Church, built in 1923.

2013年10月，青浦博物館當時舉辦的有關商務印書館和夏瑞芳的展覽。
Exhibition on the Commercial Press and How Zoen Fong at the Qingpu Museum, October, 2013.

攝於2013年10月青浦博物館。館內當時正舉辦關於商務印書館和夏瑞芳的展覽。
Exhibition on the Commercial Press and How Zoen Fong at the Qingpu Museum, October, 2013.

史濟良（左）和周松在青浦博物館門前（2013年10月11日）。
Julian Suez (left) and Zhou Song in front of the Qingpu Museum, 2013.

2013年10月史濟良在青
浦附近的朱家角追尋130
年前外祖父夏瑞芳離開
家鄉前往上海的足跡。
Julian Suez at Cape Zhu,
near Qingpu, taken in
2013.

夏瑞芳在青浦南庫村的
這所房子裡住到10歲左
右去投奔在上海打工的
母親。周平弟（右）是
夏瑞芳妹妹的孫子，向
史濟良介紹翻新過的老
宅。攝於2013年10月。

Zhou Pingdi (a grandson of How Zoen Fong's younger sister), right,
and Julian Suez at the Qingpu family house, 2013.

青浦「夏氏小學」的原址，現已不復存在。周平弟（左）向史濟
良（中）講述當初學校的佈局，右為他的兒子周松。攝於2013年
10月。
Partial grounds of the How Elementary School, in Qingpu, 2013.

〔圖片來源〕

*表照片由斯坦福大學胡佛研究所檔案館提供。
Photo granted permission by Hoover Institution Archive, Stanford Univrsity, from its Francis E. Stafford collection.

**表照片取自《遠東工業商業活動—1924》，E. J. Burgoyne 編，F. S. Ramplin審，倫敦－上海－香港－新加坡商務百科全書公司1924年出版。
Photo from Far Eastern Commercial and Industrial Activity-1924, compiled by E. J. Burgoyne, edited by F. S. Ramplin, and (published by) The Commercial Encyclopedia Co. of London-Shanghai-HongKong-Singapore, in 1924.

A Pioneer Remembered

A Biography of How Zoen Fong

By C.M. Chao

Translated by Ben Wang & Yuan Xiaoning

Table of Contents

The Story of How Zoen Fong by Jiang Weiqiao

In Memoriam ... by Zhang Shunian (Zhang Yuanji's son)

Chronicle of the Commercial Press, 1897-1914

Acknowledgements & Foreword

(All surnames in this section are in CAPS.)

Finding the appropriate words to describe or document an event, a person, a deed, an idea, or facts, whether perceived or real, is a huge commitment and even more so when writing a book. To pen a biography of HOW Zoen Fong, my maternal grandfather, encompassing his vision and legacy, is even a larger commitment. Mr. C.M. CHAO, the author, took on the challenge of digging into historical documents dating back over 100 years. His insight and analysis of the environment and situation to my grandfather's deeds are nothing short of extraordinary and fascinating.

My special gratitude and thanks go to the three principals of the Renwen Society of the China Institute in America, New York City. Dr. Yong HO, Mr. Ben WANG, and Mrs. Gwynne TUAN. Their vision and commitment to sponsor the writing of this book convinced me that this project would take off and be completed.

My thanks to the Hoover Institution Archives of Stanford University for its permission to use the historical pictures of Commercial Press and HOW Zoen Fong taken by Mr. Francis E. STAFFORD a century ago in Shanghai. These precious pictures were donated by Professor Ronald E. ANDERSON, a grandson

of Mr. STAFFORD, to the Hoover Institution. Mr. York LO the author of the book written in Chinese, 東成西就 (*East and West*, its English title), published in 2012 by Joint Publishing (Hong Kong) Co., Ltd., gave some information about the HOW family which I did not know before. In particular, Mr. LO uncovered some details of the work of my own father in the US and southwest China during the Japanese war, when I was less than 10 years old. Thank you, York.

I express my personal appreciation to Mrs. Diane T. WOO whose suggestion to Renwen Society for a commemoration of my grandfather eventually led to the writing of this book. Also thanks to Mrs. SONG Lu Xia, Shanghai, China, for reconnecting me to long lost relatives in Qingpu, my grandfather's childhood hometown.

The encouragement of my seven 'HOW' cousins has been a driving force for me to stay on this project. Special thanks to Mr. Louis CHIANG, one of the cousins, who gave me much advice throughout the project. Many thanks to the cousins who shared the expenses of producing this book.

I would also like to thank Commercial Press of Taiwan for publishing this book on my grandfather whose life and that of the Commercial Press were inseparable. It is a real honor to have the support of the Commercial Press.

Finally, I salute my mother, who died in 2006 at age 100. Throughout the years, she had given me bits and pieces of family

details. Mother's emphasis of the HOW family's love and support of each other was always the central theme. That, in turn, instilled in me the importance of the extended family of the nine HOW siblings of her generation and the eight 'HOW' cousins in mine. Mother, I hope I have captured the essence of what you seeded in my head. May your and the HOW family spirit be preserved for and by the family, for generations to come, 流芳百世.

Julian SUEZ, a grandson of HOW Zoen Fong

January 16, 2014

New York

Transcribing Chinese Names

There are currently two common ways to transcribe Chinese names: the Wade-Giles system and the Pinyin system. The Wade-Giles system was developed by Sir Thomas Francis Wade of Great Britain in the mid-nineteenth century and was modified by Cambridge University Professor Herbert Allen Giles. This system makes it easier for English speakers to pronounce Chinese sounds, but it is not an accurate reflection of the sounds. In mainland China, the Wade-Giles system has been replaced by the Pinyin system, which was developed in 1958 with the purpose of introducing standard pronunciation of Mandarin to school children. This system is for the most part used in this book to transcribe Chinese names of people and places. Exceptions are made, however, for some well-known and established transcriptions of names, such as Chiang Kai-shek and T.V. Soong, in order to avoid confusion. There is a third type of spellings that is based on neither Wade-Giles nor Pinyin. These are the spellings in pre-Pinyin times that were done in the way individual saw fit, either by local dialect or otherwise, such as How Zoen Fong and Julian Suez.

Chinese family names precede given names and that is also what is rendered in this book. However, for people who adopted a Western given name, we followed the convention in English by placing the given name before the last name, such as Julie How and Bill Hwa.

Introduction

Back from the Future, 2014 Manhattan to 1914 Shanghai

One day in the summer of 2012, five people were having a meeting in a small classroom at the United Nations Headquarters in New York. The five people were Yong Ho, Coordinator of the Chinese Language Program of the United Nations, Ben Wang, a language teacher of Chinese at the UN, Ms. Gwynne Tuan of the Renwen Society, myself, and the pivotal character, Julian Suez (Shi Jiliang, in Chinese). Piled up on the table next to the five attendees were old pictures, magazines, books, and copies of old documents, all of which were from a century ago, or more.

The somber subject of the discussion at the meeting was the following: a man of distinction, a legendary publishing house, a proposed book of connected historical and personal anecdotes, which can well be a chronicle of a cultural reform in the history of China. The man in point is How Zoen Fong[1], one of the

---

1　The Romanized name of How Zoen Fong, based on the Shanghai dialect back in the days when there was not an official Romanization system for the Chinese sounds, was used by the master himself. The official Pinyin (Romanization system of the Chinese language) today is Xia Ruifang. Also see Page 71. With the exception of the names of the protagonist and his immediate family members, which are all Romanized based on the Shanghai dialect, Pinyin is used on all other proper nouns throughout this translation.

founders and the first general manager of the famed Commercial Press in China. All the materials on the table were rarefied and memorable historical documents that chronicle the life of How Zoen Fong and tell the story of how in 1897 he, with two brothers of a Bau family, founded the Commercial Press at the Dechang Lane on the south end of the North Jiangxi Road (later location of the Chinese Kenye Bank) in Shanghai.

Tattered and scattered as the old documents might be, they nonetheless provided the five of us at the meeting with a clear and bright picture of what once took place in the old Shanghai in the twilight years of the 19th century, and the tears, sweat and blood How Zoen Fong shed in his assiduous and indefatigable effort to found a publishing and printing house during the years of wars and extreme chaos in China.

With his role equivalent to today's CEO of a great enterprise, How Zoen Fong was possessed of a rare instinct of perspicacity of recognizing great talents, which prompted him to recruit and hire the erudite scholars who were also writers to work in his publishing house, an unprecedented establishment in those conflicting years in China when the old and corrupt Qing Dynasty was in quick decline and the new-born Republic was still in its raw and nascent stage: a new age indeed in which How Zoen Fong was in the firm conviction that a publishing and printing house would be the sine-qua-non in helping promote education and disseminating new knowledge at this critical

moment for a ravaged old China.

It was with this very belief and goal that the Commercial Press was founded. It should be abundantly clear that printing was far from being the main business of the organization. Publishing worthy and important educational textbooks in English and other reading matters, on the other hand, was its primary interest and concern. Because of this conviction in the mind of one of its founders, How Zoen Fong, the Commercial Press has since its inception nourished the people of China with a rich feast of Western culture and civilization, which resulted in its impact on the cultural development in China across two centuries.

On January 10th 1914, as How Zoen Fong was leaving the headquarters of the Commercial Press, he was shot by a gunman. Due to the gunshot, he was taken to the Renji Hospital where, despite desperate rescue efforts, he died in a matter of minutes. He was only forty-three years old.

There were flying speculations at the time as regards the motive of his assassination, with none of them proven to be true. The most credible one was that in those tumultuous years of political upheavals with warlords blatantly going about their evil and venal deeds and a general by the name of Yuan Shikai, who had once served the Qing monarchy, proclaiming himself to be the new emperor in Beijing, the Governor of Shanghai, Chen Qimei, a revolutionary who helped overthrow the Qing Dynasty in 1911, asked the wealthy and famous businessmen in Shanghai,

including How Zoen Fong, to support him in staging a second revolution (after the 1911 revolution) against the warlords and General Yuan. But How declined the request by stating that he was in the belief that politics should be separated from business, which so ired Chen that he allegedly ordered the assassination of How. In the mind of Chen, murdering How Zoen Fong would send a proper warning that other wealthy and influential members in the business world had better show him the support he needed, or else.

At the time of How Zoen Fong's tragic death, the Commercial Press had been only 17 years in existence, yet the foundation that he had laid for the Press was so solid that its goal and vision never faltered and the Press sustained instead through many later years of raging storms in China, and has remained to this day a cornerstone in the world of publishing circle to millions of readers in China, Hong Kong, Taiwan and beyond.

The modern educational reform has been among the most successful reforms since the final years of the Qing Dynasty. During the long process of the educational reform, the Commercial Press has played the vital role of promoting reading and learning by continually editing, compiling, publishing and printing all kinds of textbooks as well as other reading matters on different subjects. For much of the first half of the 20th century, the Commercial Press introduced more textbooks to the Chinese people than any other publishers in China.

Back to the five-member meeting in New York, 2012: so how can we bring this long forgotten man of such tremendous importance in culture and learning back to this current world of the 21st century? And THAT is the very point in question. Julian Suez, one of the attendees, is a grandson of How Zoen Fong. "My one fervent but unfulfilled wish has been for people of the young generations in my family and for the whole world not ever to forget my grandfather and his extraordinary accomplishment," Julian states with a mixture of resignation and anxiety.

The five of us reached a unanimous agreement: the glory of the past must be maintained and remembered forever, and How Zoen Fong's accomplishment will not be forgotten.

And so it was, we arrived at the decision that was to piece together all the anecdotes in the life of How Zoen Fong into a bilingual biography in both Chinese and English, tracing from Manhattan in 2014 back to the old Shanghai in 1914: a biography for posterity. A biography in both languages should provide a good reading experience for readers of the two languages. The title of the biography would be "A Pioneer Remembered – A Biography of How Zoen Fong" to be published in 2014 to commemorate the passing of this legendary pioneer 100 years ago.

Personal Reflections

A biography of How Zoen Fong should once and for all

place his name in the minds of the readers from generation to generation, and it may serve particularly well the young Chinese readers as a poignant book on the history of China from the late 19th century to the 21st century, reading which may enrich their knowledge about what trauma and turbulence China as a country had gone through during the final years of the Qing rule and the bumpy road of decay inside the country and attack and invasion from the outside thereafter.

And, if this biography and How Zoen Fong's journey of glory can arouse the Chinese young readers' national and cultural awareness and thus get to find their identity more positively, I will not have written it in vain.

A Cause Célèbre, A Cold Case

An unsolved case of assassination during the dawning years of the Republic; possibly involving Chiang Kai-shek, among other big names of the day.

Late in the afternoon, about 6:30, on January 10, 1914, an assassination took place in the international concession zone in Shanghai that made headlines in the media and shook the entire city of Shanghai. The victim was How Zoen Fong, General Manager of the Commercial Press (CP). All efforts to save his life failed. How died of a gunshot soon after he was taken to a nearby hospital. He was only 43 years of age.

How Zoen Fong's assassination remained one of the most shocking and mysterious unsolved cold cases during the early years of the Republic of China. His funeral procession and services were grand events and was a top news item of the day, and prominent names such as Chiang Kai-shek and Chen Qimei (among others) were mentioned as possible suspects involved in How's tragic death.

One of the founders of CP, How Zoen Fong was the man who turned a mere family printing shop into the most prestigious

publishing house in China. At the time of How's death, CP, in existence for 17 years, had been well groomed by How into a fine modern company with fine rules and policies. Other than the printing plant and offices for editing and translation in Shanghai, CP had expanded to other major cities in China with 21 branch offices, 4 branch mini-offices and one retail bookstore. The Press had become a company of 750 staff members with a capital that reached $2,000,000[2].

As a company of both printing and publishing, CP focused on the publishing of textbooks in both Chinese and English, a revolutionary idea in those early years of cultural exchanges between China and the West. This in turn opened Chinese readers' minds toward Western culture and thus exerted great influence on the new development of interactions between Chinese and Western cultures in the ensuing centuries.

The accomplishments of How Zoen Fong impacted not only printing and publishing, but also education, communication, among other cultural aspects – he was an immensely influential and perspicacious man in the newly established Republic, who, by initiating and introducing new textbooks to schools and students, brought about a fresh cultural and educational scene to China, markedly different from that in the old dynasties.

---

2 Unless otherwise indicated, the dollar sign ($) refers to the Chinese currency used at the beginning of the 20th Century, also known as the "silver dollar."

Gunshots from the Assassin Shocked the City of Shanghai

The assassination didn't take place in a typical dark and stormy night of a murder drama, but rather at a time of tumultuous political change. The murdered was not a casualty in an open war between states, but a victim of a sinister plot. Neither was it a killing of personal grudge; rather, it was the product of power struggle and insidious conspiracy.

In a relaxed mood after a hard day's work on January 10, 1914, How Zoen Fong stepped out of the headquarters of CP on Henan Road (also known locally as Chess Board Street) in Shanghai's International Settlement, a district of concession of more than one foreign force. He was all ready to get into the horse carriage that was waiting outside of his office building to take him back home.

Something was odd that afternoon. Hu Youqing, the young carriage boy, thought to himself. The horse was as strangely jittery, and Hu was overcome by an unknown anxiety. Pulling the reins in his effort to calm down the horse, Hu said to his master How Zoen Fong, as the latter got into the carriage, "I don't know why, Boss, but the horse has been in a state of jitters tonight, as never before." Hardly had he finish these words when suddenly a masked man came charging at them from across the street. In his hand he was holding a dark gun with which he pointed at How Zoen Fong and pulled the trigger. Shot in the chest, How clutched

at the wound, blood oozing out through his two hands. In pain, How tried to retreat back into his office building, but he dropped on the ground in agony after moving just a few steps.

The loud popping sound of the gun shot stirred some of the workers at CP. Dashing outside to find out what was happening, they saw their General Manager shot and lying in a pool of blood right in front of their office building. While How made a pitiful and ultimately failed attempt to get up, some workers of CP helped How up, as some others phoned and notified the hospital. How, sensing life was slipping away from his body, struggled to open his eyes and tried in vain to leave some final words to the workers who were holding him – but not a sound was uttered, despite the slight movement of his lips.

When How was taken by car to the Renji Hospital located in the western part of the British concession—this was the nearest hospital to the Press and one of the most prestigious Western hospitals in China in the early days of the 20th century— great rescue efforts were made by the staff of the hospital. Meanwhile, How's wife and other family members were notified, as were some of How's close associates who helped manage business affairs at CP, such as Zhang Yuanji, the Bau brothers, Gao Mengdan, among others. But by the time How's shocked business partners dashed to the hospital, How had passed away amid the heartrending cries of grief of his wife and other family members. How Zoen Fong, a giant in the publishing world in

China, no match for the bullets of unknown dastardly foes, fell prey to assassination in a world of political tumult and power struggle.

The Brave Young Carriage Boy

The carriage boy, Hu Youqing, 16 at the time, helplessly watched the entire scene of the assassination of his master, but when the gunman started to flee, he jumped into action. Swiftly jumping into the driver's seat of the carriage and shouting a sharp, loud command to the horse, he gave chase to the assassin. Pursued by the boy in the carriage, the desperate gunman ran as fast as he could, but when he was completely out of breath and saw that his pursuer was closing in, he raised his gun and shot into the air in an attempt to scare the pursuer into giving up the chase. Just as the assassin was shooting the gun, however, young Hu's carriage caught up with him. In another flying swoop, Hu jumped down from the carriage and pounced on the gunman and started to beat fiercely on him with his fists.

No match for the young and virile Hu, the gunman raised his gun toward Hu's head and pulled the trigger. Pushing away the hand that held the gun, Hu turned his head from the barrel of the gun and managed to dodge the bullet from hitting his head, even though it brushed his earlobe. Blood streamed down Hu's entire face and neck. With no time to check if he had hit the target, the gunman got up and continued his flight. Little did

he expect his pursuer, with blood all over his face and body, to also leap up and continue his hot pursuit. In the distance sharp whistles of the police could be heard.

When the chase reached the corner of the Guangdong Road, known locally as the Fifth Road, a policeman, badge number 511, who was standing on guard, heard the gun shots and soon saw the chase party running toward him: a man, with a pistol in his hand being pursued by a younger man. Quickly, the policeman hid himself behind his guard stand and, when the man with the gun ran past his post, he dashed out and caught him. When the gunman realized he had been caught by a policeman, he threw his gun to the roadside to get rid of the murder weapon. No sooner had he thrown away the gun, however, did Hu, the carriage boy, hurry to the spot and pick up the gun. Crazed with anger for his master's assassination, Hu pointed the gun at the assassin and shot at him. The bullet narrowly missed the gunman, and instead nearly hit another policeman hurrying to the scene. Mistaking Hu for an accomplice of the assassin in the melee, the policemen arrested both Hu and the assassin.

When Hu Youqing was cleared of any wrongdoing, the police discovered that the assassin was named Wang Qingrui, whom they detained in the police station. Meanwhile, CP bailed out the young hero Hu, who had with great bravery tried to catch his master's assassin.

The tragic assassination and the nabbing of the gunman

were reported in detail in all the major newspapers in Shanghai. The date of the tragedy also appeared in the prominent Shanghai Daily: Sunday, January 11th, 1914, in the 3rd year of the Republic of China.

The Mystery of Instigators and Plotters Surrounding the Assassination

The assassination of How Zoen Fong was at the time a shocking case of crime that shook up the entire city of Shanghai. His funeral service and procession were rare events of somberness and funereal pomp. CP put together a collection of epitaphs and messages and poetic couplets of condolences from both inside and outside of China. The legendary literary master Zhang Taiyan sent a couplet of condolence that reads:

> *Gloriously intrepid in exposing the evil,*
> *your spirit will not pass on with the flesh;*
> *Lived ever so vigorously for the good and just,*
> *your wisdom and compassion shall endure.*

Cai Yuanpei, another legendary man of letters and president of Beijing University, wrote a brief biography of How, in which he stated: "A pious Christian, Master How was a brilliant man of self-cultivation, extremely kind and compassionate in how he treated all others: truly a man deserving peace, happiness and

longevity. For a man like Master How to be the tragic victim of an assassination, it surely seems that there is no heavenly justice. Now that the Master has passed on, the enterprise he has established with painstaking effort is, however, flourishing, and it will exert an everlasting influence on culture and education in the development of our country. It can truly be said that the Master shall never really leave this world."

The board of trustees of CP passed a resolution to have a bronze statue of How Zoen Fong erected and dedicated to his memorable deeds and achievement, but the proposal was gently declined by How's wife, Tsui Nyoh Bau. She suggested to How's close associates, such as the Bau brothers, Zhang Yuanji and Gao Mengdan, that the money for the statue be donated to schools, kindergartens and orphanages instead. That, she thought, would be a much more appropriate thing to do.

A loving couple, How and his wife Tsui Nyoh had a son, named Bang How, as well as eight daughters. After a few family meetings, also attended by close friends, the family decided to have a school built in the fond memory and commemoration of How Zoen Fong in How's impoverished and backward native town, Qingpu. The school was named the *How Elementary School* upon completion.

Following How's assassination, despite the anger expressed not only by the family of How, but also by all those who knew or knew of him, all attempts to find the instigators

and plotters behind the assassination failed, largely because of the rampant evil power of the warlords who were much hated by the masses in those days, but were feared even more. As some signs of the motive for How's assassination pointed to this band of warlords, none would dare to point fingers at any of them. Wang Qingrui, the assassin, confessed at the trial that he had been hired and paid a large amount of money to carry out the assassination. Other complications of involvement were revealed during the questioning, to the point that a deep mystery developed surrounding the true perpetrators behind the scenes. The assassination became a cold unsolved case, long after the gunman Wang Qingrui was sentenced to death and was executed, throughout the century and up until today.

At the time of How Zoen Fong's death, speculations and rumors as to the motive of the assassination abounded in China, many of which appeared in written articles. A truer answer may be found in "The Chronological Events in the Life of Zhang Yuanji," in which the following theory of the murder of How was advanced: "(How's assassination occurred) because How, not long before his death, had formed a united front with many prominent business leaders in Shanghai against the plan of Chen Qimei, Garrison Commander of Shanghai. Chen's plan proposed setting up a military base in the district of Zhabei (literally, the North of the Sluice) in Shanghai, and thus instilled deep resentment in Commander Chen, which led to the eventual plot to

destroy How by assassination."

A longtime staff member at CP, Hu Yuzhi, supported the above theory. Zheng Xiaoxu — another prominent staff member at CP who had once served as an imperial envoy in political affairs to the Hunan province under the Qing rule, before settling down in Shanghai after the founding of the Republic – wrote in his diary, "Before his assassination, How had received letters of warnings and threats, which stated that How would pay dearly for causing Chen Qimei's plan to set up a military base in Zhabei to be aborbed."

The phrase "Zhabei" referred to an old sluice of the Suzhou River to the northwest of Shanghai, which was built during Emperor Kangxi's reign (late 17th century). In the 13th year (1734) of Emperor Yongzheng's reign during the Qing Dynasty, a new sluice was built to the southwest of Shanghai, which was named Xinzha (literally, the New Sluice). Areas surrounding the two sluices were quickly developed into popular urban areas, and Zhabei was considered a significant strategic point in military affairs in the defense of Shanghai.

After 1899, the International Settlement in Shanghai had expanded to the eastern border of Zhabei, whose western and southern borders were only a river separated from the Settlement. The district of Zhabei had already become a boisterous and bustling urban area quite comparable to the Settlement on its borders. With the flourishing of the area, both commercial and

industrial businesses increasingly thrived.

A company of rapid growth, CP in Shanghai, under the brilliant management of How Zoen Fong, had moved to a 12-room house on Beijing Road in the second year of its existence. In 1902, a new printing establishment was built on North Fujian Road, with a separate business office on Henan Road. In 1903, an editorial office was established on Boone Road. In 1904, CP bought more than 300 acres of land on Baoshan Road in Zhabei, where its main publishing plant was moved, in 1905. In 1906, a large sales building on Henan Road was completed. Before How Zoen Fong's assassination, a spacious, reinforced concrete printing building was added to the plant, besides several smaller buildings. In 1924, 10 years after How's death, the impressive library and club building was completed.

All the buildings built or bought by CP were Western-style edifices of unusual architectural splendor, more extraordinary even than all the beautiful Western-style buildings in Shanghai at the time, which further attests to the vision and grandeur of its general manager, How Zoen Fong.[3]

---

3   The following are general descriptions of the architectural styles of all the buildings of the Commercial Press erected between 1902 and 1923. See photos on pages 189-190 for buildings in the Commercial Press Compound, in Zhabei District, Shanghai.

Plant Buildings (Industrial modern style) in Zhabei
This group of buildings was in the "pre-modern" style. Most of them were built with bricks, steel, reinforce concrete and large glass windows. The exterior facades were simple without many ornamental elements.

In 1905, after the plant had been built in Zhabei, the Press had, in addition, built residential houses near the plant for its staff and workers. Later, during the Sino-Japanese war in December, 1932, Zhabei was heavily bombarded by the invading Japanese army, resulting in the burning and total destruction of many buildings, including the publishing plant of CP. Another memorable historical event of the heroic battle of the defense of Shanghai by 800 courageous and patriotic Chinese soldiers against the Japanese army in 1937 – in which all of the 800 Chinese soldiers literally fought to their death — also took place in Zhabei.

Sales Office Building (mixed styles) on Henan Road
This building was in three different styles. The top level with flat roof and half arched windows was Roman in character; the middle levels with plain walls and large glass windows had the "modern" look; the street level had a Chinese style storefront.

Club and Library Building (French style) in Zhabei
The Mansard roof and windows in the mid-levels were in French style. The bottom level was in mixed types of porticos.

School Building (mixed styles) in Zhabei
The building was symmetrical and formal in appearance with two traditional Chinese styled tilted wing sections. The middle portion of the building with covered open balconies looked like the French style. The openings of windows of different sizes and styles in the Chinese sections were without any specific style.

Editorial Building (French style) in Zhabei
This was a French Colonial Styled building with open balconies and raised level.

Administration Building (mixed styles) in Zhabei
The upper level was plain modern like the Sales Office Building, while the street level had portico with Greek columns.

Motives behind the Assassination

Three characters, Chen Qimei, Yuan Shikai and Chiang Kai-shek, were most likely to have played leading roles in the hostility and hatred against How Zoen Fong that culminated in his murder, due to military affairs that led to a series of incidents at Zhabei. The incidents took place during the famous Second Nationalist Revolution in the modern history of China, after the Republic of China was founded in 1911. The Second Nationalist Revolution was also known as the "War Declared by the Nationalist Revolutionary Force against Yuan Shikai and His Army."

Having emerged from obscurity, Yuan Shikai was promoted by the Qing ruler, after the anti-Qing revolution in 1911, to serve as Grand Councilor to the Qing monarchy, whose chief mission was to hold a number of peace talks with the Nationalist revolutionary force formed by Dr. Sun Yat-sen, which in turn led the revolutionaries to mistake Yuan Shikai for a progressive sympathizer of the revolution. After the demise of the Qing monarchy and the founding of the Republic, Yuan persisted in pursuing the presidency of the new republic. To prevent more civil wars and bloodshed in China, Dr. Sun Yat-sen yielded the presidency of the Republic to Yuan Shikai, while the other revolutionaries of the Republic and patriotic military leaders resolved to get rid of Yuan, whom they all came to see as a

dangerous egomaniac with his heart and mind obsessed with power and material gains. Later, not content with the position of a mere president, Yuan plotted to restore the political system back to a monarchy and eventually set up his own small court of henchmen who helped make him Emperor. Yuan Shikai died of fear and agony due to his great number of political foes, who discovered Yuan's dark and insidious nature and his anti-revolutionary activities. He was on the throne for only 3 months: a truly bizarre page in the dawning years of the Republic.

In his non-stop struggles with the Nationalist revolutionary forces, Yuan cooked up a strategy that was designed to win support from foreign countries both morally and financially by borrowing stupendously large sums of funds, while promising a handsome repayment of land and high interest, and to foster the power of warlords in northern China so that they would remain neutral in the fights between the revolutionary army and his own force—an army consisting of soldiers Yuan recruited with false promises of monetary gains and power.

On the 20th of March 1913, the second year of the Republic, one of the founding members of the Republic and a close associate of Dr. Sun, Song Jiaoren was assassinated at the young age of 32 at the Shanghai railroad station in a plot mapped out by Yuan Shikai, as he was about to board a train to Beijing. The cause of Yuan's bitter ire and resentment against Song was that, as an influential political figure who saw through Yuan's

reactionary ambitions based entirely on greed and self-interest, Song had been traveling widely in the country giving talks and lectures, openly advocating a political system in which the president must yield his authority to the cabinet and congress.

The shock wave set off by Song Jiaoren's assassination was such that it convinced the revolutionary comrades of Dr. Sun Yat-sen to launch a military expedition to the north to finish off Yuan Shikai and his army, despite Yuan's vigorous denial that he had plotted the murder of Song.

Dr. Sun Yat-sen, in Japan studying that nation's more progressive political system at the time of the assassination of Song Jiaoren, promptly returned to China at the news of Song's murder. Upon his return, he immediately planned a military action against Yuan Shikai, an action that became known as the "Second Nationalist Revolution" in the early 20th century, following the first successful Nationalist revolution, which had felled the Qing monarchy. All the military leaders to the south of the Yangtze River joined in the Second Nationalist Revolution. One leader was Chen Qimei, who was another founding member of the Republic, and the mentor and sworn-brother of a rising star in the new republic, Chiang Kai-shek. In 1913, at the age of 26, Chiang Kai-shek, at the request of Chen Qimei, organized a loyal group of nationalist revolutionaries of particular bravery, named "Dare-to-die Corps," to carry out challenging military missions under the command of the revolutionary force. In the same year,

Dr. Sun Yat-sen appointed Chen Qimei the Garrison Chief and concurrently, the Governor of Shanghai. A close associate of Dr. Sun, Chen was also appointed the Commander-in-Chief of the Nationalist Anti-Yuan Shikai Army.

As soon as Chen Qimei assumed his posts in Shanghai, Chiang Kai-shek, as his close associate and advisor, convinced him that the first thing to do in order to destroy Yuan Shikai's military power, would be the taking of the Jiangnan (south of the Yangtze River, in translation) Ammunition Factory, which was indispensable for providing Yuan Shikai's army with its weaponry.

Heeding Chiang Kai-shek's advice, Chen Qimei appointed Chiang Commander of the 5th Regiment of the revolutionary force, whose mission was to take the Jiangnan Ammunition Factory by force. On July 23rd, Chiang Kai-shek launched his first offensive on the Factory, but it failed. Thereafter, despite repeated attempts by military maneuvers and offensives, Chiang failed to take the Factory, which was heavily armed and strongly defended by Yuan's army due to its extraordinary significance to the military,.

The battles between the Nationalist revolutionary force and the Yuan Shikai army sounded a clear alarm that echoed throughout the city of Shanghai, prompting the local business leaders to form the Committee for the Protection and Defense of Shanghai, which sent an official letter to the two battling parties,

appealing to both armies to initiate an immediate armistice to spare Shanghai from being a battleground and to keep it a neutral city of peace and stability. In the letter it was stated that, "As Shanghai is a city of great business and financial importance in China, and not a battleground, and the Ammunition Factory, a factory that belongs to China in general, there is hardly any justification for the factory to become the cause of war for either the northern or the southern force. Consequently, whichever side that starts the fighting will be regarded by the people of Shanghai as foes of the people of Shanghai."

Clearly, the adamant anti-war sentiments of the entire population of Shanghai were fully reflected in this open letter, which placed the military actions of the Nationalist revolutionary army, in their attempt to take over the Ammunition Factory, in an extremely unpopular and unfavorable light.

On the 24th of July, the Nationalist revolutionary army fighting the Yuan Shikai army, led by Chen Qimei and Chiang Kai-shek, set up their headquarters in the neighborhood of Baoshan Road in the district of Zhabei. This was where the general office, translation department, printing site and the dormitory of CP were located, which meant that the entire CP would be annihilated, if more battles were to take place in Zhabei.

This serious threat on the publishing enterprise which had been founded with so much painstaking effort, labor, and capital by How Zoen Fong and his associates caused in How so deep

an anxiety and apprehension that he had no choice but to take immediate actions to prevent the possible destruction of CP. As President of the Chamber of Commerce of Shanghai, How Zoen Fong promptly called for a meeting with 16 other leaders in the business community, at which they passed a resolution to sign a petition asking for protection from the Municipal Committee of Roads, Jetties and Police. Established in 1854 when the British and American counselors agreed to have the British and American concessions merge into an International Settlement, the Municipal Committee was set up to manage and control the roads and jetties within the area. Furthermore, the Committee set up police precincts, also headed by the British or British-appointed Chinese, to maintain peace and security in the Settlement.

Once the resolution was passed, they immediately set off to deliver the petition to the Municipal Committee asking for protection of the lives and properties of all the residents and business establishments in Zhabei by having a defensive police force sent to keep a close watch on the entrances and exits of the district.

The request and petition by How Zoen Fong and his fellow business leaders were quickly approved by the British leaders in the Settlement, and with the approval, police protection was granted to the entire area of Zhabei. This action, needless to say, was like putting a strait jacket on the Nationalist revolutionary army that was hell bent on taking by force the Ammunition

Factory from the hands of Yuan Shikai, and thus gravely restricting any further military actions on the part of Chen Qimei and Chiang Kai-shek.

The reason that the British were so willing to accept and approve the petition was simply and solely because of all the potential territorial gains and monetary profits for the British "protectors" in the Settlement. As stated above, after Yuan Shikai became President of the new regime, he "borrowed" a stupendous amount of money from Great Britain, France, Germany, America, Japan and Russia, who, as creditors, became increasingly appreciative of the profits gained first from the weak and ineffectual Chinese Qing monarchy, and then subsequently from the weaker and more ineffectual Yuan Shikai.

It was a welcome and comforting thought to these nations of creditors that, China, with all her debts, would doubtlessly collapse soon into a colony divided among them. With this conviction, they handed the Chinese government a list of conditions that came as a package deal with their "generous" loans in order to protect their interests in China: they would have the right to intervene in affairs related to national security and to maintain peace in the International Settlement as well as in different concessions in cities "loaned" to them, such as Shanghai, Tianjin, Guangzhou, etc., which would give them military and police supremacy over the Chinese authority. As all of these conditions were met with the approval of the new

government, these foreign forces showed unanimous and warm support for Yuan Shikai, actively protecting all the pro-Yuan factions and answered favorably to any pro-Yuan requests, all at the expense of any anti-Yuan Shikai factions or elements.

When all of this came to bear on the actions of How Zoen Fong to keep CP and his life's endeavor, from destruction, the British approval of the petition and the decision to send forces to protect Zhabei area must have struck as a heavy blow to the Nationalist revolutionaries and instigated in Chen Qimei and Chiang Kai-shek an intense hatred and resentment, not only toward the British, but specifically toward How Zoen Fong, leader of the petition, whom Chen and Chiang must have come to view as an enemy and traitor to the Nationalist revolutionaries, and a stumbling block to their fierce struggle against Yuan Shikai.

On the morning of July 27th, 1913, the British Municipal Committee for Roads, Jetties and Police officially sent both army and police forces to Zhabei with a public announcement that the action was "in compliance with a petition and request made to the British authorities by prominent Chinese businessmen, led by How Zoen Fang, in their plea for the British to take military and police actions to protect the lives and properties in Zhabei.

A cavalry of 30 or more, and a regiment of 150 soldiers and policemen, carrying with them 6 machine artillery pieces, were led by the British police chief into Zhabei to carry out their mission, as well as to disband and dispel all the anti-Yuan Shikai

forces, which consisted of 207 Nationalist revolutionary soldiers of the "Dare-to-die Corps" under the command of Chiang Kai-shek. Not wishing to fight wars on two fronts against Yuan Shikai and the British, Chiang Kai-shek and his mentor and blood brother Chen Qimei, in anger and humiliation, gave orders to surrender their arms to the British, and withdrew the entire troops from Zhabei.

The following two days of the 28th and 29th of July saw soldiers and policemen from the British Municipal Committee patrolling the streets and neighborhoods of Zhabei to make sure that the entire area was cleared of soldiers from the Nationalist revolutionary force. Furthermore, on the 29th, policemen of the Indian Sikh nationals were dispatched by the British authorities to stand guard at the headquarters and different offices of CP to thwart any possible acts of violence.

To Chen Qimei and Chiang Kai-shek, these developments were a clear sign of a close relationship between How Zoen Fong and the British Municipal Committee, a relationship that so irked Chen and Chiang that they mistakenly considered How Zoen Fong a running dog of both Yuan Shikai and the British, someone who was actively helping Yuan Shikai foil the Nationalist revolutionaries' plans to not only topple Yuan Shikai, but to be free from any foreign intervention in their Nationalist and patriotic military activities against Yuan and the warlords under his wing. How Zoen Fong must have seemed such a thorn in the

side of Chen and Chiang that they would be only too pleased to see How wiped off the face of the earth. Their hatred for How might indeed have culminated in a plot of his assassination. Amidst all the speculations and rumors as to the reasons and motives of How Zoen Fong's assassination, the acrimonious feelings of Chen Qimei and Chiang Kai-shek toward him certainly remain the most convincing evidence that they were the culprits.

The true irony of this tragedy is that at the time Chen and Chiang had no clue that it was actually How's desperate attempt to safeguard CP, his life's work of an education enterprise, from destruction that drove him to ask for protection from the British, and that How Zoen Fong, having no love for either Yuan Shikai or the British, had dedicated his life solely to culture, publishing and education in order to build a new China, which was exactly what Chen and Chiang had dedicated themselves to do. Two years after the assassination of How Zoen Fong, Chen Qimei also died as a result of an assassination plotted by Yuan Shikai, another evil deed rampant in those years of chaos and tumult.

Having dedicated his entire life to reading, learning, publishing and education, How Zoen Fong was murdered as a man completely uninvolved in any political faction. That may be the reason why neither the People's Republic of China, nor the Republic of China in Taiwan, commemorates or even remembers the achievement of How Zoen Fong, although CP is still going

strong as a publishing house both in Beijing and Taipei, all thanks to the vision conceived and the solid foundation laid by its creator, How Zoen Fong.

Movers and Shakers, Men of Vision

An authorized biography was published after the death of Steve Jobs, CEO and the driving force behind the creation of the Apple computer, on Oct. 5th, 2011.

Born in San Francisco in 1955, Steve Jobs studied one semester at Reed College in Portland, Oregon, before he dropped out. A year after making his first Apple 1 computer with his friends, Jobs, at 21, founded Apple Inc. Business took off immediately thereafter. In 1984, the first Macintosh computer was introduced to the world. The following year saw Jobs leaving Apple Inc. because of a high-level power struggle inside the company. Jobs soon single-handedly founded NeXT Co. In 1997, NeXT Co. was purchased by Apple Inc., and Jobs returned to serve as Executive Director with his mind set on making revolutionary changes with the Apple products, which included iTunes, iPhone, iPod, iPad, among others. Tested positive for pancreatic cancer in 2004, Jobs continued to work for 7 years, until he resigned from his position in August 2011. Steve Jobs died of the illness three months later.

These are the introductory notes in a commercial on the

life and work of Steve Jobs, one of the most influential talents of our times, whose creations and contributions changed our lives. This authorized biography of Steve Jobs was advertized by Commercial Press in the New Book section of its website in early 2012.

As Steve Jobs' Apple products have brought new light to the world, the publishing house CP has changed the lives of millions of Chinese since the early 20th century and remains today as a bright star that has illumined the lives of generations of the Chinese people for over a century by bestowing upon them knowledge, intellect and wisdom.

Today, Commerial Press has also stepped into the cyber-technical world and has its own website on the Internet: CP1897. com. The initials C and P stand for Commercial Press and the number 1897 marks the year in which CP was founded. The work and mission of the Press in Beijing, China, Hong Kong and Taipei are clearly stated on this site. In Beijing, CP claims to be the publishing house with the longest history in China, which has exerted a lasting influence on Chinese culture, publication and education. In fact the founding of CP marked the dawn of the enterprise of publishing in modern China, and it has marched into this current age of cultural, communication and educational work through the latest technology to improve both the quantity and quality of their published works.

On its website, CP in Taipei presents itself as the

cornerstone in the history of the publishing industry in China, which has published more than 10,000 books of the highest quality.

And on their website in Hong Kong, CP shines as a publishing house that is not only marked by its long history, but also by its great variety of books, uniquely combining traditional fine classics with the newest communication systems and world media, all of which has also made CP one of the most distinguished publishing houses in the world in management and sales.

It wouldn't be an exaggeration to suggest that, while Apple products have introduced to mankind a new plateau of living, Commercial Press has bestowed upon all the Chinese people cultural and spiritual inspiration for the past century. And the man who created this publishing house of lasting influence was none other than How Zoen Fong.

How Zoen Fong, the protagonist of this biography, was the man, the pioneer, who conceived and created CP. Emerging from obscurity in the final years of the 19th century, he became General Manager of CP, presiding over and supervising the entire operation, including the production of books, sales, quality control, market research, publicity, policy making, etc. Simply put, How Zoen Fong was the first CEO in the true sense of the word in the modern history of China, a CEO with vision, determination and inspiration. It took a legendary pioneer like

How Zoen Fong —-who was so keenly aware of the significance of education and learning — to found the legendary CP.

Although cut short by a savage assassination, his life was distinguished by glorious and extraordinary accomplishments, a life worthy in every way of being celebrated and written about.

Chapter 1: From a Planted Seed, Sprouted a Mighty Tree

The impact of the Commercial Press (CP) weighs far more in publishing than printing, as English textbooks were an important item of its publication, which started a century-long nurturing of a new culture, in the early days of the Westernization of the masses in China. In this light, CP exerted a great influence on the cultural development and growth in China during the 19th and 20th centuries.

The success of the enterprise that How Zoen Fong founded went way beyond financial gains, with the scope of its functions covering publishing, education, culture, among others. It was a major influential force on the inchoate social scene immediately after the establishment of the Republic of China in 1911. Considering how How Zoen Fong stood as a man who helped change the life of so many people, he was indeed a kindred spirit of Steve Jobs of the 21st century.

His Assassination A Hundred Years Ago

The name How Zoen Fong (1871-1914) is practically unknown in the modern history of China, as surprisingly few people in and out of the country have even heard of this man who

single-handedly struggled as an unsung promoter of the complete modernization of his native country. It was How Zoen Fong who founded the first modern printing company in China, CP: a man not only possessed of a genius of business management and operation, but also of great gumption to bring progress and bliss to the world. This was best illustrated, when he stated, "We must take upon ourselves in educating the people as our sacred duty," which he insisted to be the goal of CP. With a vision and a hope of accomplishing his mission, he further declared, "In order to help China step into the new age, education must be the indispensable and basic requirement for the people, before a new constitution and strengthening of the country can be achieved."

Like a bolt out of the blue, his advocacy was astonishing in those twilight years of the Qing Dynasty and the dawning days of the Republic, when China had sunk into a dark pit of backwardness, destruction and corruption. As a revolutionary force in the world of culture, CP endeavored to publish textbooks in both Chinese and English in its effort to introduce new thoughts and learning, in addition to bringing in modern technology and printing machines to improve the quality of their publications.

Indeed, founding an enterprise that introduced new concepts of education, publishing and mass media to the Chinese masses, How Zoen Fong was a father figure who sowed the good and precious seeds in the modern history of Chinese culture.

Unfortunately, destiny played a fatal role in How's life, in that he was-tragically assassinated, in all possibility as a direct result of political strife and disagreement, in 1914, exactly a hundred years ago this year.

The Beginning

The school was called the Lowrie School, a school founded in Shanghai by an American missionary. The school was founded at the fin-de-siecle of the 19th century, when China was under the influence of the Western powers, long considered by the Qing monarchy as the Western barbarians, who had suddenly come thousands of miles from the West to launch an attack on China and who had greatly humiliated the Chinese by dealing them a decisive defeat. For both the Qing rulers and the millions of Chinese, it was much more than a physical defeat - it was a new-found mixture of inferiority and curiosity that seriously gnawed at their minds and spirit. With these new painful feelings on the part of the Chinese, there appeared in China a new group of religious foreigners: Catholic priests and Protestant pastors.

In the Lowrie School there was a teenage boy from the backwoods outside Shanghai, whose name was How Zoen Fong. It was a genuinely fresh experience for the boy to be in a school founded and operated on an American educational system which imparted in him a great deal of new knowledge from the Western world. Particularly impressive to him, however, were the

textbooks used in class: books with neatly printed words on snow white paper, which were shipped to China all the way from that distant country, the United States of America. He couldn't help wondering, "How on earth were they so neatly 'made?'"

Sneaking by Boat to Shanghai

How Zoen Fong was born in Nanku Village in the County of Qingpu to the west of Shanghai in 1871 to a family living in stark poverty. His father made a meager living as a vendor of sweets and could barely keep his family from starvation. Hardship compelled his mother to leave their native village for the metropolis of Shanghai to work as a maid-servant in order to help feed the family. Not too long after his mother's departure, the father quit selling sweets and opened up a small grocery store in a town called Dongjiadu on the riverbank near Shanghai. Both his parents having left, the young Zoen Fong remained in Nanku and was taken in by his paternal uncle. As soon as he was old enough to work, he became a shepherd, tending to the grazing of his uncle's water-buffalos. After working strenuously as a shepherd for a few years, he decided to look for his long-separated mother in Shanghai.

So decided, Zoen Fong set out for the river in the back of Nanku Village, where boat-woman ran a ferry business, taking paying customers across the river to the town of Cape Zhu. Quite out of breath from running to the ferry boat, Zoen Fong asked

the boat-woman to take him to Shanghai. Finding the little boy all alone without any accompanying adults, the boat-woman flatly refused. No sooner had she refused than she was shocked to watch the boy walking straight into the river while shouting, "I'll swim to Shanghai, then! Yes, swim I will!" "Oh, no, don't scare me like that, Child!" the kind-hearted woman shouted back. "Come back ashore! You'll drown, for sure! Alright, alright, I'll take you to Shanghai! Come back here!"

Once in Cape Zhu, a rather boisterous town that was the center of many cities around Shanghai, such as Songjiang, Kunshan and Wujiang, the young stowaway, Zoen Fong, mingled with the crowds and boarded unnoticed a small steam ship to Shanghai, thinking the ship would take him to the big city in a matter of minutes, just as the ferry boat had taken him across the river from Nanku. To his surprise and dismay, the trip was to take more than two long days from Cape Zhu to Shanghai, all due to the inchoate and crudely made steam ship typical of the late 19th century in China. The sight of the wide and turbulent Yangtze River was a new sight that added to his fear and anxiety for the unknown future before him. He had, also, in his young and adventurous heart the knowledge that he would most likely never be a shepherd boy again.

Alone and penniless, Zoen Fong was a miserable small stowaway hiding in one corner of the ship suffering from hunger, until finally an adult among the passengers noticed him and

alerted the crew to the sorry plight of the boy. When a member of the crew approached him, the boy slowly and hesitantly opened up to the curious questioner. Members of the crew knew about his parents and sympathized with his predicament. Promptly they offered him some food and drink, and by the time the ship docked in Shanghai, they found someone who happened to know where Zoen Fong's mother was working as a maid, and took him there.

His reunion with his mother was understandably a tearful event which moved the man for whom his mother worked, Pastor John Marshall Willoughby Farnham (1823-1917): the very man who would change the life of How Zoen Fong.

For years thereafter, the mother and son believed it was all due to the blessing and love of Christ that not only did they reunite, but also that Zoen Fong was helped and supported by Pastor Farnham, for it was almost certain Zoen Fong would have perished in Shanghai, if they had not found each other. Shanghai in 1883, the 8th reigning year of Emperor Guangxu of the Qing Dynasty, was already a tremendously large city, a Westernized metropolis in China, where many blond, blue-eyed Westerners could be spotted on the boisterous streets, sporting a superior air toward the native Chinese, a result of the Nanjing Treaty, signed in 1842, that permitted all the foreigners to carry on their different businesses with no restrictions from the Chinese regime, following China's humiliating defeat by the foreign powers in a

conflict known historically as the "Opium War (1839-1842)."[4]

Abiding by the Nanjing Treaty, the Qing monarchy would open five of her most prosperous coastal cities to England for free trading: Guangzhou, Xiamen, Fuzhou, Ningbo and Shanghai. It was during part of the treaty that China would cede Hong Kong to England for 150 years.

One historically significant social change that resulted from this national shame might have been that the Westernization of Shanghai led to its becoming an increasingly important Chinese city, not only in social affairs, but also in humanities and customs, among other aspects.

Kingdom of Heavenly Peace and the Lowrie (Qingxin, in Chinese: which means "Pure Heart") School

A native of the State of Maine, Pastor John Marshall Willoughby Farnham was a missionary sent to China from the Presbyterian Church. In March 1860, the 10th reigning year of Emperor Xianfeng, Farnham and his wife Mary Jane arrived in Shanghai, finding it not a Chinese city in the lovely early bloom spring, but instead a war-torn city rife with scenes of misery, as it

---

4   The war had been ignited by Great Britain's boldly greedy and iniquitous act of shipping and selling opium from India to the Chinese masses, which had met vehement opposition and prohibition by the Qing monarchy. This eventually led to an attack by Great Britain. Corrupt, weak and incompetent, the Qing monarchy was flatly defeated, resulting in its being forced to sign the Nanjing Treaty, the first of many unequal and unjust treaties that followed in subsequent years.

was experiencing the chaos brought on by the ill-conceived and ill-advised rise of the Kingdom of Heavenly Peace in China.

After taking by force a few provinces south of the Yangtze River from the ruling monarchy, Hong Xiuquan, the leader of the Kingdom of Heavenly Peace, was not defeated until 1864 by the Qing armies led by Li Hongzhang and Zeng Guofan, marking the end of the Kingdom, 13 years after its destructive and bloody start in 1851.

But in 1860, the civil war was still underway, and refugees by the thousands poured into Shanghai from all directions. In view of the homeless and miserable conditions under which the refugees were living, the new arrivals Pastor John Farnham and his wife Mary Jane, with their Christian spirit and human compassion, started their mission to help the down-and-out in Shanghai. They founded the Lowrie Boys' School, a Christian school to take in and educate many of the homeless refugee children, in the district of Lujiabin outside the South Gate of the city (present 597 Lujiabin Road). Between 1865 and 1868, more buildings for classrooms and an administration office as well as a Presbyterian Church were erected on the campus. In 1880, the school's name was changed into the Lowrie School. John Farnham presided concurrently as the pastor of the church on campus and principal of the school. In 1919 the church was moved from the campus to a specially built site on Dafuochang Road. Although it was no longer part of the Lowrie School, it was

named the South Gate Church[5], or the First Presbyterian Church, where John Farnham served for many years as the pastor. The Lowrie School eventually became today's Shanghai Municipal South Middle School.

In those first years of the Lowrie School, all the teachers, administrators and students would attend church service regularly. Since a pure heart must be vigilantly maintained, whether that of a teacher, student or a worker. The school was named Qingxin, (literally, Pure Heart) after this belief.

In 1861, a year after the founding of the Lowrie Boys' School, a boom in registration prompted the planning and founding of a girls' school which was named the Mary Farnham Girls' School, one of the earliest girls' schools in China. In 1918, the school's name was changed to the Lowrie Middle School for Girls, which was in turn changed into the Shanghai Municipal Number Eight Middle School for Girls in 1953. It became a co-ed middle school in 1969 and was renamed the Shanghai Municipal Number Eight Middle School.

In 1883, when the young Zoen Fong finally reunited with

---

5   The South Gate Church was also named the First Presbyterian Church in Shanghai. It was also known to the Chinese as the Qingxin Tang, which literally means "the Pure Heart Church". In 1994, a commemorative plaque was fixed to the former First Presbyterian Church building (after renovation work after years of neglect, largely due to tumultuous political and social upheavals in China) at 30 Dachang Road in Shanghai. The text on the plaque reads that the building — built in 1923 by the Presbyterian missionary church — has been marked and preserved as a landmark for its historic and architectural distinction. See photos, xxx & yyy.)

his mother, a maid at the time in the household of Pastor John Farnham, out of compassion and sympathy for the mother and son, broke the traditional rule of prohibiting family members of the hired help to move into the employer's house, decided to take Zoen Fong in. And so it was that the lucky boy was able to stay in Shanghai with his mother.

Raised in rural areas where life was marked by hardship and labor even for little boys, Zoen Fong was an early riser and took it upon himself to help his mother clean the house, the front and back yards, and to tending to the plants and flowers in the gardens, as horticulture was the hobby of the lady of the house. Impressed by the boy's good and conscientious work, Mary Farnham soon suggested to John that the boy deserved some schooling, to which John replied, "Let's send the boy to our school, then." This decision changed the course of How Zoen Fong's life.

How Zoen Fong and the Bau Family

With this brand-new experience of going to school, Zoen Fong was able to acquire new knowledge from the distant Western world, the most important of which would be the English language, which helped broaden his views and opinions of the entire world.

Furthermore, he was able to make a few friends, among whom the brothers Bau Xian'en and Bau Xianchang, as well

as Gao Fengchi. These three became particularly close to him because of their common interest and goals. Their friendship would later come to fruition in the world of publishing and printing, resulting in the creation of an unprecedented cultural enterprise in the history of China, for they were none other than the future founders of the prestigious Commercial Press. Sharing the same alma mater, the Pure Heart School (Lowrie School), they received Western education and were baptized to become Protestants. Moreover they would be deeply tied by friendship, kinship, work, and marital connections, as How Zoen Fong later married Bau Tsui Nyoh, a sister of the Bau brothers.

The Baus at the time were a well-known Westernized family among the Chinese Christians in the coastal cities of Jiangsu and Zhejiang provinces in the southeastern part of China. A graduate of the Ningbo Boys' Boarding School, founded in the city of Ningbo, Zhejiang Province, south of Shanghai by an American Presbyterian missionary, Bau Zhecai, head of the Bau family, chose to dedicate his life to be a pastor of the Presbyterian Church. Also devoted to publishing and printing, he worked as a type-setter at a small printing company headed by William Gamble, a pastor of the American Presbyterian church in Ningbo. In 1862, William Gamble, taking Bau and some other technicians with him, moved the company to Shanghai and named it "US-China Book Company." This was the cradle of CP later founded by How Zoen Fong and Bau's two elder sons.

In Shanghai, Bau met and became friends with Pastor John Farnham who invited Bau to serve as a co-pastor at his church on the campus of the Lowrie School. Farnham and Bau later co-founded the Child's Paper and the Chinese Illustrated News in 1875. Three years later, the two, with members of their churches, founded the Religious Tract Society, whose work was to write and publish pamphlets and handbooks on missionary teaching. It wouldn't be an exaggeration to suggest that Bau Zhecai was the inspirational founding father of publishing and printing, in that his devotion exerted a great influence on his three sons and his son-in-law How Zoen Fong to carry out his life's endeavor. On January 27th 1895, Bau Zhecai died at the age of 62, only two years before his son-in-law and sons founded CP.

Bau Zhecai was survived by three sons and three daughters, all of whom studied at the Lowrie School. While still students there all three sons worked part time at the "US-China Book Company," the company co-founded by their father that published and printed simple, rudimentary reading matters in English, where the eldest son Bau Xian'en (Bau Yee Ung, in Shanghai dialect; 1861-1910) studied carving out letters, the middle son Bau Xiannchang (Bau Yee Chong, in Shanghai dialect; 1864-1929) studied type setting, and the youngest son Bau Xianheng (Bau Yee Hun, in Shanghai dialect;1867-?) studied printing. Their part-time work and on-the-job training at the company gave them a solid foundation, later enabling the two

elder brothers to join How Zoen Fong in founding CP.

Working at English Papers: A Turning Point

How Zoen Fong, studying diligently and making good grades at the Lowrie School, took a course in publishing and printing at the Lowrie School just as the Bau brothers had. After the outbreak of the American Civil War in 1861, the Presbyterian Church was unable to provide much financial aid to their affiliated churches and schools; consequently, the Lowrie School thereafter added two required courses to their curriculum of which the students were to choose one: horticulture and publishing and printing matters. These courses were offered so that students could learn a trade for their livelihood after graduation. When Zoen Fong started schooling at the Lowrie School in the 1880's, he enrolled in the publishing and printing course.

In 1889, Zoen Fong suffered a big blow when his father died. Now 18, he was almost considered a grownup and was quite mature in his thinking about his responsibility in life. Realizing the financial situation in his home had worsened with his father's passing and his new role as the provider for the family, he decided to quit school and find work. Watching him struggling, a teacher at the Lowrie School, John Alfred Silsby, lent Zoen Fong a helping hand and recommended that he work as an intern and handyman at St. Luke's (Tongren, in Chinese) Hospital, which

was founded and operated by a charitable Christian organization. A rather small hospital, it required no training or experience on the part of Zoen Fong, whose job was cleaning and running errands. After working there for a year, he came to realize that his lack of any medical knowledge or training in science prevented him from having a future in the field of medicine. As he had already gained training in publishing and printing, he found a job as a word-setter at the Shanghai Mercury, an English newspaper, and soon afterward, moved on to work at the North China Daily News, another English newspaper.

Setting up a tremendously large network of news and information in China, the North China Daily News supplied free copies to all missionaries in China. In return, the newspaper would receive from the missionaries written news reports and information on all the political and social activities and movements. Additionally, the paper would run editorial commentaries and essays on Sino-Anglo relations, as well as the state of the Qing monarchy and other newsworthy topics, such as making suggestions and demands for the Qing monarchy to adopt an open-door policy with the Western and other non-Chinese powers, stating its opposition to the armed forces of the Kingdom of Heavenly Peace, among others. All these were the paper's attempts to coerce the Chinese monarchy to grant ever more special privileges to Great Britain in China. Featuring these salient topics, the paper was widely read by all the Qing officials

in charge of foreign affairs in China. Its readers included men of high position, including Li Hongzhang, the Grand Councilor.

The North China Daily News saw many tumultuous decades in China, including the fall of the Qing Dynasty and the founding of the Republic of China in 1911, the Northern expedition against the warlords in 1925, the 8-year Sino-Japanese War that ended in 1945, the civil war between the Nationalists and the Communists and Nationalists' subsequent retreat to the island of Taiwan and the founding of the People's Republic of China in 1949, and right up to the paper's termination on March 31, 1951, bringing to an end a newspaper that had lasted for nearly a century. The North China Daily News remains to this day one of the most important sources from which the historical records of Shanghai are derived.

The building of the North China Daily News was eventually taken over by the municipal office of Shanghai, which granted a permit of occupancy to the American AIA Group Limited, an insurance company. It's known today in Shanghai as the AIA Building.

Chapter 2: He had a Dream!

By the time How was promoted to the head of the type-setting section at the North China Daily News, his salary was high enough for him to support a family, enabling him to think of marriage and children. Because of his close friendship with the Bau brothers, he was able to get to know and eventually marry their sister, Bau Tsui Nyoh. And yet at this time of great auspiciousness and happiness, the young groom, who was known for his filial piety to his mother, was struck by a dark tragedy: his mother passed away the day before the wedding ceremony.

How's marriage to Tsui Nyoh was a happy and harmonious one, which further deepened his friendship with the two elder Bau brothers, his new brothers-in-law. The three of them, joined by Gao Fengchi, another close associate, would confide in one another. They loved to pass the time after work playing chess, sipping tea or simply shooting the breeze. Following church services, which they attended every Sunday, they would frequently walk to a teashop named Lake Pavilion located near the local City Buddhist Temple where, while having a bite to eat or sipping tea, they would share with each other their desires, ideals and viewpoints on current affairs, but most often they would dwell on how to realize their common dream to found a

printing company and plant.

Working at the plant of the English newspapers, they all encountered constant racial discrimination from their Western employers and superiors. Suffering daily scolding and verbal abuse, which bred increasing resentment in the young Chinese workers, compelled them to strengthen their resolve to establish their own company and printing plant. Driven by this determination, the four quietly set out to work harder and pursue an even more frugal lifestyle in order to save enough money to realize their common dream.

On April 15, 1896, these original four—How, the two elder Bau brothers and Gao Fengchi—were joined by four other friends in a small teashop by the Sanyang Bridge. With support from these dear friends, who all of shared How's ideas and beliefs, How proposed to start raising funds to cover the purchase and operating costs of a printing company. Unanimously approved by all seven attendees, they drew up a simple agreement stating that the eight of them would be the investors and shareholders of the company, with each party investing $500 yuan, or a total of $4,000 as the initial capital of the company.

And as the colorful city of Shanghai was going about its own boisterous, hustling and bustling business, a printing company, owned and operated by Chinese, would soon be founded. It would flourish, and, in time, make itself a household name on the cultural and business scene of China.

How the name was chosen

On February 11th, 1897, the year following their meeting at the teashop by the Sanyang Bridge, How and his business partners rented two rooms in the Dechang Alley of Jiangxi Road in Shanghai, in which they had three printing machines installed. Excitement filled their hearts as this preparation intensified their anticipation of operating their own plant, which at the time could only turn out simple reading matters. Nonetheless, there was plenty of hope for expansion and growth, as long as they worked hard enough with the funds they had chipped in. At 26, a bright future presented itself before How Zoen Fong.

The total initial investment for their printing shop was $3,750, with each share at $500. How and the two Bau brothers owned one share each, which came to $1,500. Another shareholder was a gentleman by the name of Shen Bofang, a pious member of the Catholic church, whose father served as a translator of French and Chinese for the local governments of Shanghai and Suzhou, and was concurrently a buyer for the foreigners in the two cities. As Shen Bofang was more well-to-do than the other members in the group, he owned two shares, investing $1,000 yuan, which brought the funds to $2,500. Yet another share went to a friend named Xu Guisheng who invested $500 yuan, with the remaining $750 divided equally among three investors, Gao Fengchi, Zhang Guihua and Yu Houdun,.

Though none of the partner-shareholders was a rich man, How was actually in the tightest plight financially. For his $500 investment, his wife Tsui Nyoh had to borrow from a classmate from the girls' school she attended. But what the eight young men lacked in business knowledge, they more than made up for in education, gumption, hope, Christian faith and an unlimited reservoir of enthusiasm. They also had a deep conviction that, united in true friendship, their dreams would surely come true. It was this very conviction that bound them closely in both body and spirit.

Work responsibilities were divided among the partners as follows: How was voted General Manager; Bau Xian'en and Bau Xianchang became the supervisors of daily printing operations; and Gao Fengchi would for the time being remain a student at the China Printing School in order to master more technology and learn more skills. With the job assignments thus settled and the three machines ready to run, they were well prepared and equipped to start their business venture.

Now came the issue of finding a name for their business. The Chinese are quite particular in having appropriate names for both people as well as inanimate objects and ideas. The question was raised by How Zoen Fong, during a break one day soon after the printing had started; he urged the partners to come up with a fitting name for their new business. Different names were suggested by all, but none were unanimously approved.

"The name of our business must have something to do with auspiciousness, fortune , success, and luck," stated How.

As luck would have it, at this point of their conversation the elder sister of the Baus (addressed by the group as Big Bau Sister) walked in accompanied by her husband. The couple had come to pay a visit and to check out her brothers' business site. Big Bau Sister—a graduate of the Mary Farnham Girls' School— was leafing through the pages of advertisements and commercials the young workers had just printed, while her husband joined in the heated discussion of naming the business with her brothers and their associates. Just then she mumbled to herself, within earshot of the others, "So, what you guys print out are all these commercials."

Her words stunned everyone and interrupted the discussion. "Commercial⋯Commercial⋯," the young men repeated the word a few times, before they exclaimed in unison, "Say, why don't we just name it Commercial Press, then!" The Commercial Press (CP), the name in English, was what they first gave their business, and, a few days later, it was translated as Shangwu Yin Shu Guan in Chinese (Business Affairs Print Book Company, in literal English). What none of them could have guessed on that memorable day was that the name Commercial Press was indeed auspiciously born and would go on to become one of the most famous and respected names in the publishing and printing industry, known both inside and outside of China for over a

century—and counting!

World's affair and the Commercial Press

To understand the birth of this new cultural technology of printing and publishing, one must look into the vision and planning of its founder, How Zoen Fong. In order to do that, one must first look at the historical backdrop of this ground-breaking business. During the twilight years of the Qing Dynasty in the late 19th century, and in the wake of the Industrial Revolution in Europe, many countries were focusing on scientific research and development under a new cultural ideology, one in which machines were beginning to take over the work of human hands. Simply put: it was a revolution that led to products being manufactured in factories and plants, replacing manual production and labor.

Starting as early as 1759, the Industrial Revolution officially took off after the invention of the rotary steam-engine by James Watt (1736-1819) of Scotland. Often called the Age of Revolution by historians, a series of successful inventions during the 18th century led Great Britain to become one of the most advanced nations and a driving force behind the Industrial Revolution. This, in turn, capitalized the country, enabling Britain to become a powerful colonizer, harnessing its new-found strength to acquire colonies all over the world by force. Before long, other European powers followed the example set

by Great Britain, industrializing their own countries, and this trend of revolutionary industrialization ultimately spread to North America in the 19th century. A direct result of industrialization was the emergence of powerful militaries and a strengthening of the economies of Western countries, which fueled their desire to control the rest of the world.

In short, the nurturing and success of the Industrial Revolution were rooted primarily in the following factors: capitalism, agricultural revolution, the significant discovery of new sea routes, the policy of colonization, new governmental laws, the spirit of Christianity, the rise of commercialism, and revolutionary breakthroughs in science and the humanities.

How Zoen Fong was born in the midst of these changes, when the Western forces were waging wars of invasion against China with the ultimate purpose of carving up China into different colonies, as the country was represented by a corrupt and scientifically backward monarchy. Meanwhile, not only was China impacted by the Western Industrial Revolution, it was also profoundly affected by a new cultural ideology brought ashore, specifically one based on Christianity. These events— all disturbing, yet many fresh—,joined forces in rendering an unprecedented and historical opportunity for the life and the lasting vitality of a publishing and printing house such as CP.

It must be noted that at the time of the founding of CP, the de facto sovereign of the Qing Dynasty was, and had been

for decades, the notoriously infamous Ci Xi (1835-1908), the Empress Dowager. A woman of enormous power, wiles and resourcefulness, Ci Xi emerged from being a low imperial consort to Emperor Xianfeng (1831-1861) to become second in status only to the Empress, after she bore Emperor Xianfeng an heir, who later became Emperor Tongzhi.

After the death of Emperor Xianfeng, Ci Xi ruled during the reigns of two succeeding emperors, Tongzhi, her son, and Guangxu, her nephew and handpicked puppet emperor. It was largely due to her extravagance for her personal pleasure and glorification when Japan and other European forces had insidious designs on seizing and colonizing China already weakened by the Opium War. These led to China's disastrous defeat in the 1894 Sino-Japanese War resulting in the Treaty of Shimonoseki (a city in Japan) in 1895, which forced China to "cede" major coastal cities to the Japanese, and to "apologize" to Japan by paying more than two hundred million taels of silver as "war indemnity." This treaty was yet another humiliating and detrimental blow to the military, the economy, the political stability and, above all, the national spirit of China. The peninsula of the eastern Liaoning in Manchuria, and the islands of Taiwan and Penghu were among the territories "yielded" by China to Japan.

Other clauses in the treaty included granting Japan the right to open whatever factory in whatever city it chose, and "opening up" major cities of Shashi, Chongqing, Suzhou and Hangzhou to

the Japanese. In short, the Treaty of Shimonoseki was one of the most blatantly unfair treaties signed in the history of China, one that not only humiliated China as a nation, but also forfeited its sovereignty.

If there was any silver lining to the national shame brought on by the decayed and incompetent Qing monarchy, it would have to be that the Sino-Japanese War and the Treaty of Shimonoseki tolled a bell of warning to the millions of Chinese masses: unless some urgent measure was taken, China would be on the verge of being carved up and colonized, and would soon be annihilated by foreign forces. Thus, there arose an acute feeling of Chinese nationalism and a realization for the dire need to overthrow the hopeless Qing monarchy, and ultimately establish a new regime with a new political system. This new national awareness of patriotism cumulated inevitably in the unsuccessful Hundred Days' Reforms of 1898, followed by other failed uprisings against the Qing, until, the 1911 revolution led by Dr. Sun Yat-sen finally succeeded in establishing the Republic of China.

Gao Fengchi, a close associate of How Zoen Fong and one of the founders of CP, wrote in his essay entitled, "The History of the Founding of the Commercial Press", "The entire country of China following the defeat in the 1894 Sino-Japanese War seemed to have learned a painful lesson and was quite united in the belief that the old examination system must be abolished and be replaced by a new and modern, or Westernized, educational

system, which afford a golden opportunity for publishing and printing houses to flourish. It must be pointed out that the success of CP is owed to a perfect blending of human effort and the bleak times China was facing."

Wang Yunwu, another man of letters quite essential to the growth and development of CP, a man who devoted more than forty years of his life to the publishing and printing house, of which he served as General Manager and Chairman of Board of Trustees of CP in Taiwan, wrote the following in an essay on the chronology of CP:

It was the 1894 Sino-Japanese War and the subsequent aborted reforms that roused the members of the intelligentsia in China to place an emphasis on education. This led to the foundation in Shanghai, Fujian Province, and Tianjin of modern schools in which foreign language study was required. Notable among those schools were the Tongwen School of Beijing and the Guangfangyan School in Shanghai.

In 1896, the year before the founding of CP, Minister Li Hongzhang of the Ministry of Justice petitioned the emperor to establish the Grand School (the equivalent of a university today) in the capital, Beijing, and Modern Schools (the equivalent of high schools) in all the major cities and counties. With the approval of his petition, modern schools were established, which helped the birth of CP, a publishing and printing house

that was quite indispensable to the interaction between new learning and the new concept and technology of publishing and printing of reading matters.

Born in the Guangdong province in southern China, Wang Yunwu (1888-1979) was one of the most prominent scholars, educators, publishers, library founders and statesmen of the 20th century China. Having studied for five years at a traditional private school, where only Chinese classics were taught, Wang Yunwu was sent to a hardware store in his teens to work as an apprentice because of financial difficulties at home. While working at the store by day, he studied English on his own by night. At 17, he entered the Tongwen School to major in English when he read a wide range of books in English and other Western languages. After turning 18, he taught English, history and geography in various schools in Shanghai.

In 1912, the first year of the Republic, Wang Yunwu was invited by the newly-elected President Dr. Sun Yat-sen to work as a literary assistant in the Office of the President, and concurrently as a bureau chief in the Ministry of Education. In 1921, Wang, at the recommendation of Dr. Hu Shih, assumed the position of Director of the Editorial and Translation Department of CP, before becoming its General Manager. Thereafter, Wang Yunwu went on to become an integral part at CP. A large number of textbooks, many series of books on different academic subjects,

and the dictionaries he compiled became household names for several generations and millions of Chinese readers. The name Wang Yunwu is now synonymous with the lofty concepts of "Education must reach everyone" and "Learning is to be free of politics and other cultural dogmas."

Chapter 3: Hot Off the Press!

In its infancy, Commercial Press had only two manual rolling printers, three pedal rolling discs and three manual pressing machines. As for staff, CP could only afford about 10 workers, all because of the lack of funds due to the difficult financial conditions, something all the founders and partners had in common. With the limited machinery and manpower, however, they could turn out work on demand and make ends meet, printing out materials such as business account books, publicity fliers, among others. It was a printing house, a humble one that they started out with.

Diligent and hardworking, How was General Manager of CP but his job also included finding new clients, procuring all materials and supplies, bookkeeping, greeting all clients and visitors, as well as editing and proofreading – in short, the company's jack-of-all-trades. Responding to his wife's urge for him not to overextend himself physically and mentally, he would constantly remind her that it was the beginning stage of their own company when everything large or small had to be handled by him and him alone. With the work ethic and attitude of a modern-day CEO, CP grew rapidly under his leadership. How convinced his partners to follow his example of not cashing out the profits

and bonuses they earned. Instead, he suggested that they reinvested them in the company in order to attract new investors and partners. Consequently, by 1901, the monetary worth of CP, which had started out at $3,750, grew to an impressive $50,000 in only four years.

Like a true entrepreneur, How was not satisfied with his success of the Press as only a printing company, because he had his eyes and heart set on something bigger and more personally meaningful: to expand CP into a publishing house as well.

"Flag People," as the Americans were Called by the Shanghai People

At the founding of CP, Shanghai was second only to Guangzhou in southern China as the most Westernized city in China. The trend of Westernization had been brought about by the multitude of new reforms and policies, which also exerted a great influence on the policy making of the publishing and printing work of CP under the leadership of How Zoen Fong.

At the time, a book was published in Chinese by CP entitled *Miscellaneous Notes on Different Social Phenomena during the Qing Dynasty* written by Xu Ke (1869-1928), who once passed the provincial examination. Xu first served in the Qing court and then as a literary secretary to the notorious warlord Yuan Shikai, and finally as an editor for CP.

The book, in which he collected and poignantly wrote

15,000 true and hilarious stories that took place in Westernized Shanghai, was also rich in documentary notes that examined and exposed the many political and social phenomena of the twilight years of the Qing Dynasty, when How founded CP.

The following is a quote from "Miscellaneous Notes on Different Social Phenomena during the Qing Dynasty":

> In Shanghai toward the end of the Qing Dynasty, the natives would call the English as 'Great Britain Man', the French as 'France Man' (some would mistakenly address the French as 'Brance Man', which was confusing the 'f' with 'b'), the Americans as 'Flowery Flag Man', and the Germans as 'German Man'. The Shanghai masses were so accustomed to these terms that if one were to call the English, the English, or the Americans, Americans, most in Shanghai would gape and be in a total fog as to what these words meant.

Fully manifesting the popular trend of Westernization and sometimes exposing the attitude of the obsequiousness of the Chinese toward the Westerners, the book, at a stupendous word count of more than 3,000,000 characters, was published in 1916.

How Zoen Fong and Xia Ruifang

On February 4th, 1892, there was a news article in the New York Times, which was based on a report sent from

Shanghai on the 28th of December, 1891, reporting that the 20-year-old Emperor Guangxu of China had started to study the English language taught to him by two young staff members in the Ministry of Imperial Education. This new curriculum was announced to the entire country by the pronouncement in an imperial edict. In the Times article, this piece of news was regarded as one of the most significant measures taken in the history of China.

Needless to say, this was a significant step taken by the Qing monarchy. Twenty years old himself that year, How Zoen Fong had quit schooling at the Lowrie School and started working as a typesetter at the British-run newspaper, the Shanghai Mercury. There is no doubt that he would have learned the news that the young Emperor Guangxu had taken up to study English even before the readers of the New York Times did.

This piece of news filled his mind with inspired thoughts as he felt deeply in his heart that if the Chinese were to catch up with their times and ever get ahead in life, they would have to study foreign languages, primarily English, in order to be able to communicate with the rest of the world. Considering himself fortunate for having studied English, he thought to himself that there must be many others who had never been exposed to English but would like to know the language. Now wouldn't it be propitiously timely for CP to publish and print English instruction textbooks? He was certain they would be welcomed by the

Chinese masses who were surely quite eager to learn.

At the time, knowing a foreign language, specifically English, was indeed financially profitable. In an editorial entitled, "On Studying Western Culture and the Urgency of Industrialization" which appeared in the Shanghai Daily on December 29th, 1896, the writer urged all Chinese to study Western culture, including languages, in order to communicate and work with Westerners, so that they might subsequently earn more income to attain a higher standard of living. The article further elaborated on the numerous material benefits that would come with mastering Western languages leading to profitable dealings with the affluent Westerners.

Materialistic and obsequious as the article was, there was some truth in it that still rings true in today's China. But it was the reality of the times, in which How Zoen Fong lived, that he decided to Romanize his full name based on the Shanghai dialect. How Zoen Fong sounded easier for non-Chinese to pronounce, which would make his dealings with foreigners much easier. After the Pinyin Romanization system was established in the People's Republic of China in early 1950's, the three syllables of How Zoen Fong became Xia Ruifang. To respect what the master chose for himself, How Zoen Fong is used in this English translation of this biography.

Success and Popularity of the Chinese and English Primer

In 1898, the year following the founding of Commercial Press, it published its very first book, the "English Primer," which almost immediately became a best-seller in China.

Before the publication of the book, Commercial Press had only taken on jobs printing documents, fliers and other reading materials for foreign companies. This did not fulfill what How had in mind for his company to accomplish: to publish and print an instructional textbook for learners of English. For quite some time he wracked his brain in vain about how and where to find his dream textbook before it suddenly dawned on him that what he was looking for might be right at hand: none other than the very English textbook used at the Lowrie School where he was first exposed to the language.

The textbook, English Primer that had been used to teach him and his classmates was also used by primary schools in India, a British colony from 1858 to 1947. Shipped from India, the book was printed in small batches by CP, until How came to realize that, without the Chinese translation of some essential parts of the textbook, it was all but impossible for any Chinese student to learn English from it. After some troubling but deep consideration, he finally decided to invite a remote relative of his, Xie Honglai, a teaching assistant at the Suzhou Institute of Myriad Studies (Suzhou University today) to translate the new

words, texts and grammatical points into Chinese, before the textbook would be published and printed in its new bilingual version. The new book had a Chinese subtitle, which in literal translation was Chinese English First Step (Chinese and English Primer, in English).

CP published 2,000 copies of the first edition of the book, with How himself taking charge of the selection of print paper, typesetting, fonts, among other details. These first 2,000 copies were sold out in only 20 days! Ye Shengtao, one of the pioneer educators of modern China, whose students included such great novelists as Ba Jin, Ding Ling, Dai Wangshu, wrote in his memoirs that the bilingual Chinese and English Primer was indeed the first textbook he had studied, when first learning English. Hu Shih, another legendary scholar, philosopher and statesman of the 20th century China, also wrote of using the book as his first English textbook. Similarly, Liang Shuming, yet another great scholar, reminisced that he had studied the same book as a teenager when he attended the China-West Elementary School, a primary school run by both Chinese and Westerners in Beijing. These are just a few examples of the important role that the Chinese and English Primer, CP's first English textbook, played in the assimilation of the English language and culture in China at the turn of the 20th century. Almost overnight, the book became a bestseller in major cities all over China.

"More editions, yes, more editions" was the unanimous

response from How and the Bau brothers, who, along with the other investors in CP, rejoiced in having found a leading partner, How, with a perfect vision and foresight in predicting what would sell on the publishing market. The unprecedented popularity of the book and the joy and encouragement from readers and partners alike prompted How to give more assignments to Xie Honglai, the translator of the textbook, to translate more advanced textbooks, eventually finishing six volumes for beginners and the advanced students. These six volumes remained bestsellers in China for more than a decade and went through as many as 63 editions. Indeed, it was this very book, the Chinese and English Primer, that helped lay the solid foundation for CP to become the leading publisher and printing company in China.

Hilarious Chinese Equivalents to Some English Words

In their attempt to cash in on the CP's success of publishing books, some smaller publishing houses in Shanghai began to copy CP in publishing illustrated books to "teach" English to Chinese readers. The method they came up with was first printing the English words and then placing beneath them Chinese characters that the publisher and author considered equivalent to the corresponding sounds in English. But this approach often had a bewildering effect on those who understood both languages, and would certainly cause complete confusion to those who understood only one or the other language. Studying

English using the examples and instructions in these books could have unintentionally hilarious consequences on the part of the publisher and the writers.

The following are just a few examples of this:

- Beneath the English word "banana," would be the three Chinese characters, "bai nai nai/白奶奶," which literally means "white grandma;"
- Beneath the English word "shirt," would be the two Chinese characters, "xiu tuo/休脱," which literally means "rest/die shed;"
- Beneath the English word "cough," would be the two Chinese characters, "ku fu/哭夫," which literally means "wail husband"!

Most of the transliterated sounds from English would sound a little closer to the original English, when and if they were pronounced in the dialect of Ningbo, a coastal city south of Shanghai in the Zhejiang province. These innovative, but rather laughable, "textbooks of English" gained much popularity in China at the fin de siècle of the 19th century, as some Chinese thought it the only way to master English, which was becoming increasingly popular, trendy, and fashionable.

Fearlessness and Patriotism of How Zoen Fong

There's a famous Chinese saying: "As times breed men of distinction, men of distinction breed times of notability." This

rings particularly true as regards the early development of CP, when its printing site at Dechang Lane on Jiangxi Road was burnt down in a fire caused by carelessness on the part of the workers. The plant, including all the machines, equipment and materials were completely destroyed. The devastation was softened, thankfully, by their earlier decision to buy fire insurance, a new measure at the time, which compensated them with a total sum that sufficiently covered the damage and loss. With the payment from the insurance company and encouragement from his partners and shareholders, How proposed to quickly find a new site to build a larger and more modern plant, and to re-open shortly with more advanced machines and equipment. How' s plan and proposal were met with unanimous and enthusiastic approval.

Soon thereafter, How had this to report to the others: that he had found a new site at Shunguang Lane on Beijing Road, a much larger site where a plant with 12 rooms for production and offices could be built. He also announced that new equipment, such as printing machines run on kerosene to replace manually operated ones, would be purchased to reduce labor and increase production speed. Again, his proposal was approved and much appreciated by the others.

Thus equipped and empowered with new and modern machines and apparatuses, the reopened CP became more productive, publishing and printing in quick succession the

Chinese-English Dictionary, and the first two volumes of Selections of Chinese and English Literary Essays, raising CP's status and prominence to an ever higher level in the world of publishing in China.

In addition to all this growth and development, How actively contacted the Catholic and Protestant churches, as well as other related organizations to recruit business to print or publish all their reading materials, especially the Bible, one of the most important books at the time, and eventually becoming the most popular book in increasingly Westernized China where the number of Christian churches and believers were growing every day.

By 1906, of the 102 different textbooks officially listed as required for students in elementary schools in Beijing, as stipulated by the Qing monarchy, 54, or more than half of the total number, were published and printed by CP in Shanghai.

In CP's infancy, it also printed two of the most progressive newspapers in China: the Modern Words Daily and the New Reformation Daily, both of which were the voice of reform and revolution. In other words, they were the voice of salvation for China. The two newspapers strongly reflected the advocacies and progressive thoughts held by famous reformers, such as the distinguished Kang Youwei and Liang Qichao. Fully cognizant of the risk he was taking by printing these papers, How went ahead and took on the challenge to print the papers. Punishment would

be beheading, as witnessed in the tragic end to a known reformer, Tan Sitong, who, as one of the six scholars and statesmen close to Emperor Guangxu, urged him to save China and the monarchy by initiating reforms. Furthermore, when the posthumous book, *The School of Compassion* by the beheaded Tan Sitong was presented to How for publication and printing, How approved it without hesitation.

The courage with which How approved and published The School of Compassion was apparently derived from his complete agreement with the tragic Tan Sitong, who had described the corruption and perversion of the thousands of years of the feudal system in China and the cruel oppression of the masses by the totalitarian rulers throughout the centuries. Tan had further condemned the way in which the armies of the Qing monarchy had flattened the force of the Kingdom of Heavenly Peace with violence and gore and other inhuman means. Like Tan Sitong, whose concern for China and its people rose high above his own safety and life, How Zoen Fong was fearless in the face of a choice between risking his life for a worthy cause or living in selfishness and cowardice by choosing the former.

Before How consented to print and publish The School of Compassion, an associate reminded him of the risk he was taking. How replied, "Have no worry. As I'm operating my publishing and printing house in the foreign concession and the International Settlement zone, I have nothing to fear from the Qing rulers."

How Zoen Fong's fearlessness and patriotism helped lay a solid foundation for CP with his lifelong dreams to save China by reforms and to advocate freedom of speech and publication. How's lofty belief was that only by reading published books concerning both the old and new teachings, and establishing a modern and advanced educational system could lead to the birth of a reformed China, both free and strong.

Chapter 4: The Printed Word, a Mightier Word

The Fostering of Soft Power in the 19th Century

Today, countries are often said to be competing against each other with their "soft power"—a new "weapon" for them to display their overall strength in the 21st century.

Throughout both Chinese and foreign history, however, the success of wars or rivalry has mainly depended on "hard power"— in contrast to "soft power"—which includes such "hard" weapons as broadswords, spears, arrows and machine guns and even airplanes and guided missiles. Indeed, man has been relying on arms to protect himself and destroy his foes. Nowadays, nations in peaceful times have begun seeking to penetrate their rivals' lines by trying to change the notions and ways of thinking on the part of their rivals through the dissemination of their own culture, thoughts, literature and arts, all of which make up "soft power". The force of such power is no less powerful than that of tanks or missiles.

The term "soft power", which did not become prevalent until the 21st century, had already found its way into China as early as the end of the 19th century when How Zoen Fong, by

establishing the Commercial Press, devoted himself to China's cultivation of "soft power" to develop people's intelligence and to improve their literacy and cultural appreciation.

One of CP's important contributions to society was the book-reading craze it created in the late Qing Dynasty and the early years of the Republic of China—a suddenly-awakened book-reading eagerness, which made a profound impact in intellectual circles. Its general manager, How Zoen Fong, backed and assisted by Zhang Yuanji and other elite scholars, managed to carry on the business of CP with painstaking effort, opening up an unprecedentedly positive atmosphere for the dissemination of knowledge and culture in modern China. In addition to the above-mentioned textbooks, which helped make basic education popular, CP also published *Yuan Fu (The Wealth of Nations)*, *Tian Yan Lun (Evolution and Ethics)* and other significant modern academic works of literature translated by Yan Fu.

Yuan Fu is the Chinese version of a monograph on economics *The Wealth of Nations* (known in full as *An Inquiry into the Nature and Causes of the Wealth of Nations*) by British economist Adam Smith. The book was deemed to be the "Bible" and encyclopedia on western economics, and reputed to be the "first systematic and remarkable masterpiece on economics". What is more, it ranks among the ten greatest works and had an enormous influence on world history. Also, *Yuan Fu* is a classic translation of great significance in modern China.

Evolution and Ethics — its full name is *Evolution and Ethics and other Essays*— is a collection of papers written by British biologist Thomas Henry Huxley. The book focused on Darwin's biological evolutionism, the first half expounding on evolution and the latter half on ethics. It was through Yan Fu's translation that the Chinese people for the first time came to know the theory of evolution and its concept of survival of the fittest in natural selection.

At the very beginning of the introduction to the Chinese version of *Evolution and Ethics*, Yan Fu pointed out the three difficulties in translating: faithfulness, expressiveness and elegance. As he noted, "a faithful translation, which is hard to achieve, is useless if it is not expressive and smooth. Hence the priority should be given to expressiveness". With this principle in mind, Yan Fu therefore selectively did some liberal translation instead of rigidly following the source text. Also in the introduction, he said, "The translator must acquire a full understanding of the original text before representing it in translation, and when the source text is elusively profound in meaning to which it is hard to find any equivalent, some explanation then can be made in the context; with such an effort, the translated version could be considered expressive and smooth, and thus also faithful.

Since then "faithfulness, expressiveness and elegance" have become the criteria for translating.

Yan Fu (1854-1921), born in Houguan County (today's Fuzhou City) in Fujian Province, was among the first cohort of students selected and sent to Britain or France for education by the Qing Government in 1877. He did exceedingly well at Greenwich Naval College (today's Royal Naval College) in Great Britain.

After two years' studies overseas, Yan Fu returned to China and was appointed chief instructor of Beiyang Naval College established by Li Hongzhang in Tianjin in 1880, and then was promoted head of the College. As the country sank into extreme peril with its defeat in the Sino-Japanese War of 1894-1895, Yan Fu, crying for political reform, wrote or co-wrote a number of essays, including *Way to A Strong and Prosperous China* (known as *Yuan Qiang* in Chinese), *Critique of Han Yu's Original Taoism* (known as *Pi Han* in Chinese), *On Saving the Nation from Extinction* (known in Chinese as *Jiu Wang Jue Lun*) as well as *A Memorial to Emperor Guangxu.*

Upon the founding of the Republic of China, Capital University was renamed Peking University in 1912, and Yan Fu became its first president, but resigned in October that year.

Yan Fu, who helped introduce China to western sociology, political science, political economics, philosophy and natural science in a systematic way, is recognized as a great enlightening thinker and translator in modern China. His enormously influential translations rank among the most important

enlightening works in the 20th century China. These include Chinese versions of *Evolution and Ethics, The Wealth of Nations,* Herbert Spenser's *The Study of Sociology*, John Stuart Mill's *On Liberty* and *A System of Logic: Ratiocinative and Inductive*, Edward Jenks' *A History of Politics*, Montesquieu's *The Spirit of the Laws* , and W. S. Jevons' *Primer of Logic.*

CP, with its far-sighted introduction of new western ideas and ideological trends into a then feudal and secluded China, helped broaden the horizon of Chinese intellectuals by presenting to its countrymen a vast and unfamiliar world, especially the outstanding translated works by Yan Fu. Therefore, its "products" undoubtedly served as a tremendous driving force for the cultural progress of modern times.

While vigorously introducing western learning into China, CP did not neglect the promotion and dissemination of Chinese culture by publishing, among others, such classics as *Lexicon* (known as *Ci Yuan* in Chinese, the first large-scale Chinese dictionary), *Collection of Ancient Masterpieces, The Twenty-Four Histories* (dynastic histories from remote antiquity up to the Ming Dynasty).

Objectively, the social function of CP was not limited to its commercial activities of publishing and issuing. In fact, CP, led by How Zoen Fong and his team, played a significant role as a pioneer in the buildup of China's "soft power" and its modernization drive.

How and his team proved themselves worthy of high respect by shouldering social responsibilities, and trying to meet the needs of their countrymen during those turbulent years.

Zhang Yuanji, Member of the Imperial Academy (known as Hanlin in Chinese), Fled to Shanghai

Far-sighted intellectuals of the late Qing Dynasty and the early Republic of China, seeing their enfeebled country threatened by the hegemony of Western power, were convinced that it was a top priority of non-governmental institutions to wake up and enlighten the public through education. Therefore, news-reporting and publishing, which, as we know, are the function of mass media today, became a new form of education.

However, in this society plagued by economic depression and illiteracy, the educational function of journalism and publishing was substantially weakened. Therefore the sector which needed heavy investment witnessed rather few successes.

Thanks to How's determined and wise management, CP in Shanghai built up a good reputation and enjoyed public praise. It soon stood out in the publishing industry. In addition, it became an ideal arena where patriotic intellectuals—generally writing-savvy but management-illiterate individuals committed to saving the nation with culture— could bring their intelligence into full play by realizing their ambitions. How Zoen Fong, holding talented people in high esteem, eagerly sought the employment

or extended employment of Zhang Yuanji, Cai Yuanpei, Gao Mengdan, Jiang Weiqiao, Du Yaquan, Hu Shih and Wang Yunwu, among numerous others.

In 1898, witnessing his country becoming increasingly enfeebled, Emperor Guangxu was determined to do something and embarked on the Hundred Days of Reform (also known as the Reform Movement of 1898).

Among the participants of the Reform was Zhang Yuanji (alternatively named Jusheng), a member of the Imperial Academy, who was born in Haiyan County, Zhejiang Province. He successfully passed the highest imperial examinations in May, 1892, together with Cai Yuanpei, Ye Dehui, Shen Baochen and 21 other fellow countrymen who also were to become famous.

Before the Reform, Zhang was appointed as Hanlin Bachelor and served as Zhangjing (a role equivalent to the minister's assistant) in the Department of Foreign Affairs and Trade (known as Zongli Yamen in Chinese), which was renamed the Ministry of Foreign Affairs following the Peace Treaty of 1901. The first Foreign Ministry of China thus came into being.

During the Reform, Emperor Guangxu appointed Kang Youwei as Zhangjing of the Department of Foreign Affairs and Trade, and Tan Sitong, Yang Rui, Liu Guangdi and Lin Xu as his assistants, all of whom participated in the Reform.

At this time Zhang Yuanji was responsible for collecting new books in the Department of Foreign Affairs and Trade for

Emperor Guangxu who, eager to carry out the Reform, was reading widely to absorb new knowledge, and came to know about this petty officer, as those books he submitted bore his post and name.

The diehards headed by Ci Xi, the Empress Dowager were strongly opposed to the Reform. They staged a coup on September 21st, 1898, locking Emperor Guangxu up in Yingtai (within today's Zhongnanhai Compound), and executing six scholars and statesmen close to the Emperor in the Reform, including Tan Sitong, their leader, while abolishing all the measures set up during the Reform.

On September 28th, 1898, the six reformers were publicly beheaded, intimidating the other scholars who had participated in the Reform jittery every day, as if in imminent danger of death.

It is said that Emperor Guangxu once advised Ci Xi, who was dismissing one government official after another in the capital, to remove Zhang Yuanji from his post as a petty officer. Therefore, Zhang Yuanji was dismissed, knowing that the Emperor was trying to protect him.

Actually, it was his survival in the Reform Incident that made it possible for him to later come across, get to know and eventually make friends with How Zoen Fong, with whom he managed to usher in a new era for CP.

After his narrow escape in 1898, Zhang Yuanji quickly left the capital for Shanghai where he was taken care of by

Sheng Xuanhuai, founder of Nanyang Public School, at the request of Li Hongzhang, who had once tried to draw some outstanding reformers over to his side and thus had had friendly correspondence with Zhang.

Nanyang Public School, founded by Sheng Xuanhuai in Shanghai in 1896 and affiliated with China Merchants Group and Telegraph Administration, comprised a normal school, an attached primary school, a secondary school and a college, with Sheng Xuanhuai as its first principal. It ranked among the first universities established in modern China along with Beiyang University in Tianjin. At that time, the Yellow Sea and the Bohai Sea were known as Beiyang (Northern Seas), while areas from the south of the Yangtze Estuary (including the East China Sea) down to Fujian Province, Guangdong Province and Taiwan were all known as Nanyang (Southern Seas). It is for this reason that the school that Sheng founded in Shanghai was named Nanyang Public School.

Actually, Nanyang Public School was the predecessor of today's Shanghai Jiaotong University. Due to the Boxer Incident in 1900, some students of Beiyang University came to Shanghai by ship and transferred to the Public School. Many years later, it was restructured as Jiaotong University.

To arrange a proper position for Zhang, Sheng set up the Translation Academy in the Public School and asked Zhang to take charge.

As the foreign books they translated and textbooks they compiled needed printing, Zhang came to know How Zoen Fong, a celebrity in the printing industry.

In 1901, Zhang launched *Diplomacy*, a newspaper focusing on international affairs, and entrusted CP with its printing. In fact, CP had already printed some translated versions of western books, but they had not sold well, resulting in a loss of nearly $10,000—a considerable sum at that time. How Zoen Fong, considering the matter rather serious, went to consult Zhang with the manuscripts. "What's wrong with these manuscripts? Please check up on them", he came straight to the point.

"Leave them to me, and I'll check them", replied Zhang willingly.

A couple of days later, Zhang told How straightforwardly that the problem lay in the unsatisfactory translation.

How Zoen Fong, who had actually been aware of this problem, immediately asked him for help.

So Zhang Yuanji took the manuscripts back to be modified by students in the Academy, and once modified and republished, the new edition was indeed better received. It dawned on How that a publisher could get nowhere in the future without in-house professionals competent in compilation and translation.

How Zoen Fong, a man of great talent and vision, devoted himself to the promotion of his business on the one hand, and at the same time sought out talented people to earnestly partner with

him.

Zhang Invited to Take Charge of Compilation and Translation

How and Zhang met each other for the first time when CP was contracted to print manuscripts for Nanyang Public School. Due to his disagreement with the American supervisor John Calvin Ferguson on the totally westernized philosophy of the school's administration, Zhang felt uncomfortable as acting Principal there, and therefore tried to resign his post several times but was always refused by Sheng Huaixuan. Just then, he got acquainted with How, General Manager of CP, and talked sincerely and freely with him about the prospects as well as the actual operation of the publishing and printing industry. Having compared notes in depth, they appreciated each other's position. While How was convinced that Zhang was the talent he had been looking for, Zhang placed his full trust with the hard-working and promising young man, How Zoen Fong. On another occasion, How found himself in a difficult situation because of a cash-flow problem. Sympathetic with How's plight, Zhang talked a bank into giving How a loan with Zhang as the guarantor. This further showed his complete trust in How. While full of gratitude for Zhang, How was made aware of Zhang's influence despite his failure in seeking a public office.

At this time, CP mainly contracted the printing of small

commercial advertisements and leaflets, which certainly did not satisfy How, an ambitious man determined to open up the book printing business after he discovered that this market had huge potential in the printing of manuscripts for churches and the Public School.

In 1902, CP set up a Compilation & Translation Section, and How, though well aware that Zhang was the best person to preside over it, was not sure whether he could succeed in persuading Zhang to take the post.

In those years, the book-printing business flourished in Shanghai, a metropolis largely permeated with western culture and ethos, with such large-scale publishing houses as Dianshizhai Publishing House and Tongwen Press, all of which boasted their own editing agencies in charge of manuscript editing and revising to ensure high quality.

To preside over such editing agencies, these large-scale publishing houses usually employed the scholars who were once members of the Imperial Academy, also known as the Hanlin Academy. The Hanlin Academy was an academic and administrative institution founded in the eighth century during the Tang Dynasty by Emperor Xuanzong. As an ancient official position, Hanlin stood for the learned and competent scholars responsible for handling confidential matters for the emperor such as the appointment of the prime minister and declaring wars.

.

The entire Qing Dynasty witnessed the emergence of 6,472 Hanlins who exerted an enormous influence on Chinese society. Those who survived the Qing Dynasty continued to play an active role in politics, military affairs, diplomacy, culture, education and economy. For example, in the early days of the Republic of China, Cai Yuanpei, Minister of Education, Xu Shichang, President of Beiyang, Tan Yankai, Chairman of Wuhan National Government, and Yan Huiqing, acting Prime Minister, were all once members of the Hanlin Academy.

With long deliberation, How was convinced that any person capable of presiding over the Compilation & Translation Section would have to be both as learned as a Hanlin and fairly familiar with Western learning and foreign affairs. Zhang had all these qualifications and was the very person he had been seeking.

However, it was not the right time then to headhunt Zhang, for he had just begun his work in the Public School and would soon become acting Principal. How had to conceal this intention for the time being and wait for the opportunity.

Since someone had to be selected to run the Section, Zhang recommended Cai Yuanpei (styled Jiemin), who had also once been a member of Hanlin Academy and had been in contact with CP through book printing. At that time, Cai, progressive in thinking, was staging revolutionary activities in Shanghai and heading the Patriotic Society.

After much discussion, Cai finally agreed to act as a part-

time director of the Section, as he refused to leave the Society. All this demonstrated that How was not only a brilliant manager, but also a trend-setter. He had no hesitation enlisting a revolutionary like Cai.

Ink Bottle Incident Prompted Zhang to Join CP

It is believed that many people have visited the former address of Nanyang Public School founded in 1896 in Xujiahui, Shanghai, and that perhaps quite a few of the visitors have even studied there—today's Xujiahui Campus of Shanghai Jiaotong University.

Strolling around the campus, visitors may glimpse several culture-related landscapes including historic buildings, which bear witness to the vicissitudes of the century-old university, reminding them of those bygone days.

In 1902, Zhang, who could not stand the corrupt bureaucracy any longer, resigned his post as acting Principal of the Public School and returned to the Translation Academy. His successor, Wang Fengzao, was a conservative of the conservatives, who, as Envoy to Japan, had been trying to avert the military conflict through diplomacy even on the eve of the First Sino-Japanese War. He was deeply troubled and frustrated then and was later recalled to the capital.

The year that Wang took over, a student strike took place, which somewhat precipitated Zhang's departure from the school

to join How at CP.

Known as the "Ink Bottle Incident", the large-scale student strike was the first of its kind in the modern history of education in China, giving rise to enormous reverberations in that closed tyrannical society. On November 16th of that year, over 200 students of Nanyang Public School decided to discontinue their schooling en masse in protest against the injustice of the school authorities.

The first batch of the students who had grown up studying *Chinese Primers* in Nanyang Public School had entered the higher-level schooling by 1902. Accustomed to open education, they could not adapt to Wang's conservative teaching style. Guo Zhenying, a teacher of Chinese, even more stubbornly stuck in old practices, choosing such old-fashioned textbooks as *Collected Statutes of Great Qing* (*Da Qing Hui Dian* in Chinese) and *Records of Military Achievements* (*Sheng Wu Ji*) while forbidding students from reading any new books and newspapers, made them discontented and indignant.

Guo was also strongly opposed to the students in Class Five getting together on the weekend to discuss western freedom and peace, and therefore threatened to expel them if they insisted on the gathering.

On November 5th, as he came to his class, he found a cleansed empty ink bottle on his seat.

What feeling could an empty ink bottle cause?

An empty ink bottle might insinuate an empty mind with little learning. "Was it their insult or provocation?" Teacher Guo said to himself, thinking it must be aimed at him.

"Who did this?" he howled on the platform, furious.

"We don't know," answered the students.

He strictly ordered them to investigate but it was in vain; utterly discomfited, he shouted at Bei Yingbo and Wu Shiqing sitting in the front, threatening to punish them severely if they did not report to him within three days.

Still unable to find the "culprit", Guo felt embarrassed and was furious, thus deciding to expel three students and punishing the whole class by recording a serious demerit for their refusal to expose the misconduct, a move that immediately infuriated the class. Indignant, the students went to argue their case with Wang Fengzao; however, Wang sided with Guo and refused to overturn the decision.

Therefore, the whole class decided to explain the matter to all the other classes in the hope of gaining support for their protest of the dictatorial oppression. Wang, after learning about this, did not try to find out the cause; instead, he announced that he would expel all the students of Class Five, which instantly irritated the whole school. Student representatives were immediately selected, and entrusted to demand that the school authority revoke the resolution.

The matter having reached deadlock, all the students, whose

protest was growing increasingly intense, finally resolved during their urgently held meeting to walk out en masse in order to uphold justice and revolt against the tyrannical school authority.

Over 200 students marched out of the campus together in this strike, leaving behind an empty campus. After much persuasion, a small number of the students eventually returned to the school. Yet 145 students still refused to come back. This sudden incident, with public opinion on the students' side, hit the headlines of many significant periodicals and newspapers. Under the circumstances, it was dawning on ex-Principal Zhang that his departure from the school was imminent.

At one point the School authorities asked Cai Yuanpei, a teacher highly respected by students, to mediate in an effort to persuade them to continue their studies in the School.

Cai, who cared about the students and sympathized with their feelings, still tried to talk them into returning to campus. With the student representative's promise to call off the strike, Cai went immediately that very night to see Sheng Xuanhuai, Supervisor of the Public School. Sheng, however, shunned him on the pretext that he was otherwise engaged.

The next morning still saw no result. All the students gathered on the playground, waiting for the final reply, but the reply never came. So they walked out of Nanyang Public School class by class at about 10 o'clock in the morning. Cai Yuanpei, always democratic-minded, resigned in anger and left the school

along with with the students.

Cai took students to the China Education Association for help, and immediately founded the Patriotic Society, where the dropouts might continue their learning with the support of Zhang Binglin, Principal of the Association. This was why Cai could not work full-time for CP when Zhang Yuanji recommended him to How Zoen Fong.

Modern education turned millions of ignorant youth in China into pioneers in pursuit of democracy and freedom. Before too long, graduates from Nanyang Public School such as Cai E, Shao Lizi and Huang Yanpei played a pivotal role in the political arena of the late Qing and the early Republican years. It was during the same period that Zhang Yuanji and Cai Yuanpei published a complete set of textbooks through CP and fulfilled a dream of popularizing the new education that they had pursued.

The progress of history is propelled by both followers of fine traditions and trail-blazers for future generations. In this context, the educational reform in modern China promoted by How Zoen Fong, Zhang Yuanji, Cai Yuanpei and other team members of CP, undoubtedly generated the first wave of China's drive for modernization, breaking off the fetters of the past with an irrepressible momentum.

Resigning from Office and Accepting How's Offer

In face of the Public School system, which, just like

Yamen (the government office in feudal China), featured endless bureaucratic entanglement and infighting, Zhang felt as if he was again caught up in the treacherous officialdom in Beijing, thereby prompting him to think that he might as well leave the school.

On the other hand, How Zoen Fong felt this was really a God-sent opportunity, knowing that now was the time to engage this talent for CP.

Therefore, How, after exchanging greetings at dinner with Zhang one day, came straight to the point, "Since you cannot bring your talents into full play in the Translation Academy in the School, why not join us at CP and work together for a bright future?"

Zhang, though willing, wanted to test How's sincerity and thus asked How whether he could afford to employ a highly-paid man like him, Hearing that, How was overcome with joy, for How knew there was no problem that money could not solve; moreover, no matter how much he had to pay, such a talent as Zhang was worth it.

So, to show his sincerity, How generously offered Zhang a salary three times more than Zhang received from Nanyang Public School. Zhang was deeply touched.

Needless to say, both enjoyed themselves while they dined that day. More importantly, their negotiation laid a solid and time-tested foundation for CP, for Zhang finally resolved to join the Press after carefully weighing pros and cons, as well as

psychological adjustment. Though he was by no means rich, he invested a small amount of money in CP by pawning some of his wife's jewelry.

From the beginning of 1902, with How in charge of printing and Zhang in charge of compilation & translation, they devoted themselves to enlightening the public and cultivating talents for the country by compiling textbooks and reference books, systemizing ancient books as well as introducing western learning, and thereby achieving glorious accomplishments in the boosting of cultural education in China.

Before he died in 1959, Zhang had acted successively as Director of the Compilation & Translation Section, General Manager, Supervisor, Director and Chairman of the Board of CP.

Ever since Zhang joined CP, How had been frequently consulting and discussing with him—that respect for people of virtue and ability also facilitated How's success—and agreed to focus on publishing cultural education-related materials, which was a complete change in CP's original direction—a change that not only brought the Press much more profits, but also greatly enhanced CP in terms of its social influence.

Social influence, intangible but fairly powerful, cannot be purchased with money, nor can it be grabbed by political force; instead, it must rely on the trust and recognition of the public. Therefore, one cannot win favorable social influence without a reputable image in people's minds based on one's positive

contributions to society.

Cai Yuanpei as Europe-based Contributing Writer

There was an anecdote concerning Cai Yuanpei and CP, which demonstrated their legendary relationship, as well as the graces and humanistic spirit of a traditional Chinese scholar and a refined businessman.

It was in 1906 when 38-year-old Cai Yuanpei, who had earlier missed the opportunity of government-funded overseas study, submitted his application to Sun Baoqi, Qing's envoy to Germany, to study there while working part-time in the embassy. At that time, Cai, who had a large family to support, was indeed in financial straits. To his disappointment, Sun only promised to offer him $42 each month, and the embassy would just provide him with room and board, but no salary.

Having found it very difficult to make a living abroad, Cai felt obliged to ask his old friend Zhang Yuanji to help him apply for financial support from CP. Then general manager How Zoen Fong, holding Cai's talents in high regard, decided to make an exception in this case and readily agreed to back him, offering him a part-time job as a Europe-based contributing writer and translator with a payment of $3 and $5 per thousand words respectively for translating and writing. Part of the payment was sent to Cai in Germany, and the rest to his family to cover their living expenses.

It was recorded that the monthly payments reached as much as $100, more than double the amount provided by Sun Baoqi.

As a result, Cai was able to concentrate on his studies without financial worries in Europe; furthermore, his part-time writing job rewarded him with abundant work, of which *Outlook on World and Life*, *Digestion of Civilization* and other papers were published in *The Eastern Miscellany* and *Education Periodical* by CP. Later, based on what he learned in Germany and France and how it applied to Chinese culture, Cai compiled and wrote, among others, *Outline of Philosophy*, *Principle of Ethics*, *Chinese History of Ethics*, and *Self-Cultivation in Secondary School*, all of which were published by CP.

Today, in Yixia Garden of Shanghai Humanities Memorial Park, where invaluable artifacts of one hundred Shanghai historical figures are collected and exhibited, a group of exquisitely lifelike figure sculptures are certain to attract visitors' attention. They are none other than those of Cai Yuanpei and Zhang Yuanji.

During a time span of 48 years of association, the two men cooperated in good faith to nurture the public with a feast of enlightening knowledge, and indeed they deserve to be recognized as epoch-making figures in the history of the cultural development of modern China.

Cai Yuanpei was praised by Mao Zedong as "a giant in the academic world and a role model for the whole society" and

Zhang Yuanji was complimented by Bing Xin as "a master in disseminating knowledge".

The group of sculptures in Yixia Garden were installed on March 6, 2004. Zhang Renfeng, the eldest grandson of Zhang Yuanji noted on the occasion that the two forerunners practiced what they preached and made a great contribution to the education and culture of the 20th-century China. While viewing the sculptures, Cai Zui-ang, Cai Yuanpei's daughter, remarked that they bore a remarkable resemblance to the two great men, capturing their spirit to great perfection. These two pioneers would have been quite pleased had they seen the earth-shaking transformation of today's China and the progress in its culture and education.

Chapter 5: A Legacy Borne from a Dream

China's educational reform in the latter part of the 19th century had been among the most successful reforms since the twilight years of the Qing Dynasty, and the most powerful driving force for the reform was credited to the compilation, publication and popularization of modern textbooks, a business undertaking in which the Commercial Press (CP) played a leading role.

During the years of the chaotic and declining Qing Dynasty and the raw and nascent Republic of China, it was an outstanding contribution to the Chinese nation for CP, a small private publishing house to achieve such accomplishments. The significance of the contribution lay in its motto—"Promoting Education to Enlighten the Public". How Zoen Fong, who, perhaps, might not realize this political intention of "benefiting future generations", did lay a solid cornerstone for China's modern civilization.

China had been a latecomer in terms of its basic education in modern times. In 1896, Liang Qichao included in his *Reform Overview* a series of education-related essays: *School Overview*, *On Imperial Examinations*, *On School*, *On Normal School*, *On Women's Education*, and *On Children's Education*—a move

which could be regarded as the beginning of modern China's advocacy of westernized education. As he pointed out in *School Overview*, Liang strongly called for enlightening the people with schooling, stressing that education was vitally interrelated with the fate of the country.

The year 1900, the first year of the 20th century, witnessed the Eight-Power (Great Britain, America, France, Italy, Germany, Japan, Russia and Austria) Allied Forces directly threatening Beijing after capturing Dagu Port and Tianjin in revenge for the Boxers' besieging embassies and killing churchmen with the countenance of Ci Xi, the Empress Dowager. The foreign powers launched a general assault on Beijing early on the morning of August 14 with the Russian troops attacking the Dongzhi Gate, the Japanese troops the Chaoyang Gate and the American troops the Dongbian Gate. At eleven that morning, the Dongbian Gate fell with several American troops first entering the outer city. Following their arrival in Beijing at noontime, the British troops launched an attack on the Guangqu Gate, which they entered around 2 pm. By 9 pm, the Russian troops had entered the Dongzhi Gate and the Japanese troops had entered the Chaoyang Gate.

Facing inevitable defeat, Ci Xi forced Emperor Guangxu to join her in her panicked escape to Xi'an. The Boxer movement came to a crushing end.

Occupied Beijing saw the Allied Forces violently burning

imperial palaces and gardens, slaughtering Chinese and pillaging treasures in the Summer Palace. Ci Xi had no choice but to send Li Hongzhang and Yikuang as representatives to sue for peace and to sign the Boxer Protocol, a symbol of China's national humiliation that would never vanish. The Boxer Protocol imposed a huge debt on China such that China had to pay various countries an indemnity of 450 million taels of silver (under the exchange rates at the time, 450 million taels was equal to US 335 million gold dollars) over a course of 39 years with an annual interest of 4%. In addition, foreign powers were allowed to station troops in the Chinese capital and at some strategic locations, rendering the country defenseless. This humiliation inflicted tremendous damage to Chinese national pride and self-confidence.

The Boxer War enabled the Chinese people to clearly see the corrupt and incompetent Qing Government, thus prompting support for the revolution against the Qing rulers.

The Boxer War landed so tremendous a blow to the arrogant Empress Dowager—who controlled the political situation in the final years of the Qing Dynasty, and issued the imperial edict of *Political Reform* (known as *Yu Yue Bian Fa* in Chinese) with an unprecedented resolution on January 29, 1901.

The entire imperial court of Ci Xi came to an understanding that they might take things easy in the process of abolishing the imperial examination system, but could lose no time in promoting new learning.

Emperor Guangxu, more resolute in revitalizing China through reform, issued one imperial edict after another in the summer of 1901 to urge the civil and military governors of various regions to develop western-style schools, ordering that universities, secondary schools and primary schools be set up in all provincial capitals, cities and counties respectively, together with abundant private tutorial schools (called *qimeng* school), apart from the reorganization of existing universities in the Capital.

New Textbooks Flourishing at the Beginning of Modern Education

During this period of reform, there were not many western-style institutions. Those that were established tended to mainly focus on language and skill training.

While vigorously developing western-style schools, Ci Xi, at the suggestion of Zhang Zhidong and Yuan Shikai, also encouraged Chinese students to study overseas. Owing to historical and geographical factors, the number of Chinese students going to Japan skyrocketed after 1901, peaking at 12,000.

The widespread establishment of the new schools and the increased interest in studying abroad had also brought about changes in society and culture. Those who had received the new-style education were referred to as "new intellectuals", who, in

increasing numbers, emerged as the social mainstream, replacing the traditional gentry.

Finally, the year 1905 witnessed the abolishment of the imperial examination system, which had been implemented in numerous dynasties spanning thousands of years since the Sui Dynasty (581-618). Not until then did private schools begin to grow in popularity with various schools specializing in teacher training, industry, law and politics, as well as military affairs, among others.

This golden opportunity was seized by CP just in time. At this time, people of noble aspirations across the country were launching education-oriented reforms.

Having anticipated China's dramatic change—western-style schools would certainly emerge and gain ground in response to the inevitable abolishment of the traditional imperial examination system--How Zoen Fong, Zhang Yuanji, Cai Yuanpei and other partners of CP decided to embark on compiling new-type textbooks badly needed in China.

After the Hundred Days' Reform, both the government officials and the masses were anxious to blaze a new trail in such traditional teaching materials as *The Three-Character Primer*, *The Book of Family Names* and *The One-Thousand-Character Primer*, which had been used in China for thousands of years without changes or any attempt to make changes. The cause, as some people believed, had to be attributed to the imperial

examination system.

In 1897, the same year as How Zoen Fong and three others founded CP, Sheng Xuanhuai set up a primary school affiliated with Nanyang Public School. Chinese, mathematics, geography, history, and sports were taught in the primary school which had an enrolment of 120 students aged between 10 and 18.

It was in that affiliated primary school that a set of *Chinese Primers* (three volumes in total), the first of its kind in modern China, was produced and published by Nanyang Public School in 1901.

Previous to this period, students had been learning Chinese for thousands of years from Confucian classics as well as from books written by sages and men of virtue. But after 1901, they could own real textbooks of Chinese. Regrettably, the contents were mainly copied from western books, and as far as the diction was concerned, these textbooks could not free themselves from the classical literary style.

In the history of Chinese education, it was the *Chinese Primers* that demonstrated for the first time a modern awareness of disciplines, facilitated the updating of values, and the knowledge hierarchy, and accelerated the transformation of the common sense system of the Chinese people in modern times.

As private tutorial schools were widely established in 1903, teachers nationwide, who were vexed at the lack of suitable textbooks, shared the wish of having quality textbooks as soon as

possible. This desire promised bright prospects for the publication of the *Chinese Primers*. These tutorial schools were predecessors of the modern schools for children, or what we know today as the kindergartens and elementary schools below the third grade.

At that time, quite a few publishing houses were eager to have a try at producing new-type textbooks, and CP would certainly devote itself to printing and publishing these.

General Manager How Zoen Fong, keenly aware of this business opportunity, held a shareholders' meeting immediately to come to an agreement on raising more funds for textbook compiling and printing. "This is the chance of a lifetime that we must seize and we should seize it ahead of other competitors. The chance waits for no man." He said excitedly at the meeting.

How, after raising a considerable amount of money in very little time, embarked at once on the path to his grand goal. However, adequate capital did not necessarily mean success. Knowing very well that he could not possibly achieve greater development with his education level, he began to actively hunt for talented people to join him, which resulted in the engagement of such literary giants as Zhang Yuanji, Cai Yuanpei, Gao Mengdan as well as Jiang Weiqiao when How was the general manager, and, after his death, Hu Shih and Wang Yunwu, among others.

How *New Primary School Textbooks* Came into Being

Let's look into CP in the early 20th century to get a close look at how its *New Primary School Textbooks* came into being.

General Manager How Zoen Fong asked Zhang Yuanji, who presided over compilation, to seek competent professionals to compile new textbooks, and they finally managed to have Du Yaquan, a teacher in the Shaoxing Sino-Western School, join them at CP.

Zhang divided the office into three sections— Chinese, English, and physics & chemistry, an arrangement similar to that of current secondary school curricula, with the three sections respectively under the charge of Gao Mengdan, Kuang Fuzhuo and Du Yaquan. There is an interesting anecdotal story about these scholars. Although they were renowned experts in their respective fields, they could not communicate with each other, as each spoke a different dialect; Gao originated from Fujian, Kuang from Guangdong and Du from Shaoxing. They either had to reply with the help of a translator or resort to the written language.

Since the compiling and printing of primary school textbooks involved a huge investment, How and Zhang, under enormously heavy pressure, began to take cautious steps to launch the new project after employing Du Yaquan, knowing that they had to devote themselves, heart and soul, to their work.

After months of planning and compiling, the first volume

was completed and sent to the press in the summer of 1902. It pioneered the use of regular scripts with each lesson on a new well-illustrated page, and thus it was known as *Elementary Literature with Illustration*. Comprising six volumes, one for each half-year term for private tutorial school students, the set became just as popular and sold just as well as the *Chinese and English Primer*.

This was one of the first carefully written and compiled sets of Chinese textbooks. "With its high quality in compiling, the book has changed the cursory compiling style of the entire publishing industry", said Cai Yuanpei admiringly.

Elementary Literature with Illustration, the textbook that has crossed the centuries

In 2012, one hundred and ten years after *Elementary Literature with Illustration* was first published by CP, a Chinese website specializing in selling and auctioning rare books posted a rare book online that was once a "textbook used in the Qing Dynasty" for those who were interested to browse. This rare book in fact was none other than Volume 3 of *Elementary Literature with Illustration* published by CP in 1901, before the Nationalist revolution in 1911. The following are a few example lessons of the textbook with illustrations.

Lesson 1 Colors of Blossoms

"There are peach blossoms in the garden; the colors of the blossoms are different shades of red.

There are plum blossoms in the courtyard; the color of the plum blossoms is white.

There are chrysanthemums in the pots; the color of the chrysanthemum is golden."

Lesson 2 Ladies of Beauty

"See the countenance of this lady; she can indeed be called a beauty.

See the countenance of this lady; is she not also a beauty?

Now see the countenance of this lady; can she not be called a beauty?"

Lesson 8 Walking Together

"The man is walking with his younger brother. When an elder brother walks with his younger brother, the younger brother follows the elder brother. The elder brother walks in front, followed by the younger brother. When a man is walking with his younger brother, he, the elder brother, leads the way and the younger brother follows."

Lesson 13 Glass

"Windows made of glass allow light to shine in; lamps made of glass stay lighted in the wind; mirrors made of glass enable one to see oneself."

In 2012, another Chinese website of rare books auctioned off Volume 6 of *Elementary Literature,* which was compiled for the 5th and 6th grades of the primary schools. The following are selected texts from two lessons as examples of what students of those grades studied at the time.

Lesson 1 Confucius

"During the Spring and Autumn Period (722-481 B.C.), Kong Qiu (Confucius, in English, 551-481 B.C.) was born in the Changping County (the present-day Shandong Province). Grown to be six-foot tall and well steeped in the Classics and the high teaching of the Rite, Confucius served at different official posts for the State of Lu, his birth state. It was a period of mini-states with lords and aristocrats in the central eastern part of China. These mini-states were often warring with each other. Born into the State of Lu, Confucius first served there, then in the States of Qi, Wei, Chen, Cai and Chu, often met with hostility and was mistreated in all the states. It was in the State of Cai that he was stranded and imprisoned. This was a period of political strife with wars among the mini-states. The geographical area of these states

cover the present-day provinces of Shandong, Henan, Anhui, Hubei and Hunan.

Finally, the powerful Lord of the State of Chu intervened. Confucius and his disciples were freed and returned to his home in the State of Lu, which was in chaos, suffering under the reign of the inefficient and corrupt Lord of the State of Lu. Disillusioned, Confucius declined all requests to serve in the government. Instead, he retired to focus his energy and talents on more learning of the Classics and Music. In the meantime, he took in more disciples from near and far, reaching as many as an astounding three thousand. Confucius died at the age of seventy-three. All of his disciples were in deep mourning by his burial site for three years, before they dispersed and returned to their respective native lands."

Lesson 46 Education for Women

Women, like men, are Homo sapiens, but many men consider them so inferior in every aspect that they are good only for sewing, needlework and culinary chores. This view of women has led to the statistic that educated women compose less than one percent among the Chinese population. How egregiously wrong of men who do not realize that it is only when women are learned and intelligent can they become wise and good wives, and only wise and good wives can in turn bring up wise and good children in later generations. For it is a natural

propensity that men/fathers regard their children as if they were only blood relatives of their wives, and by the same token, the children receive their common education (savoir faire and modus operandi) mostly from their mothers.

All of this results in the fact that if the mothers are learned, intelligent and good, it is rare that the children will grow up to be wicked and unlearned ignoramuses. To further elaborate this point, if the mothers are learned, intelligent and good, their children will strive to be like them. Now, if the whole world can come to see all this clearly, need one emphasize more the utter significance of the advocacy of equal education for women?

From the above two selections from the texts, it should be crystal clear what the central theme of the textbooks published by CP was: to inspire students and readers with modern and *avant garde* messages of life and learning in general.

In 1904, Du Yaquan, a scholar and writer, wrote nine other textbooks: three of them with the title of *The Modern Textbook on Model Behavior as a Sagacious Man* and six of them entitled, *The Modern Mathematics Textbook*. All of these were for a long time widely adopted and used by primary schools in China. These textbooks have been praised by educators and literary critics of today as cornerstones in the 5,000-year history of Chinese culture.

A great number of academic researchers of the modern and current China have unanimously agreed on and endorsed the invaluable contribution of CP to Chinese culture under the guidance of How Zoen Fong. In an essay on the research of the development of academics written by Shi Chunfeng, which was published in the academic magazine of the Beijing Teacher's University, the following quote speaks volumes of the opinion of the author, a member of the intelligentsia in China:

The textbooks published by the Commercial Press have had a lasting and indelible influence on the cultural and academic scenes in China, as well as on Chinese students and readers, for the past decades, up to this day.

The principle goal of CP in its founding days, the educational concept and themes of their publications, including the choice of the contents of the textbooks, has endured and served as models for the editorial effort and publication of different textbooks in today's publishing houses. What makes it all the more remarkable is that through the long and chaotic years in war-torn and catastrophe-prone modern China, CP, a private (as opposed to state-owned) publishing house, managed by independent individuals dedicated to culture and the publishing enterprise, has so endeavored to sustain the spiritual life and the learning spirit of the Chinese people by providing them with much needed cultural nourishment. It goes without saying that

such an astonishingly magnificent publishing house is sure to be an everlasting inspiration to all posterity in the area of culture and learning.

Chapter 6: Corporate Conscience and Responsibility, 1914

In 1902, the same year as the publication of Du Yaquan's *Elementary Literature with Illustration*, the Qing government issued the *School Charter*, the first state-issued document on the educational system in modern China. It covered the charters for private tutorial schools, primary schools, secondary schools, higher schools, universities in the Capital, and an entrance examination, specifying the objectives of these schools in nature, length of terms, admission requirements, and curricula in a 20 year period. The document aimed to develop students' skills in the disciplines of politics, literature, business, science, agriculture, industry, or medicine, etc.

Though the *School Charter* failed to be implemented, it served as a great mobilization call for promoting modern education in China, which was welcomed by the whole country. The compiling and printing of modern textbooks undoubtedly was the most important link in the new education system. The urgent need on textbooks was in line with the national educational focus and the trend of the times.

Painstaking Efforts in Compiling the *New Primary School Textbooks*

The lack of experience and examples to follow constituted the major difficulty in compiling primary school textbooks. How Zoen Fong, pondering anxiously, found it difficult for scholars, though wealthy in knowledge, to compile a practical textbook for children with no existing rules to follow.

At that time the foreign investor of the Commercial Press (CP) was none other than the famous Kinkodo Book Company of Japan, which developed modern textbooks for compulsory education during the Meiji Restoration, in Japan. It had experience in this kind of endeavor.

Through Manager How's arrangement, Zhang Yuanji engaged the Japanese partners to share their experience with the CP colleagues. The decision was that the textbook would be compiled by the CP team of four, led by Zhang Yuanji modelling after the Japanese texts with the national conditions of China taken into account. This textbook was to be translated by Liu Chongjie who had returned to China after his studies at Waseda University. Fifteen of 15 monthly sessions were held during 1903-04.

Through these lengthy sessions, CP finalized an epoch-making set of compilation guidelines cognizant of the fact that teaching materials had to be convenient for children's studies and

appropriate for their psychological and intellectual development. The guidelines were formulated by the CP team in these sessions where any concept would be discussed and debated in detail A set of rigorous principles were established some of which became exemplars for textbook compilers of later years. In Jiang Weiqiao's memoirs on the CP team effort, he documented the set of strict rules for selected Chinese characters and the number of strokes in each lesson or volume.

To ensure a high quality, they would not finalize any lesson without unanimous agreement of all four in the team—using this strategy of compiling by brainstorming adopted by How, Zhang, and their associates.

"No lesson would be finalized until the best of all versions was selected, reviewed and revised to perfection." This comment was quoted from Cai Yuanpei's eulogy to How after his assassination. From this statement, it can be clearly seen that CP had taken great pains to compile and print this new textbook.

Jiang Weiqiao, a member of the CP team, recalled that CP's *New Primary School Textbooks* ranked among the best in terms of both form and content—this was not a boast, rather a proven fact.

In addition to striving for perfection in compilation, How Zoen Fong, as an expert printer, was constantly devising new ways to present this fine content with quality printing. CP chose writing paper made of bamboo based on a new principle:

durability over beauty. The usual reflective white paper might be harmful to children's eyes.

The first volume of the *New Primary School Chinese Textbooks* reached the market on April 8th, 1904, and were sold out within just a couple of days. Jiang Weiqiao recorded in his diary on the excellence of the new textbook. First, once this volume came out, similar texts from other publishing houses gradually went out of print. Secondly, the textbook was written in near common language, soon to be imitated by other private printing houses and by the, then, Imperial Ministry of Education. Jiang's pride was obvious. By 1906, the ten volumes of this set of textbooks had all been published.

In Volume One, several instructions were made, teaching schedules, strokes of new characters, and the number of new words in each lesson. It also specified equal importance on moral, intellectual and physical education in the selection of materials. Illustrations and large font characters should be highlighted in layout and design. More valuably, How Zoen Fong even took into account the paper used for printing.

Hence, it was evident that General Manager How and all the CP scholars, for the publication of *New Primary School Chinese Textbooks*, worked hard to bring about as perfect a product as possible. Anything that was wrong or fell short of standards would be rejected even if it had consumed a lot of time, labor and money. Zhuang Yu, one member in the CP team, noted

why CP, with this set of excellent textbooks of carefully selected materials on a wide range of subjects, surpassed any other textbook of its time to become the best choice for primary school students. That is why CP succeeded.

Later, new textbooks for advanced classes were completed, totaling ten volumes on other disciplines. At the same time, the *New Secondary School Textbooks* were also published, selling well nationwide.

As Wang Jiarong, senior expert with CP, pointed out that this set of 32 textbooks in 156 volumes for 11 subjects in primary and secondary schools, was the most comprehensive of its kind in China, with a circulation of 80% nationwide from 1904 thru 1911. With this set of new textbooks, How Zoen Fong and others at the helm succeeded in leading CP into the mainstream of the times and making it a trend-setter up to today. CP has now spanned three centuries!

The West's Attention to CP's Promotion of Educational Reform

Christian missionaries flocked into China, after the Opium War. They set up numerous missionary schools sparsely scattered across the country, without a systematic organization. In 1887, a missionary named Calvin Wilson Mateer delivered a speech on China's education in the First Mission Conference held in Shanghai by Christian missionaries in China. The speech was

recognized as a milestone in the history of missionary work. The conference set up the School and Textbook Series Committee (renamed Educational Association of China later) in charge of textbooks on very diverse subjects as mathematics, astronomy, measurement, geology, chemistry, flora and fauna, history, geography, Chinese, music, etc. to exert a direct influence on textbooks in China. The Committee had its official publication, the *China Report,* serving as the Western nations' window on Chinese affairs. Its special column in 1904 on "textbooks of the Commercial Press" referred to the *New Primary School Textbooks* as CP's "fist" products, meaning the most competitive products. The report, after its in-depth analysis, regarded these CP textbooks as vital to the educational reform, which would revolutionize schools in China.

Another report in 1907 mentioned the publication of CP's textbooks as "one of the most significant events in the past few years", that Chinese children were breaking the fetters of traditional classics and flinging themselves into new literary works of fun and knowledge. Convinced that a kind of "Japanesque patriotism" was being aroused among the Chinese people who had suffered so much due to foreign invasion and corrupt Qing rulers, the report suggested that the ideological trend of revolution was under way, as the line between patriotism and revolution had started to blur. As some scholars hold, CP and its *New Primary School Textbooks* ushered in "the Age of

Textbooks", a vital starting point in shaping China's modern education.

Calvin Wilson Matteer, born in 1836, was a minister of the North American Presbyterian Church. Graduating from Divinity School in 1862, he came to China the following year, preaching in Tengchow (today's Penglai), Shandong Province. Before long, he set up a private school at a small temple in town, giving poor students free schooling. The school, formally named Tengchow College in 1872, was the first modern institution of higher learning in China, and became the predecessor of Cheeloo University as it expanded. Mateer spent nearly half a century on missionary work in China before he died in Qingdao in 1908.

Numerous "Firsts" in Modern Publication History

CP, China's first modern publishing house, created numerous "firsts" in the history of Chinese publishing and even culture, of which the most important are listed as follows:

- Published the first monograph on grammar: *Ma Shi Wen Tong* (1898);
- Published the first English textbook in both Chinese and English: the *Chinese and English Primer* (1898);
- Published the first English-Chinese dictionary: the *Commercial Press English-Chinese Dictionary* (1899);
- The first to print books with paper matrix (1900)
- The first to systematically introduce western academic

works (1902);

· The first to use the copyright stamp (1903);

· The first cultural enterprise to take in foreign funds (1903);

· The first private enterprise to employ foreign experts and technicians (1903);

· The first to systematically compile and print the *New Primary School Textbooks* and other modern textbooks for primary and secondary schools (1904);

· The first to set up a series of modern magazines, including *The Eastern Miscellany* (1904);

· The first to use collotype printing (1907);

· Published first bilingual dictionary compiled by Chinese scholars: *An English & Chinese Dictionary* (1908);

· The first to use electroplating copperplate printing (1912);

· The first to use automatic typecasting machines (1913);

These are CP's "firsts" before 1914 as listed on the company's website (Cp.com.cn); the "firsts" after 1914, though similarly plentiful and remarkable, are omitted here, since How Zoen Fong, the protagonist of this biography, was assassinated that year.

The First CEO of the Republic of China with Traits of Creative Management

Emerging from the obscurity of being an apprentice, How Zoen Fong became CP's General Manager, a novel and trendy title in China in the 19th century when a person in charge of a business was usually called Dazhanggui (shopkeeper) or boss. Having presided over and supervised the entire operation of the Press, including sales, quality control, market research, publicity, policy making, and more, How Zoen Fong could be considered China's first ever CEO in every sense of the word, a CEO with vision, determination and inspiration.

Holding talented people in high esteem, General Manager How thirsted to recruit and hire them, as he was well aware of the importance of talent to the development of his company. For competent staff members, or those who made great contributions, How provided not only high salaries but also thoughtful care, such as room and board, tea and hookah. Therefore, it was rather difficult for other publishing houses to lure anyone away from CP.

According to the 21st century theory of leadership, all successful general managers or leaders should have certain shared traits and behaviors. It is because of those personality traits, like lofty aspiration or ambition, that a leader may achieve success.

Modern psychologists have been exploring one question—

what traits should an innovative leader have? The concept of being such a leader did not exist at end of the 19th Century, in How's time.

At the beginning of the book, How Zoen Fong is compared to Steve Jobs, a legendary figure in the electronic revolution of the 20th century, in terms of his outstanding contributions to cultural communication in modern China. If we go further, we may find similar leadership traits of the two CEOs living almost a hundred years apart.

Researchers at Harvard University spent six years on an in-depth study of the traits shared by innovation-minded leaders by interviewing more than 300 senior managers. Would they have gotten the same answer if they had asked How Zoen Fong or Steven Jobs directly?

According to the study, entitled "The Innovator's DNA" and published in the *Harvard Business Review* in December, 2009, innovators, compared with those without creativity, uniquely boast a most essential ability: associating-that is, the ability to associate seemingly irrelevant questions or thinking of different fields.

From 1901 to 1902, How Zoen Fong made unremitting efforts to recruit Zhang Yuanji to be the Director of the Compilation and Translation Section until finally he succeeded: he opened up the market for foreign books; and he entered the school textbook market. We may conclude that his creativity lay

in his ability to keenly associate the political situation with urgent social needs. He saw his chance, and he took it.

A recent issue of *Newsweek* with Steven Jobs on its cover tells his life story as well as how he guided Apple to its peak, and concludes ten outstanding principles of Jobs' creative management, familiarly known as the "Ten Commandments". Specifically,

1) go for perfect;

2) tap the experts;

3) be ruthless (Jobs took pride in scrapping products that were not received well);

4) shun focus groups (Jobs, holding that people will not know what they want until they see it, once spent months testing a product himself as the "focus group");

5) never stop studying;

6) making hard things simple;

7) keep your secrets;

8) keep teams small (the team for Macintosh involves 100 members, and no more);

9) use more carrot than stick;

10) prototype to the extreme.

It is indeed inappropriate and unfair to impose the "Ten Commandments" on How Zoen Fong, who would have acted differently in different times with different products and competitors. However, with a deeper analysis of How's operation

strategies and skills, we may well find some traits conforming to the "Ten Commandments", such as attention, excellence, perfectionism, and elitism, among others.

It is particularly worth mentioning that CP, under How's leadership, established the fine tradition of recruiting elites and striving for perfection. How deeply valued talented people, offering them high salaries, and thus managed to engage such learned men as Zhang Yuanji, Cai Yuanpei, Gao Mengdan, Jiang Weiqiao, Ye Shengtao, Hu Yuzhi, Hu Shih, Zheng Zhenduo and Wang Yunwu.

It is due to those talented people, How Zoen Fong's keenness to seize opportunities at a time of change, and his pursuit of perfection that CP has been very successful and has served as a leader in China's publishing industry and in culture over the past one-hundred-plus years. (JSuez: please smooth out this paragraph, removing unnecessary words. A simple sentence, ELEGANTLY written will be more powerful than this set mouth of words.)

Ambition and Courage—Establishment of the Earliest Sino-Foreign Joint Venture

During the late Qing Dynasty and the early Republic of China, China's cultural and publication center was not Beijing but Shanghai, as Shanghai was one of China's five treaty ports at that time. These port cities contributed to the accumulation of

commercial benefits and to the development of the publishing industry, thus making these cities hotbeds of ideological reform as well as the cradle for its dissemination. As a result, Shanghai became the quintessential port city where Western ideologies and lifestyle, including conspicuous consumption, became prevalent.

Under these circumstances, while sparing no effort to introduce modern Western ideologies and culture into China, the Commercial Press also assimilated new ideas of capitalist business management.

With the diligent and wise management of How Zoen Fong, CP exceeded other publishing houses in scale and scope of business, making itself the earliest modern establishment in China, even if judged by today's standards.

In fact, CP was also the first Chinese enterprise to attract foreign capital.

In October, 1903, CP, with How at its helm, signed a contract with Kinkodo, the prestigious Japanese publishing house, transforming CP into a joint-stock corporation limited, with a capital of $200,000, equally injected by the two sides..

As a result of the expanded capital, CP immediately bought land in the Zhabei District of Shanghai to build new plants and workshops, purchased new machines, and introduced foreign technologies, especially the new printing technologies featuring color lithograph, halftone and collotype—the earliest photographic lithography, also known as "glass printing" due to

its use of thick glass as the base.

In business management, CP was gradually transforming itself from a family business into a corporation based on a modern enterprise operating model.

The decision maker for such changes was none other than How Zoen Fong, General Manager of CP.

Kinkodo, the biggest of the four major textbook publishing houses in Japan during the Meiji Restoration, played a key role in providing CP with the concepts and experience of modern textbook compiling and publishing. Thus equipped, CP outshined its rivals in the commercial textbook market amid fierce competition.

CP compiled and published a number of important textbooks, such as the *New Textbooks of Chinese*, consisting of ten volumes. This set of textbooks sold over ten million copies, exerting an enormous influence on China's education. It could easily be said that the publication of these textbooks was the cornerstone for CP's success in becoming China's leading publishing house and top institution of cultural communication.

By analogy, the cooperation between CP and Kinkodo, which established a Sino-Foreign joint venture, was also an important factor contributing to the success of CP.

After the Revolution of 1911, the Japanese committed increasingly ruthless atrocities in China, laying bare its ambition to invade China, triggering a nation-wide, anti-Japan sentiment.

Consequently the CP-Kinkodo joint venture was frowned upon by the Chinese people. This situation prompted CP to eliminate all Japanese interests at all costs.

How Zoen Fong, himself, shouldered the task of persuading the Japanese publishing house to give up its shares. How then traveled, many times, between Shanghai and Japan to negotiate with the Japanese stockholders, despite the challenges of traveling and communications. Eventually, CP over-compensated the Japanese investors to buy back all Japanese interests in CP.

In a document *In Memory of Mr. How Zoen Fong* written by Zhang Shunian (Zhang Yuanji's son), the narration and evaluation of the above event were described as follows:

> Mr. How showed an admirable foresight concerning the successful 10-year cooperation between CP and Japan's Kinkodo. In 1903, the head of Kinkodo wanted to establish a publishing house in Shanghai, with which CP would find it hard to compete, as the Japanese possessed advantages in printing technologies. So How chose to set up a joint venture to take advantage of the Japanese capital, technologies and talents, thus further developing China's national publishing industry. In the joint venture, How insisted that the Chinese side would take charge of daily operations, personnel management and administrative affairs, while the Japanese would be represented on the board to exercise supervision only. During this period,

when China was being invaded by foreign powers and was on the decline, this joint venture might have been the only one that adhered to the Chinese sovereign interests.

In 1913, How Zoen Fong went to Japan to sign the agreement on Kinkodo's withdrawal its shares from the joint venture. On January 10 of the following year, *Shen Pao* (申報, a Shanghai newspaper) carried a notice, announcing that CP had bought back all the shares held by the Japanese, making the publishing house wholly owned by Chinese investors. This achievement was also attributed to the indomitable perseverance of the respectable How Zoen Fong.

On January 10, 1914 when How Zoen Fong was reading the announcement in *Shen Pao* in his office, he was finally able to let out a deep sigh of relief.

On the same day, as he was walking out of his office on Henan Road to board his horse-drawn carriage for home, How was fatally shot and passed away instantly without uttering a final word.

On January 31, 21 days after How's death, CP convened a board meeting reporting on the withdrawal of the Japanese interests:

CP was founded with a small capital investment in 1897. In 1903 when a Japanese business intended to set up a publish-

ing house in Shanghai, CP, finding it difficult to contend with a foreign establishment due to its inadequacy in compiling expertise and printing technologies, was obliged to establish a joint venture with equal investment of $100,000 each. Nevertheless, it was stipulated that personnel and administrative affairs were in the Chinese side and Japanese interests should abide by Chinese commerce regulations and laws. As the capital increased and the business scale gradually expanded, CP grew rapidly in experience, technologies, and profits. In fact, from that time on, most of the additional equities had been held by the Chinese. At the end of 1913, the Chinese held about three quarters of the equities while the Japanese held only about one quarter, namely, 3781 shares. Therefore CP enjoyed complete decision-making power, without any interference from the Japanese shareholders.

However, the fierce competition in the publishing industry prompted CP's rivals to slander our publishing house, using the pretext that the Japanese still owned shares in it; these slanders seriously affected CP's further expansion. For example, the Qing's Imperial Ministry of Education excluded CP from the printing of textbooks for secondary schools, citing the fact that there were Japanese investors in CP. What's worse, a newspaper announcement from Jiangxi Province blatantly accused CP; many in the academic circles in Hunan Province made unfriendly remarks about CP; and the Examinational Committee

of Hubei Province, under the excuse of CP's Japanese equities, refused to let its publications enter its market – to name only a few. Whenever such incidents took place, the leaders of CP management team suffered indescribable psychological pain and went through trouble to resolve them. Therefore the board decided to reclaim all the Japanese-held equities without convening a shareholders' meeting to discuss the matter due to its urgency. CP asks its shareholders for understanding.

The successful withdrawal of the Japanese equities from CP should be credited to General Manager How's efforts. Just as CP was freeing itself from the jostling of its competitors, General Manager How was unexpectedly assassinated in front of his office on the same day that CP issued the announcement. This is indeed CP's most unfortunate event, for which all the shareholders must be saddened.

How Zoen Fong lived during the waning years of the Qing Dynasty and the dawning years of the Republic, a most tumultuous period of time in Chinese history fraught with uncertainty and strife. How Zoen Fong was not only a witness to the vicissitudes of his time, but also a mover and shaker of this historical period with his extraordinary vision, resilience, courage and fortitude. Even though he died a premature death, the foundations he laid for CP resulted in a publishing empire that are continuing to thrive in contemporary China, Taiwan and Hong Kong with a readership none other publishers can match.

With an indomitable spirit in the face of adversities and risks, he pioneered a brand-new industry of publishing and education that changed the lives of millions of the Chinese. In this sense, he ranks among such greats as Bill Gates, Steve Jobs and Mark Zuckerman.

100 years has elapsed since the passing of How Zoen Fong. On the occasion of the centennial, one cannot but think of the two verses that Li Bai, the great Tang poet, dedicated to another towering poet of his time, Meng Haoran, his hero, by comparing Meng to a lofty mountain:

【高山安可仰，徒此揖清芬】

"High mountain you are,

    too high to gaze in reverence;

We can do no more

    than breathing your pure fragrance."

These two verses are a fitting tribute to How Zoen Fong, a pioneer and a giant in the modernization and advancement of culture and learning in the history of China!

Epilogue: Flowering Branches Bearing Fruits

In order to commemorate How Zoen Fong after his assassination, the board of the Commercial Press (CP) had originally planned to erect a bronze statue of How, but How's widow, Bau Tsui Nyoh (1873-1938), who believed that her husband's aspiration had been to help young people with their education, declined the offer politely. Instead, it was finally decided that a school named How Elementary School would be built in How's poor hometown— Qingpu County.

Surviving How Zoen Fong were his wife, 41-year-old Bau Tsui Nyoh, a 17-year-old son and eight daughters, the youngest of whom was only two years old. The sudden death of How, on whom his beloved wife and children depended heavily, emotionally devastated the heart-broken family. However, Bau Tsui Nyoh, with her strong Christian belief, resolutely shouldered the responsibility to raise and educate her nine children.

To provide financial support for her children's education abroad, Bau Tsui Nyoh rented and mortgaged the family' s 12-room house to pay her children's tuition fees and living expenses.

How Zoen Fong and Bau Tsui Nyoh's only son and the

oldest of the nine children was Bang How (1897-1976), whose style name was How Siao Fong, meaning junior How Zoen Fong (a naming method paralleling that from England and the US in which the son inherits the name of his father). Upon his graduation from St. John's University in Shanghai, he went to the U.S. to study in the Wharton School of Finance and Economics, receiving a Master's degree in Business Administration in 1920.

Bang How's Wedding – Soong May-ling as Bridesmaid

Bang How's wife was Rose Ng-Quinn, a daughter of an eminent Hong Kong family. In their Western-style wedding in Shanghai, one of the beautiful and stylish bridesmaids was Soong May-ling, later to become very prominent in Chinese history. It could not have possibly occurred to the bridegroom, Bang, that Soong May-ling would later marry Chiang Kai-shek! It was an uncanny historical episode that would go down in history.

In 1922, Bang How returned to China. To contribute more to CP, he went to England and Germany to study the printing industry there. When he returned to CP, he first worked in the Import Department, and later successively assumed the posts of secretary for the Production Department and the Operation Department, then as director of the board in 1925 and manager in 1927.

On January 28, 1932, the Japanese army attacked Shanghai's Zhabei District. China's 19th Army Corps stationed

in Shanghai fought back in resistance. According to statistics, the Incident inflicted heavy losses in Zhabei District, damaging as many as 4,204 Chinese businesses and 19,700 buildings to ruins, amounting to a loss of 1.4 billion dollars.

All the buildings of CP, situated in Zhabei District, were also bombed, Bang undertook the important task to salvage them. On August 1, 1932, CP's business along with those of thousands of other enterprises resumed operations from the ruins, demonstrating Chinese national resilence and perseverance.

When CP resumed business, Bang How was assigned the director of the Issuing Section. In the mid-1930s, he changed career to join Shanghai Commercial and Savings Bank (SCSB) to develop its insurance business. Bang How and his wife and daughter eventually left China in the late 1930s to settle in the U. S. In the 1950s and 1960s, he protected the interests of SCSB in the U. S. In 1971 when he moved back to Hong Kong, he was invited to serve as a board director of Hong Kong's Shanghai Commercial Bank and that of Taiwan's Shanghai Commercial and Savings Bank.

Bang How died in 1976 at the age of 78. Being the oldest of How Zoen Fong's nine children, Bang took fatherly care of his younger sisters, as their father had left them too early. He also showed loving care for his nephews and nieces.

Bang How's only child was Julie Lien-Ying How (1926-1982), a gifted graduate from Columbia University. She

was an expert in contemporary Chinese history and would later compile *Documents on Communism, Nationalism, and Soviet Advisers in China, 1918-1927* (published by Columbia University Press in 1956) with the American scholar, Columbia University professor, Dr. Clarence Martin Wilbur. This book was an important literature for both the CPC（Communist Party of China）and the U.S. in the study of the CPC's history.

Julie How was mentioned by historian Tang Degang in his article *On Reminiscences of V. K. Wellington Koo*:

> *In the early 1950s when the Communist Party succeeded in its revolution, a number of Kuomintang's important person-ages, including Hu Shih, Li Zongren, Kong Xiangxi, and Chen Lifu, migrated to the U. S. Accordingly, Columbia University put forward a plan known as 'the Oral History of China.' and set up a relevant research office staffed with only two research-ers—me and Miss Julie How, who was a graduate at Columbia, excellent in English but less so in Chinese* (Actually Julie How could speak fluent Shanghai and Cantonese dialects, Mandarin Chinese as well as French according to the author.) *She was assigned to interview Kong Xiangxi at first and then Chen Lifu while I was assigned to interview Professor Hu Shih and then Li Zongren.*
>
> *Mr. V. K. Wellington Koo was a qualified witness to many of the important historical events, as he was a longtime states-*

man in China's political arena. When he was a grand justice in the Hague International Court, he had only a three-month-vacation at his New York home every year. Therefore Columbia University hoped that we could interview him during his vacation. As I was then busy interviewing Li Zongren and could not take time off, Julie How was the first to interview Mr. V. K. Wellington Koo.

What should be mentioned here was that Julie How interviewed Chen Lifu, a nephew of Chen Qimei, the suspect behind the assassination of How Zoen Fong. It is said that during the interview when Julie keenly asked about this unsettled historical case, Chen Lifu evaded her question and vaguely hinted at something else.

Thanks to the oral interviews, Julie How became well acquainted with many of Kuomintang's celebrities, such as T.V. Soong. At the wedding of his eldest daughter Laurette Soong, Julie was one of her bridesmaids, which later manifested in the intimacy between the How and Soong families.

Julie How's husband was Hwa Chunghou (William Z. Hwa, or Bill Hwa), born in Dangkou Town of Wuxi in 1918. In 1941, Bill Hwa received his master's degree in engineering from the Massachusetts Institute of Technology for his work on the internal combustion engine. His father, Hwa Yizhi, was a famous businessman, educator, collector and philanthropist in China's

modern times,

Following his retirement in 1998, Bill Hwa started a family project in his hometown in Wuxi to renovate the Hwa Filial Son Temple, a clan temple in eulogy of filial piety at the foot of Mount Huishan. For his deeds, his clansmen wrote his biographical notes, in which his marriage to Julie How was mentioned:

Bill Hwa had a legendary marriage. In his youth, he studied in America during the Second World War. Due to the war, he was unable to return to China, neither did he want to get married and settle down in the U.S. When he returned to China at the end of the war, the youthful marrying age had slipped by him. The years of instable domestic situation that followed and a transient life deprived him of any serious consideration of marriage. Not until he was 53 years old did he finally find love. In 1971, Bill Hwa married Julie How after they had been friends for many years. Julie How was a born beauty and grew up in the U.S. It was when Mr. Hwa worked in the Universal Trading Company office in New York that he came to know Julie How whose grandfather was the founder of CP in Shanghai and her father was a director of Shanghai Commercial and Savings Bank (SCSB).

Julie How, who spoke fluent Shanghai and Cantonese dialects, English as well as French, was a talented woman with an extraordinarily good memory. After graduating from Vassar College, she went to France for further education. Later on

she completed her Master's degree at Columbia University, specializing in Chinese history, especially in the study of Chen Duxiu's thoughts and the history of the Communist Party of China. She then became a well-known expert on Chinese issues. After their marriage, Mr. and Mrs. Hwa travelled extensively enjoying cultures and history of different parts of the world. Unfortunately, Julie was diagnosed with cancer only a few years after her marriage and she died in 1982 at the age of only 56.

Happy Lives for How Zoen Fong's Eight Daughters

All of How Zoen Fong's eight daughters graduated from McTyeire School for Girls in Shanghai and most pursued further studies abroad.

How's eldest daughter, Mary Mo-Li How (1900-1957), studied for a time at Simmons College in Boston, but returned to China without completing her education to marry Huang Hanliang, a manager in Shanghai Commercial and Savings Bank. They ultimately divorced.

How's second daughter, Ruth Loo-Tuh How (1901-2005), graduated from the New England Conservatory and returned home to China to become a music teacher. She had a legendary marriage because she married the man who had divorced her aunt: her ex-uncle Ping-Wen Kuo (1880-1969).

Ping-Wen Kuo (Hongsheng, his style name) was born in Shanghai, and graduated from Lowrie School, Shanghai,

where he taught for one year, after graduation. He worked in a customhouse, a post office and a bank successively in the following nine years, before going to U.S. In 1908 he studied at Wooster College in Ohio, where he received his Bachelor's degree in Science in 1911. He then went on to obtain his Master's degree from Columbia University's Teachers College in 1912, and later acquired a doctoral degree in Education there in 1914, making him the first Chinese national to get a Ph.D. from Teachers College. In August, 1914, he returned to China and was appointed by CP Chief Editor for *Webster's Dictionary*. In 1915, he served as director of the Teaching Administration Office in Nanjing Higher Normal School, and became the President of the School in 1919. Kuo actively devised a plan to establish China's second state-funded university, Southeast University, based on the School. In 1921-1925, he was appointed the first president of Southeast University.

Before the May Fourth Movement in 1919, China's institutions of higher learning, except church-run universities, did not enroll female students. On April 7, 1920, Nanjing Higher Normal School decided to put an end to this policy. Thus Ping-Wen Kuo discussed with Cai Yuanpei, Jiang Menglin and Hu Shih, and agreed on the recruitment of female students nationwide.

Ping-Wen Kuo Became a Son-in-Law

Ping-Wen Kuo, helped promote Sino-American cultural and academic exchanges to an unprecedented level by relying on the connections he had established when he studied in the U. S.

In May, 1926, Prof. Paul Monroe of Columbia University, and Dr. Hu Shih established the China Institute. Ping-Wen Kuo became its first president. The Institute was financed from the Boxer Indemnity funds, and after three years the Institute would be provided with a $25,000 (USD) subsidy, proposed by John Dewey. Aimed at encouraging cultural exchanges between China and America, the Institute always invited well-known Chinese celebrities to lecture or perform in America, giving publicity to Chinese education and culture.

There were two special achievements worthy of mentioning during Ping-Wen Kuo's tenure as President of the Institute:

1) Under Kuo's leadership, the China Institute organized the splendid exposition of the China Pavilion in the 1926 Philadelphia Expo. The history of Chinese culture, the rapid development of modern education in China, and the emergence of new Chinese civilization under Western influence were demonstrated at the exposition, centered around the theme of "Five Thousand Years of Education in China". Also on display in the exposition were pictures reflecting the relationship between Confucius and Chinese education, vocational education and

economic reforms, education for the common people, and a campus model of Tsinghua University, along with various books and magazines published by CP.

2) Kuo elaborately arranged the captivating and sensational show by the renowned Peking Opera master Mei Lanfang on Broadway on February 16, 1930. This performance represented the very first time that Western audiences were exposed to the charm of the quintessential Chinese culture. The show initiated the Sino-Western exchanges in the operatic art.

The China Institute has evolved into a prominent platform for Sino-American cultural exchanges since the early years of the Republic of China. Both Chinese and American celebrities have been invited to exchange ideas, deliver speeches or hold discussions. For example, Hu Shih, a leader of China's New Culture Movement and Liu Tingfang, Dean of Theological College at Yenching University were invited to give lectures in the U.S. Similarly, many American university professors were invited to China to deliver speeches and introduce American culture.

Besides the above-mentioned Mei Lanfang, the Institute has arranged, for nearly a hundred years, many celebrities to give speeches. The list of invitees included Feng Youlan, Zhao Yuanren, Wu Yifang, Pearl Buck, Lao She and Lin Yutang. For this reason, the China Institute has served as an important stage for Chinese scholars to give lectures and to hold seminars in the

U.S..

In the 21st Century, the China Institute, with its role of promoting Sino-American cultural exchanges, continues its commitment to preserve and carry forward Chinese cultural traditions. Today, the Institute is becoming increasingly active in building itself into an important bridge for Westerners wishing to learn Chinese culture, art, language and even to establish commercial relations with China.

With a view to providing a broader platform to showcase Chinese culture in mainstream American society, the China Institute formed the Renwen Society in 2003 with Ho Yong and Wang Ben as its co-chairs. The Society has already presented over 300 lectures covering literature, opera, painting, calligraphy, etc. Many speeches were given by brilliant celebrities such as C.T. Hsia, Kenneth Pai, Yu Qiuyu, Zheng Chouyu, Wang Anyi, Zhang Chonghe and Shu Yi from mainland China and Taiwan— activities highly regarded and complimented on in both Chinese and American cultural circles.

In 1931, Kong Xiangxi invited Ping-Wen Kuo to serve as the managing director of the International Trade Administration. Returning to China Kuo entered the banking world. In 1945, he was named the deputy director and secretary general of the United Nations Relief and Rehabilitation Administration (UNRRA).

Ping-Wen Kuo died on August 29, 1969, in the U.S. After

her husband's death, Ruth continued to work in Washington until her retirement. Ruth was very active in the Sino-American Cultural Society, an organization Ping-Wen Kuo founded in Washington, D.C. In addition, Ruth co-founded the Organization of Chinese American Women to promote awareness of Chinese American women in the American society. Ruth was always the center of the How family activities. She was very loving and generous to her nieces, nephews, and their families. She was also active in musical groups with Chinese-Americans in the Washington, D.C. area. In her later years, she carried forward her late husband's educational ideas by setting up Ping-Wen Kuo Scholarships in Taiwan's Chinese Culture University, Chung Yuan Christian University, and New York's China Institute. She also made a generous contribution to How Elementary School in Qingpu, China, when it was re-opened after the Cultural Revolutions in the late 1980s in memory of her parents.

How's third daughter, Louise Loo-Yee How (1903-1983), furthered her studies in the Oberlin Conservatory of Music in Ohio. She married Frank Ling in Shanghai and they had a son, Bobby Ling (1937-1962). Frank Ling was a son of Shanghai's richest and most distinguished family from Taiwan. Ling family's prosperity was attested by the Ling Family Garden, in Taipei, which was said to have been modeled after the Grand View Garden depicted by Cao Xueqin in *A Dream in Red Mansions*. Once dilapidated due to the damage of war and vicissitudes

of time, the Garden has been renovated and is now a famous Taiwan tourist attraction. The Ling Family Garden is considered a precious historic heritage and a treasure embodying Taiwan's traditional architecture.

How's fourth daughter was Loo-Mei How (1904-2001), an outstanding student at the Julliard Conservatory of Music. Like the other seven sisters, she had refined musical skills as her mother, who often sang hymns while playing the organ in the Pure Heart Church.

When Loo-Mei How was in the U.S., a cousin of hers introduced her to Nelson Y. Chiang, a graduate from Cornell University, majoring in Civil Engineering. After their return to China, they were soon married and had two sons, Louis Chiang (1931-) and Paul Chiang (1934-). Moving to Taiwan with the Chinese Nationalist Government, Nelson changed his profession to manage tourism business. As General Manager of China Travel Service under Shanghai Commercial and Savings Bank, he participated in establishing the Tianxiang Hostel, the predecessor of Silks Place Taroko, at the time when Chiang Ching-kuo was building the cross-island highway.

Julian Suez's Grandfather Once Served as Consul General in New York

How's fifth daughter, Rhoda Loo-Ya How (1905-2006), graduated from the University of Shanghai. In 1932, she married

Albert K.Y. Suez and gave birth to their only son Julian Suez (1933-) – a key figure of this book. His grandfather Iuming Suez was a diplomat, serving as Consul General in New York in the early years of the Republica of China.

When asked why his English surname is Suez, not "Shi" in mainland China (Pinyin), "Shi" in Taiwan, or "Sze" in Hong Kong, Julian explained: "When staying in foreign countries as a diplomat, my grandfather, whose assumed name was Shi Ai-shi (史藹士, in Chinese), found that Westerners had difficulty in pronouncing his surname, the Chinese character '史', so he ran his assumed name of "Shi Ai-Shi" together to become Suez as his English surname in a flash of inspiration. That's how SUEZ came into being."

Julian's father Albert K.Y. Suez is well regarded as a pioneer in the development of China's auto industry. For many years he worked as manager of the Kunming Auto Plant and thus could not be with his family in Shanghai. As a result, he and his wife Rhoda How were alienated and divorced in 1948. Their only son Julian Suez was brought up by his mother. After graduating from the Massachusetts Institute of Technology, Julian joined IBM in 1962 and worked in its offices in New York State, Hong Kong and Beijing, until he retired in 1993. He now lives in New York and continues to work in IBM to receive customers and make business arrangements involving China.

How's sixth daughter was Loo Yuin How (1906-1972).

After graduating from the university of Shanghai, she also studied at the Julliard Conservatory of Music. She and her husband Paul Huo Chin Yin, who was engaged in trading in the U.S., had two sons and one daughter: Robert K. Yin (1941-), Theresa Yin Michna (1947-) and George K. Yin (1949-).

Their second son George K. Yin is a professor of law at University of Virginia. He served as Chief of Staff for the Joint Committee on Taxation in the U.S. Congress from 2003-2005. Julian Suez acknowledges the achievements of every cousin, but he considers cousin George, youngest in the generation, to be the most accomplished in the United States Government among all in the family.

Uncle-in-Law of How's Seventh Daughter –Wang Zhengting Used Twin Oaks Residence in the U.S.

How's seventh daughter, Lydia Loo-Ing How (1909-1968), married Wang Kungfong, whose grandfather was Wang Youguang, the earliest Chinese pastor of Ningbo's Anglican Church. While Pastor Wang's 2nd son was Wang Kungfong's father, his 3rd son, Wang Zhengting, was a high-ranking diplomat in the early years of the Republic of China.

Wang Zhengting was one of the plenipotentiaries to the Paris Peace Conference in 1919, and served successively as Deputy Prime Minister of the Beiyang Government, the Nanjing Government's Minister of the Foreign Ministry, and Ambassador

to the U.S. In 1938 Hu Shih replaced him as Ambassador to the U.S. The Twin Oaks residence he rented as his official mansion later became the Embassy for the Republic of China, and today the building has been turned into the Taipei Economic and Cultural Center. Furthermore, Wang Zhengting was the first IOC (International Olympic Committee) member, thus winning him the reputation as Father of China's Olympic Games.

Theodore Tso-ting Wong's Murder Shocks the U.S.A

Loo-Ming How (1911-1999), How Zoen Fong's youngest daughter, was only two years old when How died. Later, she married Wilfred S.B. Wong, who was also the youngest child of his family. They had a son, Wilfred Y.M. Wong (1935-2013) and a daughter, Winifred Wong Chase (1938-). Coincidentally, Wilfred S.B. Wong's father Theodore Tso-ting Wong was murdered in his prime, also at the age of 43.

In 1908, the U.S. government, after covering its actual loss, put aside the remaining funds from the Boxer Indemnity into the scholarship for gifted Chinese students to study in America. In addition, the U.S. and the Qing government reached an agreement to establish the Tsinghua School as a preparatory institution for the scholarship program. Among the 72 students admitted nationwide by Tsinghua School in 1909, Zhao Yuanren ranked second, and Hu Shih, fifty-fifth.

The Boxer Indemnity refers to the indemnity of the Qing

government for the Boxer Uprising that took place in 1900. As was mentioned in Chapter 5, the Eight-Power Allied Forces, after capturing Beijing by assault, forced the Qing rulers to sign the extraordinarily humiliating Boxer Protocol. It required China to indemnify the invaders with 450 million taels of silver, or 50 grams per capita for each Chinese citizen at that time. Later, the British government and the American government, among others, declared to "return" the balance of the indemnity that had not been paid, to be used for setting up schools, libraries and hospitals in China, and as academic grants or scholarships for students to study abroad. In 1909, the first cohort of students was selected and sent to the U.S. after the American government initiating the "return" that year. Zhao Yuanren and Hu Shih took the examination that year and were part of the second cohort.

At that time, Theodore Tso-ting Wong was appointed by Tsinghua School to work in Washington D. C. as Supervisor of the Chinese students studying in the U.S. His primarily responsibility was for their daily life and studies. In 1911, he was promoted to President of the Washington-based branch of the School. During the decade he worked there as Supervisor, hundreds of excellent students completed their studies and returned to China, among whom were Mei Yiqi, Zhao Yuanren, Hu Shih, Zhu Kezhen and so on.

Zhao Yuanren wrote in his book *From Hometown to the U.S.A*, "When I came to Washington in the District of Columbia,

I got in touch with our supervisor Theodore Tso-ting Wong as well as Li Gang, who later acted as a secretary of Tsinghua University in the 1920s."

On a winter day in 1919, Wong's office was robbed by two Chinese students. When their request to "borrow" some public money was refused by Wong, they then killed him, as well as his secretary, Wu Bingxin, and an assistant, Xie Changxi, who rushed to the scene on hearing the gunshots.

The news of the triple murder was reported as it appeared in the headlines of major media such as the *Washington Post* and the *New York Times*, for days on end. It shocked the U.S.

The murder case was soon settled in the U.S. court; the two criminals were each sentenced to 25 years' imprisonment. However, both were released on parole several years later. The two convicts were said to have shown sincere repentance to an American religious group during their visit to the prison. The group succeeded in their clemency argument plea with the US Justice Department which commuted their sentences.

Since Wong was killed for the protection of public money, the authorities granted his family a pension, and shipped his body back to Shanghai in an American copper coffin. The remains were interned in the Jing'an Cemetery for foreigners (today's Jing'an Park).

The Wong family, closely connected with western Christianity, was early founder of St. John's University in

Shanghai, and Theodore Wong's brother-in-law, Francis Lister Hawks Pott, was none other than the founder of St. John's School (the University's predecessor).

Final word by Julian Suez

While fostering the spirit of respecting culture and valuing education, he strove not for fame, but for the benefit of future generations.

Julian Suez is the son of Rhoda How, How Zoen Fong's fifth daughter. Julian lived with his mother in grandmother's house with two aunts and cousins, the Chiang brothers, before and after grandmother's death in 1938. Having never seen his grandfather, in Julian's mind, his grandfather was a little more than the gentleman in the large old photograph, yellowing with antiquity, hung in the living room of his grandmother's home. Grandfather's past was told to him in bits and pieces: random fragments of remembrance.

Julian does remember how the How family lived frugally yet always emphasized the importance of education. Christian faith and love of music were parts of the family life. On frugality, Julian remembers how grandmother would tell the grandchildren how grandfather's only business attire was washed every night to be worn the next day to go to work even when CP was beginning to be successful.

"When I was less than 10 years old, each time I heard adults speaking of grandfather, I often felt somewhat mystified and scared, as they always spoke in an exceedingly low and cautiously fearful voice about grandfather being shot dead by bad men, and that we should talk as little about it as possible in order to avoid further disasters."

"My mother told me that she remembered little about her father, as well, for she was only 8 years old when her father passed away," Julian added. Julian's mother did tell Julian a couple of things she remembered:

As Commercial Press was very successful in the first decade of the 20th Century, CP had a few reserved seats every night in a box at a Chinese opera theater for her father or other CP managers to entertain clients. However, the How children were never allowed to use those seats, not even when the seats were not used for business purposes. And the children would not be interested in the Chinese Peking Opera anyway, since the family were all trained to appreciate Western music.

Her father would always bring a few baskets of fresh fruits to his children, no matter how late he would work.

These episodes, though minor and insignificant, did tell how grandfather's love and care of his young family of 9 children and the family's emphasis on Western culture.

Then what motivated Julian to have a biography written for his grandfather?

Julian said that he had had a very blurry knowledge of grandfather until he began to understand the complex operations of a giant Western corporation after he had worked in IBM for a some years in his fourties. It occurred to him one day that his grandfather was truly "the one I cannot help holding in high esteem and admiring." Since this remarkable man had broken the fetters of thousands of years of tradition, taking the lead in introducing Japanese capital and advanced technologies, while at the same time keeping practical management power in an age of closed-mindedness.

As Julian knew very little about his grandfather. "I do not understand why such a great man who contributed substantially to the development of culture, education and the publishing industry in modern China is so little known to the world that he is even unfamiliar to his own descendants. Therefore, I feel obligated to publish a complete record of his stories so that the world may come to know him, or at least, we descendants of the How family will know about this ancestor who made outstanding contributions to modernize China."

That is the hope and longing deeply rooted in Julian's heart.

"Unfortunately, my cousin Julie How died an early death at the young age of 56, so that none of our family members is surnamed 'How' today. What a regrettable thing! But even though no cousin in our generation carries the name How, we always consider ourselves the 'How' cousins. We, the few 'How'

cousins know that we must let our next generations know how a great entrepreneur our grandfather was."

Reviewing merely from the historical perspective with all the emotional factors excluded, Julian is still convinced that How Zoen Fong, though unfamiliar to him, is well worthy of admiration on account of his contributions to the country. "He should be presented to the world so that the public can know him and recognize his great merits," Julian added.

That is history's evaluation of him; how then does Julian view How from a historical perspective?

"My grandfather, who did not receive higher education, was not much of a scholar, nor an extraordinary general or statesman; rather, he was just an ordinary person, or at best a businessman in the publishing industry. It is indeed not easy to define his position in history," Julian replied with a little hesitation. "If we look at him in another way, however, we may find that it was extremely extraordinary for a not well-educated man to succeed in undertaking the reform of textbooks which benefited people's education and the national rejuvenation. What extraordinary wisdom and great vision the man had! Indeed, my grandfather was neither an emperor nor a grand councilor: ruler of an entire nation. Yet, quite unlike those Machiavellian statesmen who, despite their selfish and insidious backstabbing activities that would lead to bloodshed and misery to the country, claimed themselves great achievers and saviors to the masses.

How Zoen Fong, my grandfather, on the other hand, strenuously devoted his life to bring knowledge and wisdom for the benefit of China and its people in aspects of culture, learning and education. Therefore, it would be better to recognize his personal life value than to place him alongside traditional historical figures. His management of CP went well beyond publishing and profit-making. He, together with Zhang Yuanji, Cai Yuanpei, Wang Yunwu, and others, fostered the universally cherished spirit of respecting culture and valuing education; they did it silently, for what they strove for was not fame, but the benefit for future generations."

In Julian's mind, what How Zoen Fong contributed to the Chinese nation was a feat of feats; thus the so-called "historical positioning" could never adequately reflect his selflessness, broad-mindedness and great vision.

"Although Mr. How Zoen Fong left us 100 years ago, but he will live in our hearts forever. What deserve our reverence are neither his wealth nor his brilliant feats, but his lofty ambitions and great vision, thus his legacy and spirit of wisdom, integrity, innovation, and entrepreneurship," Julian said soulfully.

Appendix

The following are three centennial-old biographical articles in memory of How Zoen Fong written by Cai Yuanpei, Jiang Weiqiao and Zhang Shunian (Zhang Yuanji's son).

How Zoen Fong, General Manager of the Commercial Press by Cai Yuanpei

The printing industry of China began in the Five Dynasties, and evolved through the Dynasties of Song, Yuan, Ming and then Qing. The books to be learned during these times were mostly Confucian classics, and were only crudely printed due to the underdevelopment of the printing industry.

In the Qing Dynasty, the Chinese began to follow European, American and Japanese educational systems, resulting in the abolishment of imperial examinations and the establishment of new-style schools, as well as in the use of textbooks. Though committed to compiling textbooks in their spare time, teachers were confined by their limited time and energies and could not perfect the textbooks. Meanwhile, printing houses, profit-oriented and inadequate in capital, only purchased cheap teaching

manuscripts and coarsely printed them out.

Only in the last 20 years of the Qing Dynasty, there emerged printing houses with relatively affluent capital. Equipped with editing sections where education-minded people could be engaged in compiling quality readings, the publication industry started to influence education. Actually it was CP that took the lead in this field.

The founder of the Press was How Zoen Fong from the Qingpu District of Shanghai, who later served as General Manager of CP until the end of his life.

How Zoen Fong—style name Cuifang—was poor in his childhood. He studied in Qingxin School which had been established by the Presbyterian Church. He served his apprenticeship as a typesetter for The Shanghai Mercury, then worked successively for the North China Daily News and The China Gazette. With the capital and experience he had accumulated from these businesses, he, together with Bau Xian'en, his wife's elder brother, founded CP, which started to translate and publish books in both Chinese and English, bearing the name the *Chinese and English Primer*, which proved to be very convenient to English learners.

After the Hundred Days of Reform (also known as the Reform Movement of 1898), many reformers studied in Japan and hurriedly translated Japanese books into Chinese and then tried to sell their translated works. How Zoen Fong bought a lot

of those books and sought professionals to distinguish the fine from the crude rather than publish them indiscriminately. He never hesitated to cast away inferior works.

As suitable textbooks were badly needed after the Boxer Incident in 1900, How Zoen Fong raised funds to set up of the Compilation & Translation Section, with Zhang Yuanji as its Director. CP also spent a lot of money purchasing works by Yan Fu, Wu Guangjian and How Cengyou, while also publishing dictionaries, novels and magazines. Nonetheless, CP's focus was on the compilation of textbooks for primary schools, which was then a pioneering undertaking in China. Even though many scholars converged to do the job, it was no easy task. In CP's compiling process, several versions of a text would be provided and only the best would be selected for further reviewing and revision; all contents would be previewed, analyzed and synthesized with prudent circumspection; and all the editors strained their hearts and minds to do their work.

Apart from the textbooks, painstaking efforts were also made in the compiling of teachers' books, which did not sell as well as textbooks. Surprisingly, the teachers' books published by CP were appreciated and welcomed in educational circles, while the teachers' books published by other publishing houses were far inferior, and could not compete with those published by CP. This result prompted all the other publishing companies to learn from CP and improve their operations, thereby making a profound

impact on the academic community.

In 1914, How Zoen Fong was 43 years old and had managed CP for 17 years. On January10 of that year, How was murdered in front of the Issuing Section office, tragically ending his avid devotion to the publishing industry. Those who knew about How felt deeply grieved indeed! How left behind a wife, Tsui Nyoh Bau, a son, Bang How and eight daughters.

How Zoen Fong, refined both internally and externally, believed in Christianity. He should have lived out his life to the utmost, but was unfortunately cut down in his prime. Could this be called the oversight of God? Though How died, the mission he began is thriving, exerting an everlasting influence on education. His spirit will live forever in our hearts.

The Story of How Zoen Fong by Jiang Weiqiao

How Zoen Fong—style name Cuifang—was born into a peasant family in Qingpu County, Jiangsu Province. When he was nine years old, his parents were forced by poverty to put him under a relative's roof while they themselves, having sold their land and house, went to Shanghai to set up a stall at Dongjiadu Dock.

One day when his mother came home to get something, the sensible 11-year-old How Zoen Fong asked to go to Shanghai with her, but she disagreed and sneaked away. When he'd realized that his mother had gone, he chased after her, knowing that she

would go to Zhujiage first. He pursued her, but was stopped by the river. Luckily there happened to be a boat passing by. He begged to be ferried across the river, but the boatman refused his request because he was so young. So he cried: "If you do not take me, I will jump into the river and drown myself."

The boatman eventually sympathized and let the child board the boat. Upon arriving at Zhujiage, he met his mother on the quay. She was moved by her son's determination and finally agreed to take him to Shanghai. At that time in Shanghai, the Presbyterian Church had established the Lowrie School and its affiliated primary schools. Those who had performed well in primary schools for two or three years could be admitted into the Lowrie School, in which both language and vocational skills were taught free of tuition and boarding expenses.

How Zoen Fong's parents sent him to a primary school, where he studied for three years. He was then enrolled into the Lowrie School and studied there until his father died, when young How was 18 years old. To lessen his poor family's economic burden, he decided to get a job to support himself. Through the connections with a supervisor at the Lowrie School, he got a job in Tongren Hospital.

Tongren Hospital was a charitable institution, which was also established by the Presbyterian Church. Since it was only a small charity hospital, it only recruited staff who did not have medical qualifications, and thus they could only work as

assistants. How worked in the hospital for a year and then left for the *Shanghai Mercury*, a newspaper where he went to learn typesetting in English.

Several years later, How Zoen Fong got a job in the *North China Daily News*, where his salary was sufficient for him to be self-reliant. At this time, he was about to marry his colleague's younger sister Bau Xianjun, but on the eve of their marriage, How's mother died. He then went to work for the *China Gazette*. As he was skilled in typesetting, he was paid well. Later he and his brothers-in-law pooled over $4,000 to set up their own printing house. In 1896 CP was founded in Shanghai. How was then 26 years old.

As there had been no well-established printing industry before in China, How Zoen Fong went to Japan to research the industry in person and then tried to imitate what he had learnt in Japan. This would give a new look and stimulus to CP. Since the period of the Hundred Days of Reform (also known as the Reform Movement of 1898), the entire printing industry had been developing quickly due to the popularity of new books and newspapers. Especially after the Boxer Incident three years later, the establishment of new schools was mushrooming. Considering that the basis of national education was primary education, How attached great importance to the textbooks for primary schools, thereby establishing the Compilation & Translation Section. Meanwhile, far-sighted How called for more investment to

expand CP, but no one responded. In 1903 a big opportunity presented itself when several Japanese men came to Shanghai with a huge amount of capital, intending to invest in the printing and publishing sector in Shanghai.

As China was backward in compiling expertise and printing technology, How Zoen Fong decided to cooperate with the Japanese to build a joint venture. Thus, CP was transformed into a limited joint-stock corporation with the two sides holding half the equities each. Nevertheless, it was stipulated that the Chinese side was in charge of personnel and administrative affairs while the Japanese shareholders were to abide by Chinese commerce regulations and laws. By then, compiling expertise and printing technology had developed rapidly, bringing CP more profits, so that it was able to establish more branches across the country employing over three thousand workers. At the end of 1913, 17 years after its opening, CP's capital had increased from the initial $4, 000 to around $500,000, with the Japanese investors holding only about one fourth of all the shares. At that time, prompted by the idea that that such a big company should be owned solely by Chinese and not by foreigners, How resolutely went to Japan to negotiate with the Japanese shareholders, and managed to buy back all their shares which he then sold to his fellow countrymen.

On January 6, 1914, CP signed the agreement on the withdrawal of the Japanese-held equities. On January 10, 1914, the newspapers carried the announcement on the signing of this

agreement. On this very day, however, How Zoen Fong was shot and fatally wounded in front of the company's Issuing Section. He was rushed to Renji Hospital and died there without uttering a last word. He was 43 years old.

How Zoen Fong was broad-minded, decisive and innovative, and he knew how to judge and use talents. That was why he was able to build up a big company from a small initial capital investment and make a profound impact on China's industry and education. Moreover, as a pious Christian, he adhered to the religious doctrine by being kind-hearted and lenient, treating his rivals nicely and loving his countrymen dearly.

How Zoen Fong also cared about his family members— How had raised his younger brother How Ruifeng since their parents had died when they were young. How was only a small boy, but he arranged a satisfactory marriage for his brother, who, in turn, regarded How as a father and How's wife as a mother. Owing to his standing and reputation in the business community, How was elected a Director for the General Assembly on Business and held that position for three years, during which he was highly regarded for his dedicated service and successful settlement of many commercial disputes. Also in his lifetime, he tried his best to improve public welfare, as exemplified by his attempt to build a school in his hometown.

How received his schooling in the Lowrie School, so he,

together with his schoolmates founded the Alumni Association, and raised funds for the expansion of the School. They later changed its name into the Lowrie High School. Apart from the Qingxin School, other schools such as the Aiguo Girls School, Shanggong Primary School and several orphanages all received donations from How. On the day of his funeral, thousands of people, acquainted or unacquainted with him, attended the service, shedding tears for the loss of this great man.

In Memoriam ... by Zhang Shunian (Zhang Yuanji's Son)

The founding of CP was in response to the needs of the times, reflecting the awakening of the Chinese nation and the hope cherished by the people. Such awakening and hope was precisely the basis for its tremendous growth. When you look back at CP's centennial development, you will find that those pioneers and their wisdom, courage and vision are indeed unforgettable and deserve respect and admiration. Among those pioneers of CP, Mr. How was the most outstanding in terms of courage and vision.

How Zoen Fong—style name Cuifang—was one of the founders of CP. During his time as general manager, CP developed from a small family printing plant into the largest publishing company in China at that time.

Since my childhood, my father has often told me stories about Mr. How. I have been deeply impressed.

Mr. How was initially a typesetting worker and became familiar with printing technology. Then How, together with Bau Xian'en, Bau Xianchang and Gao Fengchi, established CP with printing as its main business. But he was not content with this situation. As he was influenced by the trend during the Reform Period, How shifted his focus on publishing. In order to publish books, CP created the Compilation & Translation Section — a really remarkable feat at the beginning of the 20th century. How asked Cai Yuanpei and my father successively to be the Director of the Section, which laid the foundation for CP to become the leader in the publishing industry in the following decades. Gradually CP printed several publications that led the modern ethos—publications such as Chinese versions of Western masterworks translated by Yan and Lin. Gradually the ethos of academia was changing with Western culture, then spreading across China. Therefore, in my opinion, How Zoen Fong was not only a pioneer in China's new-style publishing industry, but also an open-minded entrepreneur with great vision and courage.

My father once said: "When How Zoen Fong invited me to be the Director of the Compilation & Translation Section, I asked him to make the development of education as our mission. How agreed and promised me he would." From the systematic compiling of new textbooks to the publication of the *Series of World Empires*, the *Series of Books about History,* the *Series of Books on Law and Politics* as well as all kinds of dictionaries,

CP always adhered to the principle of enlightening and educating people, which was also the basis of my father's friendship with How.

In 1906 when Lu Xinyuan from Wuxing, who owned a library named the Song Building, planned to sell all his collected books, How Zoen Fong, after consulting with my father, wanted to spend $80,000 to buy all of them for the Compilation & Translation Section. How courageous and daring How was, because at that time, the total capital of CP was only several hundred thousand dollars. My father was deeply touched. It was a pity that How failed in his attempt, as all the books were taken by Seikado Bunko Library, a Japanese plutocracy. This fully demonstrated How's sincere promise of "making the development of education his mission" and his patriotic sentiment to preserve the motherland's cultural classics.

How Zoen Fong showed an admirable foresight in the successful 10-year cooperation between CP and Japan's Kinkodo. In 1903, the head of Kinkodo planned to establish a publishing company in Shanghai. CP found it hard to compete with the Japanese as they possessed advanced printing technology. So How decided to set up a joint venture to take advantage of the capital, technology and talents of the of Japanese for the development of China's national publishing industry. In the joint venture, How insisted that the Chinese side take charge of daily operation, personnel management and administrative affairs,

while the Japanese side only exercise supervision by assigning members to the board. During the time when China was being invaded by foreign powers and was on the decline with her fate in jeopardy, this joint venture might have been the only one that adhered to the Chinese people's sovereign interests.

In 1913, How Zoen Fong, on behalf of CP, went to Japan to sign the agreement to withdraw Kinkodo's stock. On January 10 of the following year, Shun Pao (a Shanghai Newspaper) carried the announcement that, having returned all the equities held by foreigners, CP was solely financed by Chinese people. This successful move was mainly attributed to the indomitable perseverance of the respectable How Zoen Fong. But on the very same day of this announcement, the 43-year-old How Zoen Fong was tragically assassinated. I clearly remember that day: I was sleeping in my mother's bed with a high fever. Suddenly somebody came in to tell us the news that How had been murdered. My entire family was shocked. Later, whenever my father referred to Mr. How, he would feel dejected, an image that has been kept fresh in my memory.

In the *Biography* of *How Zoen Fong, the General Manager of CP,* Cai Yuanpei eulogized: "Though How died, the great mission he initiated is thriving, exerting an everlasting influence on education. His spirit will live forever in our hearts !"

CP has trudged this rugged road for over a hundred years, and is now embracing the new century with an even brighter

future. May Mr. How rest in peace!

Chronicle of How Zoen Fong

1871   Born in Nanku Village, Qingpu County, Shanghai.

1882   Walked out of Qingpu in search of mother working as a housemaid in an American missionary family in Shanghai.

1884   Attending Lowrie School, where he met fellow students: Bau Xian'en, Bau Xianchang, 2 brothers, Gao Fengchi and others.

1889   Quit school to work as handyman in St. Luke's Hospital upon father's death.

1890   Joined *Shanghai Mercury*, later joined *North China Daily News*, both English newspapers, as a word setter.

1895   Marriage to Bau Tsui Nyok; mother died just before the marriage.

1897   Founding of Commercial Press in Shanghai.
       Birth of only son, Bang How.

1900   Birth of #1 daughter, Mo-Li How.

1901   Met Zhang Yuanji for business consultation (Zhang joined Commercial Press in 1902).
       Birth of #2 daughter, Ruth Loo-Tuh How.

1903   Birth of #3 daughter, Louise Loo-Yee How.

1904   Birth of #4 daughter, Loo-Mei How.

1905   Birth of #5 daughter, Rhoda Loo-Ya How.

1906   Birth of #6 daughter, Loo-Yuin How.

1909   Birth of #7 daughter, Lydia Loo-Ing How.

1911   Birth of #8 daughter, Loo-Ming How.

1914   January 10: Front page news on newspaper in Shanghai (申報): Commercial Press is a 100% Chinese-owned enterprise.

       January 10: Assassinated in front of the Commercial Press office on Henan Road, Shanghai, at about 6:30 p.m.

Chronicle of the Commercial Press, 1897-1914

1897   How Zoen Fong, Bau Xian'en, Bau Xianchang and Gao Fengchi founded CP in Shanghai

1898   CP published *Ma Shi Wen Tong*, the first grammar book that blended Chinese and Western learning, and the *Anglo-Chinese Royal Reader*, the earliest books in both Chinese and English.

1900   CP printed books with paper matrix for the first time.

1902   Zhang Yuanji was hired; the Compilation & Translation Section (with Cai Yuanpei as its director) as well as the sections of Printing and Issuing were established.

1903   The first branch of CP was established in Hankou, Hubei Province (later the number of CP's branches and subsidiaries would reach over 80); CP became the first to use the copyright stamp and to compile and print the most up-to-date textbooks for primary schools under the

new educational system.

1904 CP launched *The Eastern Miscellany*, which was published until 1948, making it the magazine with the longest-running circulation.

1905 CP set up a tutorial class to train teachers for primary schools. It also founded an affiliated primary school.

1907 CP established Shanggong Primary School.

1908 CP published the *Dictionary of Physics* and *Dictionary of Chemistry*, the earliest publication on technical terminology.

1909 CP founded a tutorial business school.

1910 CP established a tutorial society for teachers, as well as Yangzhen Nursery School; *Novel Monthly* was launched.

1914 CP opened its Hong Kong branch.

Extracted from "Chronicle" at the website of the Commercial Press (Hong Kong).